THE OBASINJOM WARRIOR

The Life and Works of Bate Besong

T0319181

Emmanuel Fru Doh

Langaa Research & Publishing CIG
Mankon, Bamenda

Publisher:
Langaa RPCIG
Langaa Research & Publishing Common Initiative Group
P.O. Box 902 Mankon
Bamenda
North West Region
Cameroon
Langaagrp@gmail.com
www.langaa-rpcig.net

Distributed in and outside N. America by African Books Collective
orders@africanbookscollective.com
www.africanbookcollective.com

ISBN: 9956-792-01-2

© Emmanuel Fru Doh 2014

Dedication

To my grandsons
Baylin, Aiden, and Kaleb

Praise and Glory to God Almighty

Table of Contents

Preface

Bate Besong (also fondly referred to as BB) was among the second generation of Anglophone-Cameroon writers whose works deal with crucial issues facing the nation as a whole, but more so their part of the twin-nation in particular as Anglophone-Cameroonians take a second look at their union with the French-speaking part of the nation, La République du Cameroun. Besong, however, is in a class of his own not only because of his avant-gardist approach but also because of the artistic value of his works and the venom with which he goes after his targets.

In spite of the fact that this is a study on Bate Besong, I have treated each work as an independent text. My reason is simple: a reader interested in just one of Besong's texts, for example, can go directly to that section without having to go through the whole book into order to weed out what he or she needs.

There is the need to observe here that some of Besong's works, especially his poems, are repeated in different collections especially those volumes presenting selected poems. An example is the volume *Just Above Cameroon* which is a volume of selected poems, most of which have appeared before in other collections. In this case, I have included *Just Above Cameroon* in this study as one of the volumes Besong published, but I have appraised only the lone poem in the volume, "Druidical Rites" (34) that has not appeared anywhere else before. The bottom line is that I have treated poems in their original volumes and left them out whenever they are repeated in another volume which is a collection of Besong's poems. In such newer volumes, I have carried out a study of the newer poems only. This applies to his plays also. I have not treated his volume *Three Plays* as a trilogy since some of the plays—*Beasts of No Nation* and *The Banquet*—had appeared earlier on as independent works before being presented in this volume as a trilogy; accordingly, they have been treated independently. From this volume, therefore, I have treated only *Once Upon Great Lepers*, the only new play in the trilogy. Again, because it was not always possible, there is the need to point out that whenever cited, the structure of dialogues, that is how they appear on paper, is kept as closely as possible to the original in the given play.

I have benefited in my preparation of this text from my personal experience of Bate Besong's life, especially the foundational years of our working lives, and from the views of others who got to know him well in later years when distance and other obligations kept us apart. Accordingly, beyond members of those early years with whom we hung out during those days of the literary rebirth in Cameroon like Francis Wache, Ba'bila Mutia, Nol Alembong, Bole Butake, Tangye Suh Nfor and a host of others, some of whom are now deceased, I am indebted to the likes of Nwalimu George Ngwane, Douglas Archingale, and Dibussi Tande to name a few, whose writings—publications or blogging—honed some of my opinions of Bate Besong. To Dr. Augustine Enow Bessong, I remain grateful for your patience and the help you offered that yielded forth answers to occasionally perplexing cultural issues. To my friend Susan Sandoval I am thankful for your reactions to sections of the work.

Special thanks are due my family as a whole, but especially my wife, Ita Doh, and our daughter Fiona-Emma Doh, the other two in an almost empty nest, for their overall support and understanding.

Introduction

It was the morning of March 8, 2007, when the dawn of a new day was eclipsed by horrendous news: Dr. Bate Besong, one of Cameroon's foremost and equally controversial literary icons had perished in a ghastly accident during the early hours of the day, just a few hours after the launching of his last collection of poems, *Disgrace: Autobiographical Narcissus & Emanya-nkpe Collected Poems*. This was a tragedy so surreal that life in Cameroon, Anglophone Cameroon in particular, came almost to a standstill as word spiraled from person to person, from house to house, from country to country; even our professors from the University of Ibadan with whom I was still in touch called to refresh their memories of the one involved. This was before pictures of Besong in past days were disseminated. Besong, in the company of close associates, was en route to Cameroon's capital city, Yaounde, for a visa to the United States. They were all invaluable members, ideological and categorical representatives of the Anglophone community: Dr. Hilarious Ngwa Ambe, Besong's former student and subsequently colleague at the University of Buea, Thomas Kwasen Gwangwa'a a Cameroon Radio Television (CRTV) director and producer, and Samson Tabe Awoh, a cab driver and true member of the proletariat. They all perished. As a result of such tragedy, one could not help but scan the past in an effort to see how far Besong had come, and if it be the case, where things went wrong or otherwise.

Had there been nobody else, George Ngwane's seemingly premature declaration (for so it felt at the time) might have come across differently, but this was not the case; there were a good number of Anglophone heroes already. There was E. M. L. Endeley, P. M. Kale, Bobe Ngom Jua, and Albert Womah Mukong, to name a few, especially Mukong who had virtually given up his life fighting for the Anglophone cause and as a result spent the best part of his years languishing in Ahidjo's political prisons all over Cameroon. As Ngwane himself points out: "Bate Besong's literary journey therefore begins from the South West Province, charting a course from where S. A. George, P. M. Kale and Motomby Woleta stopped. These people represent to him the unsung heroes of the South West Pantheon..." (*Symbol* 9). Again, it was about this time that other symbolic Anglophone movements and personages were emerging: the creation of a significantly Anglophone based political party, The Social Democratic Front (SDF) that was establishing itself as a thorn in the flesh of the francophone dominated regime of Mr. Paul Biya, followed by the convening of the All Anglophone Conference in Buea, at the Mount Mary maternity, on the 2nd and 3rd of April 1993, and the creation of the Southern Cameroon National Council (SCNC) to name a few. These frighteningly audacious movements were executed by other extraordinarily determined and brave sons and daughters of Anglophone origin. Canute Tangwa confirms this when he observes:

> Today and in the past, the Southern Cameroons issue has raised a lot of legal and historical arguments. Legal leading lights like Gorji Dinka, Carlson Anyangwe, Simon Munzu, Charles Taku, Timothy Mbeseha, Ayah Paul, Sam Ekontang Elad as well as economists, political leaders, activists and opinion leaders like the late Albert Mukong, Ntemfac Ofege, Boh Herbert, Nfor Susungi, Prof. George Nyamndi, Mola Njoh Litumbe and so on have proffered stellar arguments.

Hence, it felt somewhat unsettling, a little too soon, rushed if you will, back then in 1993 when George Ngwane went on to title his book on a comparatively newer and younger yet raging spirit, *Bate Besong or The Symbol of Anglophone Hope*. Ngwane was conscious of the fact that the grain Bate Besong had just seeded in the somewhat freshly tilled literary and socio-political fields of Cameroon was only beginning to sprout, along with Besong's tender years, comparatively speaking, especially when pitted against the biblically accorded length of three scores and ten. Even then, Ngwane stayed his course. Hindsight, Ngwane must have been discerning or clairvoyant enough to identify in Besong, as was the case with Sundiata in D. T. Niane's *Sundiata: An Epic of Old Mali*, the extraordinary qualities that Besong possessed and was beginning to display. The passion and determination in him were driven by a mad yet justified rage consuming and channeling him to reclaim his and his people's birthright such that Ngwane was convinced these seemingly ordinary sprouts, nourished thus, would someday be towering and with a rich bough bearing down under the weight of delicious, juicy fruits in the form of refreshing, rebellious ideologies.

George Ngwane was right. Within a decade, after Ngwane's seemingly audacious title, Besong had come to personify, to many, the Anglophone cause by becoming a literary and cultural warlord and freedom fighter with his pen for a gun and his words ammunition rounds. Besong had risen to being, in a way, one of Anglophone Cameroon's foremost ensign bearers in the face of La République du Cameroun's hypocrisy; a veritable symbol of not only Anglophone hope but of the nation as a whole, with its web of problems, even if this is unacknowledged. By these means, Besong authenticated the wisdom in the Book of Wisdom that teaches us that venerable old age is not that of a long time, nor counted by the number of years.

Besong's death with those of the members of his team was a tragedy that seemed to sum up the catastrophe that Cameroon amounts to even today, years after Besong's demise. These were the things he was fighting against: a government so insensitive to the plight of the people such that while the leaders fête their ineptitude with champagne parties and repeated embezzlement of public funds, the infrastructure of the nation is left to decay; a country in which no citizen or regional office is of any consequence and so all must voyage to the capital city, Yaounde, for every possible thing one could need from the government and the diplomatic services of foreign nations. It has all amounted to a form of waste and total lawlessness otherwise known as Cameroon.

Bate Besong, mindful of the circumstances in Cameroon at the time, had, through his writings, rippled and muddied so many waters in so short a time, almost as if in a haste, only to die so suddenly and too soon, it will seem, given that he was only fifty-two when his life was cut short by this ghastly motor-accident. Apparently, Besong had approached life haunted by a premonition that he might not live that long, as his message to his people was, for some strange reason, so urgent. Otherwise, why is it that at a time when his contemporaries talked about and rejected poor publishing standards as an option, Besong did not seem to care in so far as his works could be published even without international standard book numbers? His, indeed, was a life with an obvious purpose, it would seem, that smacked of urgency, a purpose he quickly identified even as a young man and set to work to achieve or else blaze a path into the heart of the matter—the survival of the oppressed, especially the Anglophones in Cameroon—for those left behind to deal with. Besong was not alone in this fight; it was a struggle that was already in place before him, and is still thriving after him, but that which made the difference between him and his predecessors and contemporaries was the degree of his bitterness and determination. Besong seized his hour without even the government thinking any harm of him until it was too late: he had exposed to the world the workings and trappings of a chaotic system.

And so Besong wrote and wrote decrying the ills all over and virtually everywhere in Cameroon as he struggled to be the conscience and advocate of an otherwise dormant people who seem to be alright with whatever is served them in their own country. As Besong struggled, calling big and small, the old and the young, the politically powerful and the weak to order, he succeeded, with such intrepidity, in making more powerful enemies for himself than he made friends. He was beginning to recognize this fact even as he himself was laying in place plans to leave the country when it happened: Bate Besong died in a ghastly motor accident along the notorious Douala Yaounde road leaving many wondering if his death was natural or programmed.

Imagine the loss, and so now, whenever I think of Bate Besong, memories of our first encounter flood my mind: it was in the English Department library at the University of Ibadan, Nigeria. Besong opened the door, stepped in and stood just beyond the threshold, taking in the scene before him as if looking for a particular person or trying to figure out if there was sitting space for him, then our eyes met, and he stared at me for a brief while as if in recognition. He turned and left without saying a word, nor did I. Neither of us knew the other well, beyond the fact of being

Cameroonians, I believe. In fact, I found out about his being Cameroonian after this encounter, but my name gave me away easily and so he might have known my nationality before I found out his. After all, there were two other Cameroonians in the Department of English at the time. Besong looked calm, but there was something that spelled restlessness in those eyes lodged behind huge reading glasses, with a close fitting sweater cap over his dreadlocks.

As time passed, our encounters were brief and far apart, but Besong remained dedicated to literary activities with other students who enjoyed writing and discussing ideas such as Afam Akeh, Onookome Okome and the likes. However, Besong ended up being really close to Okome. Onookome Okome was another restless and fiery intellectual of a graduate student then, who, like Bate Besong, seemed to have something to accomplish urgently also, or else they were both under the powerful spell of the literarily enchanting and equally challenging atmosphere consuming the Faculty of Arts of the University of Ibadan at the time—the early eighties. The University of Ibadan was afire at the time, with seemingly larger than life academics physically present and directing the electrifying currents along with the inquisitive and creative minds in their care. They emerged ultimately with challenging works which they created and distinguished scholars whom they had trained. Examples of such great and intellectually active minds from students and faculty were Afam Akeh, Onookome Okome, Harry Garuba, E. Biakolo, Pius Omole, Olatunde Olatunji, Niyi Osundare, Isidore Okpewho, Femi Osofisan, Dan Izevbaye, Ayo Banjo to name a few. In addition to these were visiting scholars like Wole Soyinka, Oyin Ogunba, and so many others whose presence or influence transformed Ibadan into the center of scholarship that it was then. There were conferences, seminars and all kinds of scholarly activities going on from the University College Hospital campus where medical students and their faculty were causing scholarly waves, through the Institute of African Studies where culture was being deciphered and interpreted, to the Department of Theatre Arts where it was all finally concretized on stage. Here, plays were performed week after week, the scholar-performers' efforts rewarded by the huge turnouts of audiences with members who were anxious to learn, enjoy, and then review the performances. The University of Ibadan was intellectually afire, with international scholars vying for limited visiting positions. Birds of the same feathers, it was only natural then that Bate Besong and Onookome Okome turned out to be good friends: their drive for scholarship was simply overwhelming as young as they were.

My relationship with Bate Besong bloomed more upon our return to Cameroon as graduates of the University of Ibadan as we reunited with a simple goal: to set ablaze the literary brush within a society so rich yet chloroformed into a state of amnesia by decades of despotic leadership and excess alcohol. We started with conferences and book launches during which we presented papers that would conscientize the public and not surprisingly so, for many have established the connections between renaissance literature and nationalism. Accordingly, Juliet I. Okonkwo observes: "...literature, especially renaissance literature has always been a close ally of nationalism..." (92). We kept to our words, and so started the literary renaissance of the early nineties especially, determined to address the ills of governance and other travails challenging the people of Cameroon; Anglophones especially. About these book launches, Dibussi Tande writes while discussing Dipoko and his demise:

Dipoko would play a pivotal role in the revival of Anglophone writing with the coming of the East Wind in the 1990s. In fact, he played front-line role at numerous book launches organized across the territory by Anglophone writers which became the venues for discussing the plight of Anglophone Cameroon....For example he was the guest speaker at the launching of Francis Wache's Lament of a Mother in Buea … and a speaker at the launching of *The Passing Wind* by Nol Alembong and *Requiem for the Last Kaiser* by Bate Besong in Yaounde on October 31 1991; a lunching that brought out the crème de la crème of Anglophone literature – Sankie Maimo, Bole Butake, Hansel Eyoh, Ba'bila Mutia, Emmanel Doh (sic) among others. ("In Memoriam: Mbella Sonne Dipoko")

It was during these years as we met and presented papers after which we assembled in one house or the other to talk about the status quo and the future, or just to celebrate the just concluded book launch that our knowledge of each other deepened, in the process exposing the scars that fueled our literary quest. There was Ba'bila Mutia, Nol Alembong, Bate Besong, Linus Asong, Emmanuel Fru Doh, Tangye Suh Nfor, Francis Wache, Mbella Sonne Dipoko, Gilbert Doho, Hansel Ndoumbe Eyoh, Kwasen Gwangwa'a, Reverend Father Humphrey Tatah Mbuy and a host of others who surfaced at these events from time to time. The first seven of this short and incomplete list seemed to amount to the core for some strange reason; at the very least they were always present for the different literary activities except on very rare occasions when invitations did not make it to their destinations on time. At last, the distances between us and the lack of effective means of communication back then, unlike today, made it hard for the group to be as effective as it would have loved to be. Given the tough economic conditions of the hour, with the government introducing measures of the Structural Adjustment Program, the members, before long, limited their activities to the different provinces to which they could easily gain access. It was during this period that the Cameroonian public, at large, discovered Bate Besong, distinguished primarily by his outlandish diction that would set the crowd at book launches, students especially, cheering while the more serious scratched their chins with puzzled looks in their eyes. Besong's students already knew him, but he was yet to be a national icon until these events were being broadcast by Kwasen Gwangwa'a on Cameroon Radio Television (CRTV), and then a legend was born.

PART I

BATE BESONG: THE MAN

Childhood and School Years

Bate Besong was born at Ikot-Ansa, Calabar, Nigeria, which was part of what used to be known as Eastern Nigeria, on May 8th 1954. His parents were Cameroonians from Ndekwai village in Mamfe, of then Southern Cameroons, and so with reunification, during which Southern Cameroons regained her independence by joining La République du Cameroon, Besong and his parents eventually returned to Cameroon. Not many are familiar with Besong's childhood years, but it is documented that he attended St. Bede's College Ashing, Kom, in today's North West Region of Cameroon, for his secondary school education. The seeds for his later love for the Rasta tradition and their philosophy were planted here in St Bede's where his artistic talents started unfurling with his love for music which led him to join and play in the school orchestra, a phenomenon that was common in those days but suddenly died out of all Anglophone secondary schools with time. According to George Ngwane, in this capacity, Besong even earned the sobriquet of James Brown after the American music icon.

From St. Bede's College, Besong moved on to Nigeria, the land of his birth, which was at the time academic haven to Anglophone-Cameroonians in pursuit of higher education, then lone University of Yaounde being a gamble with so many bulwarks in the path of students.[1] Besong earned his Advanced Level certificate at Hope Waddell Training Institute Calabar, then went on to the University of Calabar to earn a Bachelor's degree in Literary Studies. He later on studied at the University of Ibadan for his Master's degree with an emphasis on African Literature (Poetry and Drama). While an undergraduate student at the University of Calabar, Besong and another Cameroonian student Ba'bila Mutia founded a journal of poetry, *Oracle*, with Besong as Senior Editor and Mutia as Deputy Editor. It was just before graduating from Calabar that Besong published his much acclaimed maiden collection of poems, *Polyphemus Detainee & Other Skulls* (1980), with a foreword by Professor Ime Ikiddeh who was then of the University of Calabar, whereas the world renowned Chinua Achebe organized the book launch. Besong went on to contribute poems in several distinguished journals such as *African Concord*, *Quest Magazine*, *Opon Ifa*, and *Okike* to cite a few.

That upon graduating from the University of Calabar Besong decided to go through with the Youth Corp Service, a program designed and reserved for Nigerian nationals, confirms the fact that Besong at one time grappled with the dilemma of his nationality. With a Nigerian birth certificate, along with the fact that he had grown into maturity in Nigeria, experiencing those invaluable landmark high school and university years, while creating connections with world renown figures and other aggressive young scholars, was he now to return to Cameroon, his roots, just because that is where his parents came from? Cameroon then, comparatively speaking, was a political backwater festering under the survival angst of a despot who was sporadically benevolent—Ahmadou Ahidjo; a land of which Besong had, pitted against his Nigerian experience, just vague memories of secondary school mates. Even then, it is true that Besong had a fondness for Cameroonians. While in Nigeria, when he heard one was from Cameroon, Besong paused and gave such an individual a second look with something in his eyes indicative of the spiritual recognition that took place. I experienced it.

In any case, it was during this Youth Corp service that Besong met and worked with later Major General Mamman Jiya Vatsa, the poet soldier who would later on be murdered by the military regime of Major General Ibrahim Badamasi Babangida for a failed coup plot in which he was allegedly involved. Upon completing his Youth Corps service, Besong registered at the University of Ibadan for his Master's degree instead of returning to Cameroon. He was not yet ready intellectually.

Coming from Cameroon after secondary school, with the stifling dictatorship of Ahmadou Ahidjo, into Nigeria was like being released from jail. Nigeria was a freer society, comparatively speaking, with numerous universities nurturing young talents, potential revolutionaries and future leaders under the tutelage of distinguished professors. These professors were world famous and determined, after all that the west had written about Africa from a biased standpoint, to re-educate the world about Africa and her true values. These were professors determined to decolonize the African mind, professors forging on with research and making significant contributions to knowledge, along with an equally free press that benefitted from the intellectual activities from within these different citadels of learning to inform

4

the people and even incite them when necessary. Nigeria's television stations, with Nigerian Television Authority (NTA) Ibadan (established in 1959) being Africa's first television station, were already working and amounted to a huge and immediate gateway into national affairs and the larger world beyond. These stations amounted to a means for revitalizing the cultures of the land while sowing pride into the citizens about their own values, about their fatherland, unlike Cameroon's sole government operated television station, thanks to the recent appearance of a few private stations, which is still nursing only one hypocritical bilingual channel after about thirty years in service, with its main role being to extol the dictator in office. Even then, this is a channel which, with its predominantly French dubbed programs, is determined to stifle the nation's naturally endowed values by chanting the myopic and equally unpopular mantra of the ruling oligarchy. Imagine watching TV series like *Dallas* in French, yes, we did; or *Fresh Prince of Bel Air* in French, yes, we did. In the same manner, imagine that all movies coming into Cameroon's cinemas were in French in spite of the audience being English-speaking in two of the nation's ten regions, and one begins to experience a little bit of the taste of freedom Bate Besong and the likes of him experienced upon entering Nigeria as university students. It was a liberating and exhilarating experience that at once implanted the seeds of rebellion in these budding minds, especially as they were immediately exposed to all kinds of philosophies within the vivacious world of academe thriving on Nigerian university campuses at the time. There was no way such a soul could return into the Cameroonian jail house of a nation and sit quietly in the face of all the abuse heaped on the citizenry by an autocratic and equally unpatriotic coven masquerading as political and patriotic leaders. Experiencing Nigeria then meant experiencing and acquiring the spirit of freedom, change, or growth if you will. Thus fired, Besong, like anyone else determined to work hard, buried himself in his academic projects resolved to complete his Master's program in one calendar year, a choice the well-structured, goal-oriented and driven universities granted, or else one was free to take a second calendar year. This was no easy task, but it could be done, and Besong, like most of the students, did it. We were all determined to complete our programs and return to our native shores to serve our compatriots in so many different ways, if only to let them know that things could be different and better. Little did we know of the suspicion and the

5

threat of rivalry with which Cameroonians, especially those in academe, would relate to their own when they returned from foreign shores where they had seen and experienced some positive values they were anxious to return and introduce into the worldview of their beloved fatherland. That spirit has not changed much; it is still reigning supreme. Nigeria, on the other hand, receives with relish her sons and daughters who have gone out and are coming back with new and fresh ideas for their country.

I was not around when Bate Besong was awarded his degree, because I could not attend the ceremony which was my own graduation ceremony also, but it was a dream come true for him as is always the case for all graduands, virtually. He was sure that as was the case in Nigerian universities, a strong MA degree holder like himself would very easily be recruited into the University system in Cameroon given the lack of professors that was being experienced then and even today. He was yet to understand how convoluted the administration in Cameroon is and how vicious even some so-called intellectuals in the system could be, especially those threatened by the arrival of sterling young minds into their intellectual-kwashiorkor-stricken academic arena of a lone and festering university system at the time.

Bate Besong: His Career

The Cameroon nation was at a political crossroads, nor has it improved, when Bate Besong returned home from Nigeria where he had been pursuing his Master's degree: Ahidjo, "the father of the nation," had just done the unthinkable by resigning from office as President of the United Republic of Cameroon, handing over power to his handpicked successor, Paul Biya, whom he had manipulated into position to succeed him in case of any eventuality. Cameroon had gone wild with the whiff of political fresh air that hit them just by the change of presidents from Ahmadou Ahidjo who had been in power for twenty-five years, to a young, handsome, and charismatic Paul Biya, but for his voice which sounds as if he is permanently under a chokehold. The mood in the country was celebratory and full of hope with musicians, notably Jojo Ngalle, celebrating the new president and popularizing his political mottos like "rigour and moralization" and so on. When amidst unbridled praise and support for the yet to be tested Paul Biya, Jojo Ngalle shouted out in his track *"Essimo na Rigueur,"* *"Rigue-e-u-u-r!!!"* we all ululated along with his chorus, in response "u-wo-o-o-o-o-o-o-oh!" Even then little known Bate Besong was, like the rest, hopeful, for he wrote of the change in a newspaper: "The roses which were stymied by desert jackals now flower. A thousand roses now, will bloom" (Ngwane 3). Little did he know the thorns were to thrive more than the blossoming of the petals and that he would be one of those to taste, someday, of the sensation produced by the pricking of the thorns to be delivered by this regime.

Before long, Besong found himself unable to be hired with his Master's degree by the university system in Cameroon, even on condition that he went on to earn his Ph.D. This should have been the case had the bulwarks in his path been genuine and well-intentioned and the entire university set-up foresighted, given the shortage of lecturers they were experiencing. Besong was, instead, completely rejected by the system. As a result, in desperation, Besong had no choice but to take up a teaching position at the Cameroon

Protestant College (CPC) Bali where he was from 1983 until 1985. If Bali was any consolation at all, besides the gentle academic titillation it provided, it is thanks to the fact that here he met the lady who would later be his wife, Mrs. Christina Besong. Together they would later bring forth six children, three daughters and three boys: Christabelle, Dante, June, Cedella, Harold Mandela, and Eldridge Charles. In the darkness of Besong's frustration designed for him by his crypt of a home country, Christina was the ray of hope at the end of the tunnel. Another harvest at Bali was in the guise of a colleague from Holland, Mr. Jan Deurwaader, a friend and literary guide who channeled Besong's bubbling and overflowing literary energy towards a meaningful struggle against the forces of evil athwart his path by asking him to focus more on drama than poetry. It is not surprising then that in Bali, Besong was the Editor-in-Chief of the North West English language Teachers' Journal. Bali also presented Besong with the opportunity to try his hands at directing and so in the company of another accomplished and indefatigable stage hand, Tangye Suh Nfor and his troupe The Mutual Drapoets, Besong's play *The Most Cruel Death of the Talkative Zombie* was staged at the Cameroon Cultural Centre in Mankon, Bamenda. It was at about this time too that Besong's second collection of poems, *The Grain of Bobe Ngom Jua* was published.

Two years went by before Besong received and accepted a government job offer from the Ministry of Education. Bate Besong, a foremost scholar by any standard, was hired to teach English in a government secondary school in a remote village, Mayo-Oulo, Mayo Louti Division, in Northern Cameroon. Besong was to teach English to a school that did not even go beyond the first year, to a bunch of kids who were fluent in neither French nor English. This offer had the flavor of a punitive appointment by all indications. What a waste, yet how typical of the system in Cameroon. This ethereal location to which Besong had been banished was somewhat of a blessing in disguise as it fertilized his creative genius all the more. It gave him the opportunity to see and interpret with profound understanding the forces against which he was to do battle in an effort to set right that which was already messed up in Cameroon. While teaching in Mayo Oulo, the village of the former head of state, Ahmadou Ahidjo, Besong went without his salary for years, like other Cameroonians who were newly recruited. The only Cameroonians who avoid this baptism of inefficiency are those newly recruited who have godfathers in the system who can expedite their being added into the system so that they get their first salary almost immediately, or else, like the rest of the citizenry without big names and godfathers, they can go for years without a pay-cheque. Pit this against the Southern Cameroon days when one got one's salary within the same month of being recruited, in so far as it was before the 16th of the month, and one begins seeing where English speaking Cameroonians are coming from with all their bitterness, frustration, and protestations. Most interesting of all was the fact that, as Ba'bila Mutia has indicated, Besong's dossier kept disappearing at the Ministry where he repeatedly submitted them for processing: a routine experience and one of the favourite spices of the cooks of the national broth of inefficiency within the outdated restaurant of a public service system in Cameroon. Besong must have intentionally, stubbornly refused to or else forgotten to appoint a caretaker whom he had to bribe to keep an eye on his dossier and do all to see to it that it travelled up the hierarchy for final approval, in anticipation of more bribes when he finally received his first salary. It is also possible that someone in particular was out to frustrate Besong or else he had just become a typical victim of the convoluted and equally corrupt and inefficient practices of Cameroon's public service.

Naturally, Besong became bitter and depressed and in an effort to mask his pain began drinking and smoking somewhat excessively. Besong's bitterness aggravated his stuttering, and I am convinced it is about this time that he developed a certain laughter of his I considered ambiguous, for one could hardly tell if the issue being discussed was funny or if it was a personal interpretation Besong had accorded it that caused him to laugh thus. Was he really laughing or was he poking fun at the system and his plight, remains a question only the context could help the listener answer. I am convinced, since "…not all laughter is related to Comedy" (Segal 23) that Besong was able to laugh because in his mind he had transformed the viciousness, senselessness, and illogicality of life into an absurd play in which he was starring as a modern day tragic hero after the tradition of Arthur Miller. [2] Therefore, to maintain his sanity while preventing the proclivity of self-destructing, he laughed at the absurd and nonsensical round about him; after all, laughter has an edifying, relieving, and even refreshing effect in the face of agonizing despair and bleakness. George D. Nyamndi confirms the place of laughter in Bate Besong's life thus:

9

For anyone who knew BB the man, laughter was as much part of him as a walking stick to an old man. He laughed generously, laughed loudest in adversity. In a sense, his whole being was encrypted in laughter. BB had not spoken until he had laughed; for in his expressive register the message was not in the words but in the laughter that accompanied them. If he termed his interlocutor a fool and left it at that, such a person could consider himself as anything but a fool. But if, as happened ever so often, he accompanied the remark with a sustained, voluptuous peel, then his victim stood anointed as a fool. BB wrote as he lived, draped in and inspired by laughter – wry, crackling laughter. Not even he himself escaped the wrath of his own condescension…. There is something about BB's laughter that marks its object with irredeemable stigma; something that says change or perish!

It takes an extraordinary outlook at life as a whole, for one to be able to laugh at one's misfortune and dejection. Besong was gifted enough to be able to perceive life from that unique angle ever so often, a stance that was buttressed by the confidence he had in himself, which came to the fore from time to time.

Bate Besong, nevertheless, continued writing, churning out volume after volume as if in some haste, whereas the rest of us agreed that we had to wait until we could publish as it should be done through respected publishing houses that would give our books International Standard Book Numbers (ISBN) and therefore international recognition. A system unfortunately noted for frustrating good writers from Africa especially as, more often than not, good manuscripts from Africa are often rejected for some rather ridiculous reason, one being that the book is too sophisticated to be from Africa. Another reason for rejection was that the potential African novel had all that a novel needed, but it was without the usual conflicts that certain books and previously published African writers had inadvertently set as the standard from this part of the world. After all, this is a part of the world forever treated with suspicion and condemned in the most ridiculous reference terms to be "sub-Saharan" indeed and at best "third world." We were virtually pioneers of a new era and did not want to be guilty of poor quality or vanity publishing which we knew was beneath us, given our world class experiences. Besong saw our point, but he felt and did otherwise: he wanted his books out there and so he went on publishing even if it meant he had to travel dangerously by canoe to Nigeria to pay and have his books published. He carried the day in the sense that knowing the caliber of scholar he was, we took his books seriously, with or without ISBNs and began treating them in our classes. It is not surprising then that *Obasinjom Warrior With Poems After Detention* was published in 1991, followed by *Requiem for the Last Kaiser* in the same year. *The Banquet* was to follow in 1994. The floodgates had burst open.

At last, Besong was brought back to life after his near death experience of a stay in Mayo Louti when he was transferred to a much better institution in every way and which could make better use of him—the Government Bilingual Grammar School in Molyko, Buea, Anglophone-Cameroon's administrative capital. From Buea, Bate Besong went to work. He became a frequent contributor to different newspapers in which he published scholarly articles that were political eye-openers to a public petrified into dormancy by fear engendered by the techniques employed by Ahidjo's discernible and subsequently Biya's less obtrusive Gestapo. Besong's articles jumpstarted a process that was choked out of West Cameroon with the demise, in one way or the other, of political consciences like Tataw Obenson a.k.a Ako-Aya, Tatah Mentan, *Fai Wotashiti* Henry Fonye, Akwanka Joe Ndifor, and the likes. Besong's audacity, one can argue, fertilized a fresh stock of journalists in the likes of Charlie Ndi Chia, Francis Wache, Ntemfac Ofege, Boh Herbert and many others of a younger generation. The literary and socio-political bough of Anglophone-Cameroon was once more flourishing as those trained at home joined in, emboldened by the forthrightness of those trained beyond the national boundaries along with the exposure dished out by the new television medium that made it possible for them to see some of what Besong and his contemporaries, in particular, had long experienced in Nigeria. It was a new day for the new deal government of President Paul Biya who was now to face a new kind of population engineered by the writing of academic warriors determined to free their country from the grasp of an autocrat bent on keeping the nation torn apart while its unqualified, unpatriotic, baffled, and sycophantic leaders thrived. It was the nineties no longer the seventies.

11

Besong had been causing socio-political ripples and so could easily be tolerated, but the ripples metamorphosed into waves especially with his politically revealing and sensitive review of George Ngwane's historically probing and astute work *The Mungo Bridge*. According to Ngwane, the review, given its tenor and interpretation of Ngwane's assertions, earned Besong "his first serious encounter with the police…a twelve-hour standing interrogation…." (*Symbol* 7). Even more serious was Besong's encounter with the police after the very successful staging of his own play *Beast of No Nation* in March of 1989 in an amphitheater at the University of Yaounde I directed by the accomplished playwright and emeritus professor of the same institution, Bole Butake. Of this performance Fon Christopher Achobang observes:

> In 1989 Bole Butake and I produced Bate Besong's 'Beasts of No Nation', epitomizing the plunder of Cameroon by unpatriotic Cameroonians. This production, watched by a furious Jean Stephane Biatcha, was seriously criticized by the government agent who reported that the play was subversive.

Not surprisingly then, en route to a scheduled interview with then Cameroon Radio Television's (CRTV) alluring anchor man, Eric Chinje, Bate Besong was picked up by the police who sought him out from within CRTV premises. True to type, the police took him to an unknown destination (some sources claim he was taken to the Maximum security prison at Kondengui, Yaounde), where it is alleged he was brutalized. He was accused of inciting the population, the Anglophone population, in particular, and disturbing the peace. Besong was later released without any explanations or apologies for police brutality or arbitrariness. Ngwane points out that a memorandum which was published by the French national weekly, *Challenge Hebdo,* NO. 45 of 31st October - 6th November 1991, had already been sent to the secret police headquarters accusing the playwright of trying to stir up a revolt among university students. A certain J. S. Biatcha addressed a similar protest to the Chancellor of the University of Yaounde which has been effectively reproduced and translated by Shadrach A. Ambanasom.[3]

Slowly but surely, Besong had transmuted into the voice of the exploited lot, a personification of the oppressed in society, but above all, the most fearless and voraciously poignant voice of the Anglophone underdog. He was now a warrior indeed, but no ordinary one as he had dubbed himself the "Obasinjom Warrior" after a Bayangi spirit-mask reputed for purging society of ills. The eyes of the population were on him and so were those of the bamboozled government.

Besong was still teaching in a high school, Government Bilingual Grammar School Molyko, Buea. He had hoped for more, not to say better; he wanted to teach in the university, a wish that would remain elusive for as long as he was without a Ph.D. Even the newly opened University of Buea would not recruit Bate Besong; he was yet to have a Ph.D. Ba'bila Mutia puts forward a more caustic view that somebody in the process had slighted Besong's Master's degree as being old. This is just a pointer at the fact that anything can go in these so-called universities managed by politicians instead of true academics along with a senate on the one hand and a respected students' union on the other. But until that day, we must not forget that this is about a woodland treed by people, in a jungle of a nation that has no rules other than the survival of the fittest after the chief miscreant parading as head of state. For which reason, ever so often, those appointed to administrative positions in these institutions tend to look at and deal with the relevant establishments as if it is their private property to (mis)manage according to their whims and caprices. In any event, they answer to nobody other than the chief reprobate who recklessly offered them the positions simply for joining his visionless and ideologically barren political chorus. This was about the time the Board of Directors of Patron Publishing House, a venture founded by three of us— Linus Tongwo Asong, Emmanuel Fru Doh, and Charles Fofang—agreed to honor Besong for his literary achievements.

When he came to Bamenda for the award, it was another opportunity for us to meet and talk with Besong, besides those moments during book launches. Besong remained clearly upset he was yet to be recruited to teach in the university because he did not have a Ph.D. We were sitting somewhere along the Mankon -Bafut road where we had a private reception in his honor. Two things about our conversation remain fresh to me until this date: after admonishing Bate Besong to stop responding to critics when they review his work, I urged him, in the face of his frustration, to return to Calabar and work for his Ph.D. which, I assured him would not be that big of a deal for a number of reasons, one and the most important being his overwhelming knowledge and experience in the field already. Besong did not say for certain if he would adhere to my advice or not; he kept mute and with a faraway look in his eyes as if seeing the wisdom in my words but wondering how long it would take him to earn his Ph.D. It was a sign that he had bought the idea otherwise he would have fought back on the spot. It was a pleasant surprise when next I met Besong and he told me he had returned to Calabar for his Ph.D. He even informed me with warmth that he had cited me in his doctoral proposal and went on to show me a bound copy of the proposal in which he referred to "Emmanuel Fru Doh, the Ibadan trained critic…." Besong was proud of our alma mater and for good reason. Ba'bila Mutia's words about Besong earning his Ph.D. confirm my convictions about his return to school for this degree which I shared with him in Bamenda: "Within a short period of time he completed his Ph.D.…." ("Besong: The Man").

With his Ph.D. in his hands, Besong's detractors, now without any seemingly genuine excuse, had no choice but to acknowledge his achievement; he was recruited by the University of Buea. In my presence, along with a few friends, he vowed to "destroy them." Besong was a wounded lion now after those who had hurt his pride. He was determined to turn them into literary game to be hunted down and obliterated. Accordingly, all hell broke loose as Besong set to work shredding literary pieces left and right and attacking anyone he considered a bulwark in the path of progress, his and society's at large. He himself had this to say of the role of the writer of his time, which, interestingly, narrows down to his fate:

The writer of my generation questions history, questions his environment, and questions people in authority. He uses his talents if I may put it crudely – to call things by their names, including the old aphorism that the emperor has no clothes. He has therefore been unpopular with the power-besotted men at the Ministry of the Education (sic). Thus, while he has won honours and literary prizes abroad, under a wastrel and nepotistic landscape, he is condemned to the ghetto of humiliation, physical abuse, and kidnappings... His name is anathema. And, like in North Korea, he meets the President's men, even in the air he breathes. (Fandio)

14

Besong was a literary tornedo in whose path one did not want to find oneself. The outcome was that he found himself with as many admirers as there were disparagers, friends as there were foes. This condition fueled rather than deterred Besong in his mission as Cameroon's cleansing spirit from Bayangi land—the Obasinjom—as he went on releasing play after play, collection of poems after collection along with scathing newspaper articles castigating those—individuals, institutions and whole nations alike—that have vandalized Cameroon's national space in any way, but closest to his heart was the predicament of the Anglophone-Cameroonian and the state of the union.

3

Bate Besong: Distinguishing Himself

Bate Besong, one of Cameroon's literary legends started like a joke: his linguistic grandiloquence always set him apart. This was the case because Besong seemed to emerge from a different world with his own peculiar phraseology. This diction of his, when combined with the fact that Besong stuttered and displayed a certain restlessness when trying to express himself, always brought about laughter, even after Besong had been known to be a serious scholar. For some strange reason, even ordinary words seemed to come across differently when used by Besong. It was possibly in how he distorted their context and meanings by associating one or the other with some Greek or Ndekwai myth, if not a personal image, or else it was in how he coined compound words out of many which like verbal flashes bemused and amused his audience as he deployed them from time to time. However, those who knew him to be thoroughly schooled forgave his edginess and sometimes seemingly fatuous or pretentious diction and struggled to get what he was saying. Meanwhile, students shouted and ululated each time Besong released one of those verbal grenades, excited by its magniloquence than by the fact or idea it communicated. But that was how Besong thought and reasoned things out; he was not being intentionally ostentatious but just being, to some, the literary aberration his training had fashioned. Besong did not seem to bother about the shouts but would go on with his presentation as if to say you are missing the point which he tried thrusting into his audience with his hands which flailed as he grasped, slashed, and pounded the air before him all in the process of marshalling his points across.

Because he was audacious enough to call to order a corrupt regime, Besong quickly rose to prominence as his popularity or notoriety, depending on which side one is, mounted. This prodigious journey was fertilized by the role of the press—the radio and television—as Besong was frequently on the air over and over during Kwasen Gwangw'a's program, "Focus on Art." The entire ambience conjured into existence a character overwhelmingly confident of himself until he could be described as foolhardy some times, a character unique in so many ways. Besong became conscious of his following and so could cultivate and weed out friends at will. He easily admired those he considered intellectually sound even if he did not say that, and seemed to recruit them as his followers one might observe, but it was with equal alacrity that he would denounce such a character if he fell foul with Besong by doing something that did not sit well with Besong's personal conviction for the nation or his literary bent. It is not surprising Bole Butake considered him "a silent volcano" and, as if in defense, said this about him:

Bate Besong was very impatient with people who tended to identify with the Regime (sic) and so regarded such functionaries as sell-outs especially if they were Anglophone. He did not only lambaste them in his essays he also tended to crucify them in newspaper articles.

In the same vein, to Kwasen Gwangwa'a, Besong had become a kind of a literary god, hence Gwangwa'a pointed out:

From the venom of his pen, the vigour of his artistic vision, the doggedness of his cynicism and an almost permanent mocking laughter, Bate Besong may seem to be feeble minded, a god, a demi-god or a dictator. To some skeptics and cynics, he may appear a dreamer.

Truth to tell, there were all these values in the man, and more, for I saw Besong weep as he pitied himself in the face of how he had been treated by Cameroon, a disposition which produced the venom he would spit in the face of his and the nation's oppressors with a certain sadistic appeal and conviction and to blistering effect. He did this while standing tall from the podium, in spite of his average height, like an Olympian. The podium was his literary throne from where he ruled, possessed by that bitterness churned forth by his plight and that of his people along with the conviction that there were traitors present, as part of his audience, and listening to him; they would then carry his message to the blighted quarters he was targeting. The very next minute he would yield into a Bacchanal embrace to drown his sorrows after a temporary cleansing had been done and the Obasinjom spirit of purgation deserts him for the time being. To Besong, inadvertently or otherwise, he had become the foremost god of the Anglophone-Cameroon's literary pantheon hence his declaration once: "I have resurrected West

Cameroon on the international podium" ("Down Memory Lane"). It is not surprising then that Kwasen Gwangwa'a saw him as the "…artist- dictator who sees every other person as a subject, a receptacle to be filled with Bostonian lore" ("Bate Besong as Seen"). How so true, for with Besong you were either with him or against him, either on his side or on that of the damned and he saw to it that your life was a living hell with his scathing articles.

As a critic, Besong was unforgiving and sometimes even ruthless when his target was one of those who made life miserable for him in any way or one whom he thought was challenging his scholarship. He disliked people he considered unqualified tampering with his works and would lash out at such individuals and their reviews ferociously. This is what he did to Menjame Njikang who, although still a student at the time, had a genuine point against Besong's writing when he accused him of obscurantism. Many were under the spell of Besong's linguistic splendor that they failed, even until today it seems to me, to realize that Njikang had a legitimate point albeit the fact, unfortunately, that he had been insulting in the way he presented it. Douglas Achingale, then also a student and mate to Besong's literary malefactor in the University of Yaounde, can still remember this traumatizing experience and captures it reasonably well from memory:

It was a rejoinder to an article written by Mejame Njikang, one of my class mates in Ngoa Ekele, and published in the now defunct Cameroon Post in 1991.

Njikang's write-up was captioned 'Bate Besong and the language problem.' In it, he rubbished BB's writings, saying that whatever message that was lodged in them could not go across because of what he described as the author's grandiloquence. He cautioned the *Association of Nigerian Authors (ANA)* Award winner to drop his pen, go back to school and learn how to write more simply.

Livid with rage, BB, then a teacher at Government Bilingual High School, Molyko – Buea, picked up his pen and did a rejoinder which he titled 'Mejame Njikang who? Query to an ostentatious iguana!' and published, of course, in the same newspaper. (Those were the legendary heyday [sic] when the Tande Dibussis, the JK Bannavtis, etc. were spitting fire in the local press).

18

As a student, I did memorize the one-page masterpiece. But today only the opening lines are still ensconced in my memory. Hear them:

'I read your literary reviews in some local newspapers and I know that you are not an intelligent man. So I am not going to invite you to tango on the sacred coliseums of literary discourse and practice.

'Perhaps someday in a free and once more communal and democratic Cameroon – and that should be after I must have sanitized your Augean stable brain with some detergents, some demi-johns of eau de javel (java water) – don't laugh, I'll try!

'I suspect you belong to that monkey monkeying cretin circus of time-serving political lakayanas and toadies who blabber like the orang outangs – they are about a pre-Gorbachev Perestroika Cameroon, a pre-Roosevelt New Deal Cameroon – brazen plagiarism in morosity!

'So in my writings, what terrifying gravamens, what genocide-like revelations swarm the goose pimples of my Anglophone Cameroonian brothers here and those in the diaspora?...'

(Oh my God! I wish I could recall the rest of those luscious lines!! For those that followed were even sweeter than the ones captured here!!!)

And do you know what? Mejame was more than devastated! After BB's rejoinder came out, the lad was walking on the campus like someone whose soul had left his body! (Langmo can again testifty).

I remember that Prof. Bole Butake invited BB thereafter to give us a lecture on African Literature, for we were preparing to take our final degree exam. On that day, Mejame, who was a habitual backbencher, sat right at the front. His tail between his hind legs, he was, in fact, the one who stood up to wipe the blackboard each time it had to be wiped.

Mejame Njikang's unusual kookiness drew BB's attention and he asked to know his name. Behold, when BB heard it, he embraced the young man in emotional fraternity, calling him 'my son.'

After the lecture, the master and the student withdrew to a solitary corner and had a close-to-one-hour tête-à-tête whose subject never filtered out to any of us who watched them with anxiety, up to this day.

That was how the two became friends until the 'Obasinjom Warrior' finally passed on. (sic)

It is not surprising then that Azore Opio, a more mature person and writer (by the time of his own encounter) who had a similar brush with Besong before they became friends says of the critic:

> A scenester, Bate Besong was fond of snatching people, especially those he was inclined to hate, and bundling them into sarcastic verse. Every mediocre, tyrant and stooge, sometimes even friend, was grit for his mill. But he was a boxer who never liked to receive jabs although he enjoyed delivering punches.

Indeed, Besong hated to be criticized negatively, nor could he stand those he considered traitors for one reason or the other. He would lash out without fear, such an individual's positions within the administrative hierarchy notwithstanding. This man was fearless. Yet the truth is Besong was forgiving as soon as his opponent repented or recanted from that which brought friction between them in the first place. Kwasen Gwangwa'a confirms this when he observes again of Besong: "Again the same Bate Besong will sometimes chant dithyrambs for persons denounced earlier but who by some acts of generosity, courage and love, impact positively on the life of the people." This, however, was Bate Besong at work and the means by which he distinguished himself in society; as a family man, he was a different person most of the time.

4

Bate Besong and His Family

Bate Besong's family was his private turf, his shrine, and only those he wanted to, met his wife and children at home. It was as if he did not want his family members to bear the brunt of his struggles accidently or otherwise, so like a jealous father and husband, he protected them. His love for his wife and kids was second to nothing, I am convinced; not even his devotion to the Anglophone-Cameroon struggle had priority of place in his heart. If Besong was bitter at the system, it was because of what it did to him: how it made it almost impossible for him to display his love for his family by providing for them what he would have loved them to have when he believed it was due. In other words he felt the system had emasculated him in the face of his family. It was as if this inability, on his part, to provide for his loved ones the way he would have loved to, made him half the man he wanted to be. His bitterness, his tears were because of this. Besong was a very emotional man and always appreciative of his friends' kindness to him. One would think a character this complex, strong, and willful in every way had to be tough, gristly, and without emotions, or was at least incapable of displaying them in public. In the literary amphitheater, true, but as a husband, parent, and friend, Besong would easily shed tears. Besong had suffered most of his life and so kindness, like bitterness, easily brought tears to this warrior's eyes.

On one occasion, it was an inner circle, and we were gathered at Nol Alembong's house in Yaounde after our host's book launch, sometime in 1991, to celebrate the event when somehow the whole ambiance struck a certain chord in this literary tiger of a man and Besong who was talking to Mutia and me on the veranda in the semi-darkness outside, thanks to an electric bulb glowing seemingly half-heartedly, melted into tears grieving the state of his family. I was in a state of disbelief to see Besong thaw, but I understood as Ba'bila Mutia tried explaining the scene to me; I understood. Who is there who loves his family who would not break down as Besong did, betrayed by his own country by being denied the opportunity to love his wife and kids as was their due, while unqualified, pilfering morons lived like lords squandering the nation's wealth? Besong's family was his everything and for his beloved country to enervate him thus before them, was not only unpardonable but too much to bear. Unlike other academics or scholarly giants who sacrificed their family for fame, as behind them are trails of abandoned children or broken marriages, to say the least, Besong joggled both his family and his work astutely. I dare suggest he would easily have given up everything else if it meant abandoning his family whose welfare was his primary concern as it became obvious whenever we sat during those trying moments when he had not been paid by his employer, the government of Cameroon, for years.

According to his son Dante, the fact that he could call his father "BB" like every other Cameroonian, was proof of how laid back his father was as a parent: a father who was also a friend, Dante pointed out in an interview with Elvis Tah. This notwithstanding, Dante Besong is quick to add that despite his father's love for his children, like most African parents, he raised his voice when necessary, as a way of disciplining them. Dante confirms his father could be complicated at times, but that was because he was human. His fondness for his family, as indicated by another of his children, comes across in the fact that he had pet names for all them, even his beloved spouse whom, according to his daughter June, Besong called Nabisco. June herself was Abo; Dante, Dantoro the Old Shark; whereas Mandela had no nickname because the father had transferred the reverence he had for Nelson Mandela onto his son. It is the consensus in his household that Besong was a loving and cherished husband and father; consequently, Mrs. Christina Besong summed up the departure of her dear husband thus: "I thank God for my husband because, having seen that he has finished his earthly duties, the Almighty decided to call him up to glory" (Tah).

Bate Besong was true to his calling as a family man and a scholar, at home or at work. Work to Besong meant being a total scholar, writer, and teacher with a purpose: a freedom fighter bent on educating, conscientizing, and finally liberating his people or else die trying, as contradictory as this may sound mindful of his love for his family. Besong took the struggle to educate Cameroonians about what is happening to them, the Anglophone-Cameroonian and his second class status especially, as personal and flung himself at this task with a reckless devotion encountered in a category of patriots who come around only once in a rare while. His every move reminded one of Achebe's brave man in *Arrow of God,* whose compound is being pointed out from the premises of the coward long after the brave man was gone as a result of his bravery (11-12). He died doing what he liked best: fighting for the underdog in society, then for Cameroonians, but specifically for the Anglophone-Cameroonian. We can only hope that someday from beyond he would be able to smile that the baton which he inherited from those who had gone before him and handed over to those he left behind, the generation of young Dante his son, has crossed the finish line with Anglophone-Cameroonians becoming equal citizens in the union or in the extreme free people on their own. He would not have made the Promised Land, but like Moses, he pointed out the way there.

Bate Besong has died, but not before leaving posterity a collection of works that tell how much this man loved his country and how much he was willing to pay for it; I dare say he paid with his life that Anglophone-Cameroonians may be treated as human beings in Cameroon even as our leaders refuse to acknowledge the existence of an Anglophone problem in Cameroon. It is our responsibility today to dichotomize his works so as to echo his ideas such that they become loud and clear to the deaf francophone-dominated governments in Cameroon while also becoming common knowledge to the Anglophone mind and beyond, so that we may stand together, the divisive schemes notwithstanding, and better our lot in order that Dr. Bate Besong may not have died for nothing.

PART II

BATE BESONG: HIS WORKS

5

Poetry

A look at Bate Besong's works reveals a different kind of poet, a poet with a technique so brash and experimentalist that it sets Besong in a class of his own in the path of those who influenced him. His poems have messages, but Besong's poetic style knows little order as he splashes his message across the page speeding and jumping from theme to theme and from image to image with more often than not an equally alienating diction. It is his diction and images that shatter virtually all effort to decipher the messages in his poems, let alone efforts at uncovering any sequence or logical development. Like the enraged spirit of the mask he was fondly associated with, the Obasinjom, Besong as a poet races from one concern to another in a breath, from one image in Africa to another from Greece within the same breath, leaving his reader gasping in an effort to catch up with the poet's intentions, messages, and technique. Besong, however, does communicate, yet one continues to wonder why he garbed otherwise simple messages in extraordinarily foreign, sometimes fine and sometimes coarse linguistic fabrics which hardly give any clue as to their origins and possible meaning. In one poem, for example, Besong is in Cameroon and in the very next line he is already in Nigeria, or in one line he uses an image from Mamfe and in the very next from Greece. The result, more often than not, is a perplexing whole on which only time and the serious association of events, names, and other historical and cultural facts can begin shedding some light. Mindful of Besong's use of language, it is consoling to learn from Aderemi Bamikunle's observation:

> Not only is language the key to understanding any literature in general, but it is of particular importance to the understanding of poetry. Of all the modes of creative writing, it is the language of poetry, particularly the form it has taken in twentieth century literary movements that represents the outermost limits to which one can stretch the use of language. Poetic language may no longer make straightforward lucid statements about its subjects. Its sentences need not obey the normal rules of grammar especially in relation to articles, prepositions, conjunctions; the structure

of its sentences may disobey the normal syntactic arrangements. (77)

Because of his rather ambitious and accordingly jolting style, Besong does not fit into the already established mold of a well-organized external structure that befittingly and easily accommodates an orderly presented subject matter. This is too much order for Besongese as in almost every way his poetry is music from a cacophonous ensemble of a wide array of dissociated and discordant choice of words and images, a puzzle from jumbled patches that ultimately emerge into an ideological quilt with a certain degree of meaning, the rest buried deep within the substratum of the poet's absurdist world. Accordingly, he is approached differently. Even though they may not all be elaborately deciphered, the point remains that Besong's poems have messages, for sooner or later it becomes obvious that if he is not lamenting, he is celebrating or else damning one thing or the other. Nevertheless, Ime Ikiddeh has presaged to Besong's audience about Besong's challenging literary disposition on introducing his maiden volume: "… that although Besong's song is large and loud they may not always hear him distinctly" (2).

Polyphemus Detainee and Other Skulls (1980)

In his first volume, *Polyphemus Detainee and Other Skulls* (1980), which is in four sections, "Throes," "Looms," "Masks," and "Wreaths," one already begins to imagine the wide range of concern displayed therein. The section "Throes," which, given this subtitle, should usher in poems on difficult, painful struggles for one's or universal values, begins with the poem "Migrant Images" (4). The poem reveals the malleable form of the human essence as people change and become dangerous because of their materialistic whims. This is illustrated in the poet's lament that even humble, obedient, and disciplined soldiers would use shrewd means to squeeze out as much as possible from struggling merchants. Besong is simply fed up with what soldiers do to people as they struggle for power and even after they seize power. Interestingly, Besong wrote this poem for Mamman J. Vatsa a poet and soldier whom General Ibrahim Badamasi Babangida's government executed after accusing him of being part of a failed coup attempt against Babangida's regime in the mid-eighties. In this poem Besong's arena is the Federal Republic of Nigeria and in this way his obscurity becomes obvious for how many Cameroonians knew Nigerian affairs so well as to know who

Mamman J. Vatsa was, and the activities of soldiers in power? After all, Cameroon has never known a military regime so why bother about the military affairs of other nations.

In "Reminiscences of a Party Thug" (6), one encounters a political party thug reminiscing. These are those people, usually young men—sometimes on the payroll of a political leader, and at other times just fanatical followers— sworn to help intimidate the political opponents of their candidate and leader. Again, this is an experience that is typically Nigerian given Besong's background. These thugs stop at nothing in their activities. Accordingly, we encounter their fraudulent practices as they stuffed "skull-stalks" (7) and men with party cards. They amount to party foundries that dish out lawlessness and are not ashamed to wound and even kill if they have to, hence the idea of salivating their "morgue tastes" (6). But these thugs are not as loyal as they want people to think because of how easily they change camps. At first they serve a party leader only to abandon him for a different master: "We changed tables, ministering" (6). Ultimately baffled by their responsibility as party thugs, the thugs sum up what their role as destabilizing factors in the dastardly and malicious game of cheating and backstabbing party politics had degenerated into: they stuffed "skull-stalks with mahogany/Tubers of Party card," so as to get cards to non-party members to vote for their party. It was all an unfortunate exhibition of manipulation and a hypocritical display of decorum, "intrigue and prudery" (7).

In "These Apparitions of Night" (8), the poet describes disturbing nocturnal necromantic rites by ambitious individuals as they interact with the dead. One gets the picture of a dead who cannot rest his haunted soul in his otherwise therapeutic tomb. Then in a sudden twist, one gets the impression of rebels being addressed as the night is described as of one of "librum-strontiums" (8), which is a respected class of Chevaliers, and the individuals are urged not to be "hollow Guerillas" (8) but to devoid themselves of the maraudic-mould and "be the crescent nugget" (8) and free themselves of all that humble them before worthless leaders gloating on Caligula who is here symbolic of tragic leadership.

Besong goes on in "Polyphemus Detainee" (9), while celebrating Wole Soyinka's emergence, unscathed by his solitary prison conditions, to lambast the powers that detained this idol of his as Soyinka worked towards peace between Nigeria and Biafra during the civil war (1967-1970). Besong then wishes that this brave venture may ultimately bring back the united nation that once was in the manner of Ogun's desire to advance humanity according to Yoruba belief: "This validity; may it rejuvenate in you for us / The communal patriarchy of Ogun" (9).[1] Soyinka, the scholar, critic, and social activist, was by any standard no ordinary detainee; hence, he is described as a "polyphemus detainee," a detainee, in other words, locked up by Cyclopes who could not see the wisdom in Soyinka's plans for his country.

Besong then leaves Nigeria and alights in his native Cameroon in "Mamfe this Time Tomorrow" (10). This is a poem with very conflicting and equally confusing images and messages particularly in the first three stanzas as one is left wondering if it is humans mourning at the destruction of another human being or nature mourning at the destruction of nature by capitalists presented as "moon-skulled vampires" draining the blood of Mamfe through the reckless harvesting of her timber, an act which will culminate in the death of the town embodied in the exploiting of its trees. The poem opens with the image of "Moon-skulled vampires" destroying "Timbers of Willows" (10) by tearing at her thrones of petals. One can, therefore, believe Besong is lamenting the depleting of timber in the forest regions which by this time tomorrow will mourn for the death of their forest surroundings. This gloomy prelude intensifies as Besong goes on to paint a decadent picture of Mamfe this time tomorrow. Then suddenly, the nourishing tubers project a different kind of picture: that of a woman's sore breast hanging down like some kind of tumor. Besong calls them "Nude stalks of pain" as by hanging this way they tell the story of nocturnal orgiastic activities intensified by the consumption of alcohol. Through the image of "Timber of willows" being destroyed (10) by "Moon-skulled vampires" (10) tearing at the succulent parts of these shrubs, Besong laments the state of decay of his native Mamfe—through the exploited landscape and the abusive and seemingly reckless lifestyle—while seeking healing, cleansing from Mfam (powerful deity) who unleashes terrible punishment on defaulters: "who unties volcanic tyrannies" (10). Mfam is the voice of the ancestors as pleas from empyrean lips seem to wonder at the tide of events in Mamfe. The poet hopes all will return to order by this time tomorrow. The poet pits the state of Mamfe against that of a thriving shrub ("Timber of willows") deprived of its beauty and well-being as nightly exploiters ("Moon-skulled vampires") tear at her resources—"throne of petals".

In "Comrade Sekou's Transformation" (11), Besong's causticity rears its head as he ridicules this otherwise exemplar of revolutionary African leadership. After rebelling against imperialist France and her Gaullist headmaster in 1958 by telling them off with "We prefer poverty in liberty to riches in slavery" (Camara), like true post-colonial African leaders, Sekou turned on his own people. Through his "Masses re-Education/Camp" (11), like Camp Boiro, Sekou Touré murdered some of Africa's greatest sons. Most painful though is what Sekou did to Diallo Telli one time secretary general of the now defunct Organization of African Unity (1964) whom he starved to death with the "*diète noir.*" The poet then goes on to explore other revolutionaries as most of them outdo each other in foolishness in the name of leadership. Besong goes from Sekou Touré, through Castro, Amin, Nguema, Botha, Muzorewa, and Mengistu to Gaddafi.

"Adrissi's Prologue at Mutukula" (13), a sarcastic poem about Idi Amin's reign, decries the torture of the citizenry under the infamous president of Uganda who is presented as plain stupid. This was a leader whose nation's economy was destroyed by his insane ways, even as he stored cadavers in his refrigerator according to his critics. Then the first section of the collection titled "Throes" leads on to the second "Looms." One gets the impression of struggles with appearance and reality here for "Looms" announces of things coming into view but distorted or indistinct and threatening also. The section begins with "Okigbo's Lament Under the Moon" (14), in which the poet laments the demise of a role model of his—Okigbo—whom he presents as the moon, a natural satellite who attends to a powerful dignitary. In his wake, shady politicians have returned to their game of corruption. The poet laments that instead of being destroyed, these personifications of corruption returned to their corrupt practices such as pitting members of society at each other's throat. Accordingly he damns them thus:

> tyrants, demented hordes, robed thugs
> bewigged senators, presidents in vaults
> bank managers party cadres flexing
> Party muscles agbada ministers
> Ourang-outangs addressing conferences of wind
> pitched against me and you (15)

In "They Hanged the Poet" (16), the rogue-politician, like the biblical Barabbas, is released into society "to use" (16) his people and environment as always, but the Christ-like poet is rejected and accused of treason against a questionably shaky constitution. The scene of the hanging is presented as the hangman approaches his task with orgiastic enthusiasm even as the priest prepares the accused for death. And after the dastardly act of hanging the poet, life goes on with indifference, with the protagonist swearing to make the victim's enemies, albeit posthumously, his footrest.

In "Our New Evangelist" (17), a poem intended to be accompanied by drumming and sobbing like some kind of a dirge, Besong grieves the reversal in the religious order. Although Christ Himself preached poverty as the manure that will effectively fertilize the lives of the religious, today's evangelists have ended up contradicting and distorting the Master's message and doing things formerly considered impossible of evangelists; hence the poet declares:

the parable is reversed:
the camel jumped

through
the needle's eye! (17)

To the poet, our new evangelists are traitors of the Messiah in other words, for they prefer and hunt for wealth instead of serving their flock in poverty after the Master. Their display of poverty is hypocritical as they are "resplendent in diamond robes and Arabian/sandals" (17). They do not worry about the sheep like their Master did, but "holiday in air-birds" (airplanes) and preach from their Cadillacs, while speedily stacking coded accounts in Zurich. The poet goes on to decry the embrace between religion and politics

for did they not quote
'give to
Christ what is Caesar's
and we chorused
give
Caesar's due to Christ? (18)

This, the poet queries, has led to the total exploitation of the poor by the rich who reserved the best overseas for themselves and the members of their families while reserving the decadent at home for the poor and wretched in society.

The section "Easter Sequence," begins with "Flutes Limit" I, II, and III in which poems the poet grieves the death of Bobe Augustine Ngom Jua who is simply referred to as "Bobe." Like Obatala, of the Yoruba pantheon blamed for creating the hunchback while drunk, Besong blames Mfam for destroying his own homestead—the metaphorical death of Jua—while drunk:

Our Bobe is no more!
Only to think

Mfam, rascally descended
With drunk-chilling shrills
Wheezing his new mint of prodigal indulgence

In his drunken insanity
Mad madliege with no difference. (22)

In "Flutes Limit" III, however, the poet inspires hope as an Easter crowd approaches Bobe's tomb, but all is dashed by Mfam's unpredictable ways. There is grieving for the demise of a hero, and hope that a miracle may be in the making, but not so as it all amounts to the stuporous blunders of an unpredictable deity. Accordingly, in "Flutes Limit I, II, III," Besong mourns the death of Bobe Jua in a series of poems loaded with the myth of creation error by the Bayangi deity, Mfam.

As if doubting or at least questioning his effectiveness as a poet, Besong sets out in "Childs Chant" (sic 25), to establish what he considers poetry to be, and who is a poet. Besong confirms that sometimes a poet could be so erratic that he comes across more or less like a lunatic:

the poet is

31

solemn like spartan fakirs
in vision more erratic, if turned so
than, Aro inmate. [2] (25)

A view some of his detractors have often aired in the background about Besong himself, than face the scathing anger of Besong's reactions to their criticism.

"Camwood on the Roads" (26) is a dirge honoring the death of a blooming young poet, Pol Ndu, and it brings to mind Wole Soyinka's own poem "Death in the Dawn" and his play *The Road*, which have bemoaned the devastating impact of accidents on African but especially Nigerian roads. Like Soyinka, one of Besong's main influences, blaming his patron deity Ogun for the bloodshed on Nigerian roads, Besong blames his own divinity, Mfam, for partaking "of the road's loot …" (26) of the likes of Pol Ndu who died prematurely. Besong thus ritualizes Ndu's death by using "Camwood" instead of "blood" on the roads, because of the sacred nature of Camwood to most Cameroonian cultures.

Enter Section three, titled "Masks," with the opening poem "And the Mortar is not Yet Dry" (27). In this poem, the message comes across when the four sections of the poem are treated as a whole. Besong is comparing the creation and emergence of a new mask of procreation through sexual intercourse. But his mask is no ordinary mask carved out of wood as usual. Instead it is of some kind of mortar reminiscent of that sexual "mortar" that yields forth offspring that forms the spirit mask when it hardens.

As a result, in section "I," the poet imagines himself as the "creator," through sex, about to create by descending into the shrine of the priestess (a yonic symbol for her vagina) for the beginning to be complete. One can only wonder then if Besong is elevating a carnal encounter into a spiritual creation dance. The sexual overtones become a lot more obvious in "And the Mortar is Not Yet Dry II," (28) which describes a heightened atmosphere of an orgiastic encounter:

White candles of overnight sex transparent camisoles
'quakes of strong perfume wreaths
b'cos the mortar is not yet dry… (28)

It is all confirmed then in the lines:

> O priestess! sole witness on perfumed leavesdown
> Clasp my heaving breath tight clasp, clasp down
> My fragrant form & harvest insides
> O Rachel of totemic scrolls too! (28)

In III, the poet continues to hope that his mistress and partner in creation will continue treating him to the creation dance as had been overwhelmingly predicted by "oracular throats" (29) against all odds. It all peaks in IV where the poet continues with brutal sexual images:

> the bruised backbone weeps
> cruised under the hind power
> of the giant turtle
> under the rubble grunt of monkey bread tree
> under the rubble insistence of the chacma baboon (30)

It culminates in the climate put forth by the last stanza which again juxtaposes sexual procreation and the creation of a mask, the realization of which process is celebrated with slit-drums grunting and xylophones blaring forth "white tornado at expectant mythcarrier" (30), the result of the hardened mortar? To Besong then, a cherished sexual encounter is like the creation of a new spiritual mask. However, the repeated lament of the mortar not being dry yet, leaves one with a perception of lack of consummation in the sense that the final product, the final outcome, is yet to materialize.

"Numistic Spells" I, II, and III (31-33), reveal a world overrun by materialism as everyone is scurrying around in search for money, material wealth, and recognition by man. In this quest, this world has gone astray so much so that there is total disillusionment and the sense of hope completely missing. The situation is so bad that even having a dream is pointless.

In "Numistic Spells" II (32), this quest for wealth has captured politicians and even the religious. It would seem Besong, accordingly, accuses even the church of standing by and doing nothing as the decadence consumes all, for he declares "…Massmakers continue to clutch pro- / Fitless hours / and so generations wail" (32).

In "Numistic Spells" III (33), Besong bewails further the decay in the country caused by a fictitious constitution that is held in place by torture and fright instead of true love and respect for one's country and compatriots. Besong himself must have feared he would die for his country—tortured to death by tyrants. It was a fear that was always at the back of the heads of a new school of Cameroonian intellectuals with their foundation in Nigerian institutions of learning of the seventies and eighties where, supposedly, they had picked up radical determination and were bent on educating the Cameroonian proletariat so as to free them ultimately from the claws of unpatriotic, egocentric, pilfering politicians. Besong's fear was not unfounded as he was molested and detained by the police for his supposedly subversive literary activities. Besong died, and although apparently not in the hands of torturers like Che Ngwa Ghandi in Bamenda during the State of Emergency imposed on the province by the Biya regime, Besong died in a most ghastly accident along the treacherous Douala-Yaounde road under circumstances that left many wondering if it was not one of those accidents always staged when dictatorial regimes begin feeling the heat of dissentious activities by the oppressed. The accident that claimed Besong's life, took along with it some of Cameroon's best in one blow, yet there was no inquiry into the cause of the accident, nor did President Biya bother to send a personal word of condolence even as the country of which he claims to be president, mourned. So Besong died, period! But as Besong himself prophesied in this poem, his "bloodied ash" (33), like a phoenix, is already arisen from the "bakery of tyrants" (33) as we continue disseminating his message against a derailed nation in the hands of a schizophrenic and bipolar leadership.

Again, Besong's anger at the exploitation of the underprivileged comes to light in "Exultations" (34). He is angry at how Pamol, a rich company that produced and marketed palm kennel oil from Lobe and Ndian areas in Cameroon, exploited the laborers here represented by his late father who has been over-worked into his grave without any recognition nor sufficient remuneration. Besong's father, his hero was "looted / at Pamol's insistence" (34). Here Besong also recognizes Mfor Aruoh's role in his life as a budding poet.

"For I Do Not Want To Think To Rethink" (35) triggered by lines from Soyinka's *Kongi's Harvest*, the youthful poet could not help remembering what he did not like recalling—those lascivious days in his life like Dipoko's in

34

Black and White in Love, when he stopped being a teen; days characterized by promiscuity and its consequences in a world ravaged by boys, men, girls, sex, disease, and cheating spouses even.

Another poem showing a rather rare soft side of the poet's is "Rachel" (37), which opens the section titled "Wreaths." From this title one cannot help but question if Besong is now about to mourn or lament or else why must he carry, if not present a wreath. The feeling of mourning or lamenting is immediately authenticated when in this poem "Rachel" (37), the poet weeps about unrequited love. His is not that lamentation brought about by distance in Ba'bila Mutia's poem "Distance" (27), which is dedicated to Liengu, once upon a time Mutia's goddess. In this poem, Mutia laments for love torn apart by distance:

> Let me slumber in my dreams
> curled in your woven selves,
> like strands of plaited hydrangea
> as I wake up
> from dreams into dreams
> as I suffer still
> from the jabs of distance,
> urging my horn into
> a jittery jive of fragments:
> And once more, in the turbulence
> of this chaotic assemblage
> my agony becomes again. (27-28)

Besong, on his part, admired and wanted Rachel, but she would not give in to him and so exorcise him of the love that like some overpowering spirit had possessed him: "O Queen can't you even touch me / With tender palms of your exorcism?" (37).

In "Flame Bearer of Dodan" (38), the poet identifies his protagonist, in spite of the latter's personal privileged position in life, with the needy class in society:

> and I of firmaments of private anguish …
> near wolverine howls of stringy morsels

35

by the demented

enzymes of penury .... (38)

In Section I (38), the poet through the use of a Greek myth, compares his persona to Prometheus, a Titan and son of Lapetus and Themis, who, because he came down from Olympus in an effort to better the lot of his creation—man—brought himself into conflict with Zeus. But Besong transforms this myth into reality and illuminates this effort as only an analogy when he declares when Prometheus came to earth as being "an ordinary mid-evening / and dark-blue October..." day (38). In Section II (38), he observes that Prometheus' descent was in response to chants of supplication as he, in Section III (38), abandons the wonderful life he once had, being a tragic idealist, to come down and help man. Section IV (39) continues to bemoan the incredible sacrifice by Prometheus to abandon the heights of it all as again echoed in Section V (39) where bored by "protocolic pseudo-sympathies" (39) Prometheus wrote thinking he is *The Shuttle*.[3] The result, of course, was, as implied in section VI (39), Prometheus' incredible punishment at the hand of Zeus. Besong's point comes to light when his title and the one to whom the poem is dedicated are taken into consideration. The poem shows that Besong considered M. J. V. (Mamman Jiya Vatsa), a once upon a time Major-General in the Nigerian armed forces, a flame bearer of the military headquarters, Dodan Barracks, which also served as the residence of the military leader of Nigeria. If it is remembered that Vatsa was killed by the government of Major-General Ibrahim B. Babangida on March 5, 1986, on charges of his alleged involvement in a failed military coup against the incumbent, then Besong's comparison of Vatsa's fate with that of Prometheus becomes as relevant as it is effective. As a major-general, Vatsa, like Prometheus, was indeed a Titan, one who towered by rank in his profession as a soldier and he had the masses at heart. Again, like Prometheus, he wrote books, and did a lot to help the struggling. As reported by Ademola Adegbamigbe,

As an accomplished poet and writer, Vatsa was able to publish eight poetry collections for adults and 11 for younger ones. Some of his book titles are *Back Again At Watergate* (1982), *Reach For The Skies* (1984), and *Verses for Nigerian State Capitals* (1973). His Pidgin poetry collection is *Tori*

36

for Geti Bow Leg (1981). His pictorial books are *Bikin Suna* and *Stinger the Scorpion.*

His literary interests transcended merely reeling out volumes of verse. *He organized writing workshops for soldiers and their families, assisted the Children's Literature Association with funds, as well as allocating a piece of land in Abuja for a writers village for the Association of Nigerian Authors.* Vatsa was so pre-occupied with creativity that he always carried jotters to the toilet, dining table and the bedroom. There were books strewn around in the family's apartment so much that, as The NEWS gathered, Sufiya once threatened to 'throw these books out.'

In view of all this then, even if Vatsa played a role in the coup attempt, it only puts his concern for the suffering human masses alongside Prometheus' for that would have been the reason he would venture any such thing being a well-paced soldier already. The result is that Vatsa found himself in direct conflict with Babangida, then powerful military dictator of the Federal Republic of Nigeria at the time, Zeus in the myth, who punished Vatsa by having him killed. Thus the effectiveness of Besong's extended metaphor of a poem.

Then there is "Ndekwai Masquerade" (40), an ambivalent poem in which an analogy is drawn between a sexual encounter and the nocturnal performance of the Ndekwai masquerade of the Bekundu society, itself a sub-cult of the secret Ekpe (leopard) society which thrives amongst the Bayangi peoples of Mamfe, Cameroon, and the Efik peoples of the Cross River area of Nigeria.

In "Bard from the Woods" (41), the poet returns to his softer and rarely encountered side as he pours his love and admiration for a distinguished damsel who is also admired by many others, but the poet considers himself a better suitor in their midst—he is "the bride's bard, singing the leopards to sleep" (41). His other distinguished qualities he declares thus: "I am the unneighing pony, tethered, in festive fires of your mind / O Queen, I am the bard from the Woods singing You" (41).

In "Bendel O Bendel" (42), Besong again returns to Nigeria as he professes his love for Bendel city in Nigeria with all its cultural values. In this section of "Wreath," Besong is at his gentlest as he laments, longs for, and praises persons and things after his heart instead of his characteristic fiery intellectual visions, trials, and judgments. Accordingly, "Wedding Day" (43) reveals the conflict within the protestant persona getting married in a Catholic Church. He attacks the presiding priest's fidelity to his vows of chastity and plans to attack his father-in-law who apparently demanded that this marriage be consecrated in a Catholic Church in spite of his son-in-law's protestant leanings.

Polyphemus Detainee & Other Skulls is certainly an extraordinary first volume, especially when it is realized that it is the work of an undergraduate student just about to graduate. The volume sweeps across society from the painful and equally difficult struggles revealed in the Section titled "Throes," through the perplexing appearance of events and the mythical in "Looms," especially with things not being what they seem to be, to the challenging views he has of life and procreation in "Masks," and finally his lamentations in "Wreaths." In this volume, Besong shows life to be quite a challenge and he is determined to face it given the diverse and equally vast influences in his personal life. *Polyphemus Detainee & other Skulls,* can then, mindful of the mythical reverberations around the name Polyphemus, be seen as an extended metaphor of what Besong considers his lot in life to be. He, like Soyinka, is Polyphemus' detainee, the brave, wise, shrewd, eloquent, enduring, and legendary Odysseus in other words, and the rest of mankind, Cameroonians especially, given his respect for other world renowned scholars like Achebe, Soyinka and the likes, are nothing much but mere "other skulls." These "other skulls" are without Besong's vision, and distinguishing characteristics like Odysseus' men with whom he has been imprisoned in this jail-house-of-a-nation, Cameroon. The rest of society, Besong's (Odysseus') men, amounts to nothing then but fodder for Polyphemus, Cameroon's Cyclopean leaders to destroy in their greed and foolishness. Besong, like Odysseus is the only wise one who can see their flaws and knows best how to deal with them: vain yet not farfetched as a potential underlying message from a scholar like Besong. Again, it would seem Besong is already at his best in this volume, with a diction and style so removed from the ordinary such that one is left awe-stricken as was Ime Ikiddeh who observes of Besong's already established poetic qualities:

If there is a unity in Besong's work it is to be found in an uncommonly vigorous sensitiveness which marks his poetic utterance on any subject. It is part of that extra sensitiveness that his poetry is a complex of the rare word, the unfamiliar turn of phrase and the startling line. (2)

As Ikiddeh confirms, the influences in Besong's young effort do not go unnoticed and are "three of the world's most 'difficult' poets: Eliot, Okigbo, and Soyinka" (2). Donatus I. Nwoga echoes Ikiddeh although limiting himself to the European influences:

> The modern European poets to whom our modern poets apprenticed themselves were difficult to understand and therefore even more difficult to imitate because their technical complexity could more easily divert the reader and imitator from the essential character of their poetry and their underlying perception of life and art. (35)

These influences notwithstanding, Besong's maiden volume revealed the juicy and equally succulent first shoots of an eventual literary baobab. After all, Sidney Burris' observation much later on, that "A young poet's early work often bears the indelible imprint of its influences..." (52) only emphasizes the role and impact of influences as common place rather than blighted exceptions.

The Grain of Bobe Ngom Jua (1985)

In the very first poem of this volume, "Their Champagne Party Will End" (12), Besong, as usual, is a bitter poet who lambasts the leaders of his native Cameroon for not only partying with the nation's wealth, but for being members of lodges—some with sinister records—determined to deplete, completely, the nation's coffers even as they make use of the armed forces to brutalize, torture, incarcerate, and frustrate a disgruntled population. The poet laments the waste by regimes without foresight as they erected "white elephant structures for a / pampered nostra" (13), a pampered gang. A good and recent example of a white elephant project is the Nsimalen airport when the Old Yaounde airport hardly needed any replacement, let alone the fact that the unfinished Douala airport is underused. The Nsimalen airport was built just to guarantee a leader who thought he would live forever that he could have a way out of the country should there be another ghost town demonstration that paralyzes the Douala airport as was the case in 1991. In any case, as the poet points out, someday it will all end, the support of puppeteer regimes abroad notwithstanding. And so to begin their downward spiral, he heaps a curse on the heads of national leaders turned bandits as they steal everything that can be stolen, from public funds within the state's coffers to electoral results: "The curse on the heads of the corrupt banditti" (12).

The opening stanza of "Facsimile of a Jackal" (14) confirms that as sadly evident from the cadavers themselves, they were badly burnt, and this must not be denied. From this one is likely to think of some form of torture in Cameroon or something to that effect, but as Innocent Futcha observes of poetry's density in content and form, it can "…sometimes lead to obscurity especially when imagery, diction and other poetic devices become too dependent on particular history and culture." In "Facsimile of a Jackal" (14), Besong is beyond Cameroon. Given that Besong wrote this poem in Kano on July 10th, coupled with his mention of Bala Muhammad, it dawns on one that Besong is lambasting events that led to the overthrow of Nigeria's second Republic, when Major Generals Muhammadu Buhari and Tunde Idiagbon took over and detained politicians and ex-politicians, only for Major General Ibrahim. B. Babangida and Rear Admiral Augustus Aikhomu to take over and free them, transforming serious national issues into some kind of a game of favors. It was July 10, 1981, with Nigeria's second republic in place, when Dr. Bala Mohammed Bauchi, one of Nigeria's distinguished political scholars and a genuine patriot (depending on which side one is), a political theoretician and practitioner was murdered and his corpse left to burn in a government residential building in Kano. The reason, in a nutshell, is that he stood and spoke for the masses in opposition to privileged northern power mongers within Nigeria. One can see then Besong's anger at the death of such a role model. Mohammad (sic) spoke up in the face of oppression; hence, tongues like his are described as "dry tongues" which "rasp, loosely" (14). Yes, he spoke freely for the truth and on behalf of the oppressed. Besong confirms the idea of this patriot being burnt when he talks about cadavers being "charred" (14). Before Mohammad's brilliance, society at large had relapsed into a lethargic state even with the ongoing hoopla, the "climacteric babel" (14) of the privileged political right-wing. Mohammad was the only one who could effectively interpret the goings on and so he had to die, murdered by "Ravening moronic spectres: / Fugue — heads, noodle

— brained" (14). Besong describes the process of burning up the corpse as "Ethered here: a sphinxed rite of Rahmadan / Allahu Akbar!" (14). Ether is, of course, highly inflammable hence a confirmation of the burning of the corpse but the motive remains sphinxlike, puzzling, to the poet, even though those who murdered Mohammad claimed to have been acting in honor of a particular emir, hence an establishment of the northern involvement by the lines "…rite of Rahmadan / Allahu Akbar" (14). These explications and implications are frightening and equally perplexing to Besong who tries to restrain his mind coming up with such dangerous intimations:

I must chill these cryptic intimations
I must unlend credibility to this putrescence
O loosening of the brain from it's (sic) moorings!
Still, I must not unbelieve me. (14)

The Besong in the next stanza goes into how the assailant whom he considers a jackal, waited for the right moment, and then with support from "his muslim pedigree" (14), struck. Yes, Besong confirms that those behind the murder of such a national gem are not only "lame-brained spectres opium drunk[s]" (14) acting from an emir's largesse, but failed revolutionaries since theirs is a parody and not the real thing. True revolutionaries and revolutions are against traitors not patriots. Besong considers the murder a "sickening awakening" (14) to Africa's political reality; he sees the murder as something fake and worthless, a "revolution parodied" (14) because it is all based on a lie since Bala Mohammad's concern, like the victimized masses, was for a just and democratic Nigeria. Richard Ali confirms:

Apart from the corruption flowing from a lack of ideals and hence fiscal restraint, Dr. Bala Mohammed communicated clearly to the common people in simple language what he saw, that the NPN and its puppeteers had no ideas and thus no policies except a vague, pitiable and eventually dangerous nostalgia for a dead Sardauna's days.

For this, he had to die.

In "The Party's Over" (15), Besong celebrates the end of the Ahidjo regime after the president announced his resignation on November 4, 1982. He looks back at how powerful members of the regime, "plunderers" (15) of our national resources used to be, especially as they had succeeded in instilling fear into citizens. But Ahidjo himself, the "shah" ended up running into exile and leaving his one-time stooges, looters of the national coffers behind. "Ah, what straw!" (15), the final notes of the poem, signal the poet's inability to comprehend that people do not seem to see the emptiness in all their ado for ill-gotten wealth.

"Grey Seasons" (16), is a rather bleak poem in which the poet laments the savageries of two governments, from Ahmadou Ahidjo to Paul Biya, which have encouraged ignorance; hence, he considers these bleak tenures grey seasons. Ahidjo encouraged ignorance by isolating the nation from the rest of the world as news was censored and only what he wanted the nation to hear was broadcast. In the process, other citizens, potential rivals and opponents, were hunted into exile, that is if they were lucky enough to escape death in a country that had been transformed into a circus with all applauding only, the audacity to challenge having been stifled, thereby transforming the nation into a cartel of "duncehood" (16). In his study of Francis Nyamnjoh's *Mind Searching*, Benjamin Hart Fishkin, was able to determine this same disposition in the Cameroonian population presented, for he observes:

> Life in modern Cameroon is equally perilous, but it is not for a fundamental lack of knowledge. Everyone knows all too well about the hypocrisy that has permeated every crevice of the capital city, Yaoundé, but all are too petrified to give voice to their criticism.
> Whether a Cameroonian belongs West or East of the River Moungo, it is clear that his or her success and survival are dependent upon a debilitating form of self-censorship. People hold back their innermost thoughts, and they are not all full-fledged members of the nation. (175)

Biya perpetrated the technique of torture with worthless party activities as they yielded nothing of benefit to the nation. When one wonders about the quenching of "monastic ires" (16), one cannot help remembering that it was under Biya's reign that nuns and priests who seemed to have known too much about his methods died mysteriously. By these means, Ahidjo and his successor, Paul Biya, had transformed the art of governance, "statecraft," into a failure, "stategraft," as their major concern became amassing personal wealth by stealing from the coffers of the state (16). Accordingly, Besong urges his comrades in struggle, like Ba'bila Mutia, to do all to stay afloat in spite of the overpowering socio-political decadence surrounding them.

"The Beauty of Exile" (17) is a poem that shows Besong addressing a friend in exile, urging him not to feel abandoned being away because through his exile they are able to see how terrible they have become, even with all those who sacrificed their lives, in some cases tortured to death in political prisons like Tchollíré; the same offenses against which they fought and gave their lives are still being perpetrated. The poet hints at the dissatisfaction of Anglophone Cameroonians at the state of affairs along with the absence of an effective leader for their struggle:

> From a long-rutted
> Ideology – very well –
> Where are the hired runners
> Who will bridge the firepower
> Of our anger across the Mungo.... (17)

From the tenor of the poem one tends to feel from time to time that Besong's "Friend" might even be Ahmadou Ahidjo, Paul Biya's predecessor, who was already in exile after clashes between them which climaxed with the April 6, 1984 coup attempt in Cameroon. Accordingly, it is appropriate to consider the poem a palinode as it reveals Besong as trying to but being unable to associate fully with a fallen dictator and arch-enemy of his whose exile enabled Cameroonians to see the ugly side of politics and governance under Biya's toddling yet power hungry regime. He writes:

> Do not say you are abandoned
> And deserted Friend
> For it is the Beauty of your exile
> That has shown how ugly we have become. (17)

Indeed one can argue that it is Ahidjo's being away from the country that revealed so much how ugly the once beautiful and exemplary African nation of Cameroon has become, with everything that looked wrong under Ahidjo escalating to megadeath dimensions under Biya: tribalism; attempts at Anglophone assimilation; waste of national resources; the collapse of government managed organizations like the Cameroon Airlines, National Retirement (Insurance) Funds (CNPS – *Caise National de Prevoyance Sociale*); and insecurity all became overwhelming under Biya thus showing us "how ugly we have become" (17). Angry at the masquerade after the departure into exile of his friend, the poet laments at the waste:

> Observe now how these same jokers
> Despoil the communal treasures
> They brush with hasty steps the torture-chambers
> Away;
> To the zombie clamour of moronic processions. (17)

In a short time Besong was already able to sense where the new regime would lead Cameroonians, especially Anglophones, hence he wrote:

> Or, soon when these same revellers
> Start running round again in circles
> Then, the stench of alien obloquies, frothing
> Ceaselessly
>
> From a long-rutted
> Ideology—very well—
> Where are the hired runners
> Our anger across the Mongo…? (17)

Accordingly the poet urges the exiled leader not to feel abandoned for it was not that long after he gave up power that Cameroonians who were already fed up with him just because he had been there for too long, twenty five years, started missing his reign. Thus he could have been away on exile, but the citizenry were with him spiritually seeing that their thoughts always went to him as Biya and his buffoons started despoiling the communal treasures and perpetrating "long rutted" ideologies. So the poet laments indeed:

Who will convert the broodings
Of these people over the past
Into bouquets to a new dawn? (17)

It was a new dawn but instead of bouquets of roses for the new dawn, as the poet had earlier predicted upon Biya's assumption into power, the people were still brooding and worse off than before even.

In "Requiem for the Sycophantic Omenologist" (18), Besong declares the impending departure of Solomon Tandeng Muna from his very long tenure as Speaker of the National Assembly. To Besong, the collapse of the Cameroon National Union (CNU) party seemed to augur Muna's unavoidable departure:

Since
The Party has gone to jail
Its profiteers will get no bail. (18)

Muna's long life and tenure as speaker of the National Assembly earned him the name Methuselah from the poet. Indeed, with the death of the CNU, Muna too was relieved of the position of speaker of the House in which capacity he had served for so long—fifteen years—that it had become his personal property in the eyes of Cameroonians. These failed political dinosaurs, like Muna, were lucky not to have gone to jail for their criminal tenures in office because it was not really a new government that had taken over as such.[4] Ahidjo had simply handed over power to his stooge-of-a-successor who went on with the same dance for governance until he clashed with his master. And so the idea of bail the poet had predicated did not come to pass as should have been the case were it a fresh government that stepped in with new ideas. A master had just handed over to his apprentice—old wine into new wine skins so to say.

In "The Iron Swallows are Gathering" (19), Besong decries the coup attempt of April 6, 1984 against the Biya regime and more so the massacre of the supposed putschists that followed, observing that it achieved nothing but send underground anger and division which portents nothing but more bloodshed, a possible civil war because "the iron swallows [are] gathering / On the cliff" (19) already.

"Makers of a New Society" (20) decries leaders of African nations as spineless given that they permit the fates of their nations to be decided in international monetary capitals of the world instead of by the local population. Typically, Francophone leaders are the greatest offenders here, hence the poet ridicules their education and training by jibing at them as "ostentatious cripples from City Halls / of Ecoles d'Outres Mer: spastic francophonie" (20). This is painfully effective when it is remembered that the French, it is said, reserved second grade education for those schools designed to train towards overseas certificates which were not locally valued but intended to be recognized in the colonies. Besong calls these second grade products from these *Ecoles d'Outres Mer* (Oversea Institutions), "tools," and accuses them of furthering the exchequers of Euro-America. To Besong, the result is anger towards these unpatriotic leaders.

"April 1984" (21) is another poem in which the poet focuses on the rather disruptive consequences of the coup attempt in Cameroon as bloodshed, in an effort to oust Biya who was only two years old in office and without any obvious blunders yet, led to more bloodshed with the captured putschists summarily tried and executed:

Artesians of death-warrants flood
forth shattered corpses
Whose brown redness

of the newly executed
print golgothas (22)

on their hadean shore...
and o if in revelry.... (22) [5]

In a characteristic geographic swing that would leave his readers gasping and lost, Besong rushes from Cameroon to Nigeria where, as he points out in a footnote, Major General Mamman J. Vatsa, soldier and poet, one of Nigeria's most educated soldiers at the time, had just been hastily executed after being

46

accused of attempting a coup against his friend and military leader at the time, Major General Ibrahim Badamasi Babangida. Again, Besong cries out against this waste which he predicts will only lead to further persecutions and death, even as he wonders how Nigeria would put an end to its series of military coups, "the incessant quotidien / of vengeful cavalries...." (22). In the case of the execution, Besong doubts Babangida's reasons behind the execution of a soldier of Vatsa's caliber, especially as it remains common knowledge hitherto, as to how close they were. That Babangida was Vatsa's best man at his wedding speaks volumes; hence, this poet's bewilderment: "Who can say Nero's purpose falters?" (23).

"The Stars Would Come Out" (24) is appropriately positioned after "April 1984," in which Besong decries the coup and resultant massacres in Cameroon and Nigeria. In "The Stars Would Come Out," he affirms the fact that the truth about these activities that led to great loss of lives—suspicious accusations and retaliations—like the stars in darkness, will come out someday. Today they are out. Listen to interviews and confessions on YouTube by those in power then, and one begins seeing the waste these murders, for the sake of political offices, were with a man like General Babangida confessing how tough a decision it was to kill Vatsa, or Madame Germaine Ahidjo confessing her husband's innocence with regards to the coup attempt in Cameroon in 1984. What a waste of valuable time, resources, and talents. Hence Bate Besong had lamented in "The Party's Over" (15), "Ah, what straw!" (15),

"The Grain of Bobe Augustine Ngom Jua" (26), besides eulogizing the brave Anglophone leader Bobe Augustine Ngom Jua, is a poem in which the poet observes the hypocritical manner in which some of Cameroons leaders pretended to mourn for this great leader who was one of the very few who could openly disagree with the dictator Ahidjo. Bobe Jua, in this guise, was like the biblical sower planting grain, the grain of fearlessness and the ability to stand up for oneself instead of always cowering in fear and applauding autocrats even as they blundered in the name of governance. Accordingly, the poet summons all to seize the moment and turn around the tide of fear and corruption. This was the grain Bobe Ngom Jua sowed. He was a metaphorical farmer sowing wisdom and resilience in the face of oppression, but his grain might not germinate if the moment is not seized and made good use of. Hence Besong warns: "*the plague on our heads / if we fail the generation of young Dante*" (poet's emphasis 27). In spite of the tendency to want to rush and allude the name Dante here to the classical Italian poet of *The Divine Comedy* fame, the truth is that Besong is referring here to his own son Dante and their generation. So Besong is warning that his generation must be careful about what it hands down to the succeeding generation, that of his son "young" Dante.

In "Prayer After the Three that Fell in Bamenda" (28), Besong expresses worry over the Anglophone predicament in Cameroon one more time. He acknowledges that it is a time of great weakness and failures and so one should be careful of yielding to other political ideas. Accordingly he prays that the dreamer and the poet may be protected because of what he has witnessed: young inexperienced soldiers, "fledgeling cossacks" (sic 28) of a sterile leader swearing to keep Anglophone aspirations from becoming a reality. He describes the times as one of dictatorship as there is tolerance for no other ideas "... climates of colossal gullibility / Shrouding over / Any other Catechism..." (28). Besong then praises the brave people of Bamenda after they resisted the regime's moves in 1983 to distort the General Certificate of Education exams usually written by the Anglophone students once a year. The Minister of Education had attempted modifying the General Certificate of Education exams to give it a semblance to the francophone baccalaureate, a move that was seen as another phase in the ongoing arbitrary efforts towards the assimilation of Anglophone Cameroonians. The decision led to fierce protestations and clashes with the police culminating in the death of students. To reiterate his admiration for the resilient populace, Besong refers to them as "cossacks" (28) because of their youthfulness and fighting spirit.

In "Exile" (29), the poet abhors treachery and so when people betray others by what they say about them, he is not a part of it as instead he anoints his lips making them sacred. He does the same with his feet by certainly leaving such environments while traitors applaud themselves.

In "Cristina" (30), the poet, in an extremely rare hand, displays his capability of loving. He declares his admiration for Cristina while prophesying that she will become the mother of his children.

Meanwhile, in "O Khalilah" (31), the poet reminisces about Khalilah's reluctant loss of her virginity; an experience which is now an "immortal memory" about which Khalilah still feels bitter (31). Besong buries his message in a repertoire of agrarian images in subsequent stanzas, all of which are metaphorical presentations of a sexual encounter.

In "Poetry Is" (31) Besong who, no doubt, met with a lot of dissenting voices about his poetic mannerisms, tells what he thinks poetry is by often highlighting what it is not, even as he confirms Bobe Jua as the voice of the Anglophone Universe. To Besong, poetry nourishes like tangerines and honey poles etc.; it is enriching, it is pleasurable. In stanza two, he declares poetry as nature itself, with goodness not evil. It is the Phoenix of Ujamaa: that is Nyerere and his Ujamaa philosophy; poetry is Soyinka not Hitler, good not evil in other words. Poetry is good music not evil; it is wise.

In "For Wole Soyinka" (33), Besong, somehow, arrays Soyinka's activities as a scholar and activist along the lines of Ogun the pathfinder who in the beginning made it possible for humans to connect with the divine, as a result of which his human protégés call for help from him in times of trouble. Thereby presenting Soyinka as a soul always out to connect human beings and bring about peace as was his goal when he set out to reject the war Nigeria and Biafra were about entering into, an effort which, instead, landed him in solitary confinement for twenty-two out of twenty-seven months during which he was incarcerated.

"Akoaya Forest Creature" (37) is a celebration of the leading journalist of old, Mr. Tataw Obenson of then *Cameroon Outlook* paper. Besong celebrates the fearless determination of Obenson as a journalist; not even the Ahidjo regime could break this leading journalist. His success left victims of his scathing pen reeling and wailing in shame.

In "Tribute to Mongo Beti" (38), Besong pays his respects to another rebel writer, Cameroon's Alexandre Biyidi Awala who used the pseudonym Mongo Beti. According to Besong, Beti echoed the voices of members of the first generation Union of the Peoples of Cameroon (UPC) political party who stood for the oppressed. Accordingly, Besong sees Beti's words as directed to future generations so that they may know the truth.

"The Night is Over" (39) laments the cyclical nature of his observations, his struggles that seem to repeat themselves causing him to recall "I have returned this way before…" (39). Alas, each time he recalls his duplicated effort, the conditions have degenerated further instead:

But alas; I have returned here,

Again and again
Into a cosmos shorn of the last shred
Of Earth
To masked sphinxes, around me,
I had never, seen. (39)

One can only wonder if Besong is giving up with the image of the night being over, overwhelmed by the repeat of the ills he has fought against over and over or if it is just adding to an already long established feeling of frustration as he re-echoes his prediction that this darkness is doomed to come to an end.

As usual, Besong's concern in *The Grain of Bobe Ngom Jua* remains the welfare of his people in the hands of an unqualified autocracy with its members running the nation aground from every angle. He laments the fallen state of the nation, nurses some nostalgic feelings for the good day of the past, before re-inventing his determination to keep the struggle to better the lot of his fellow citizens burning bright. Someday indeed the grain of Bobe Ngom Jua will germinate and bring about the elimination of darkness, the dawn of a new day when Cameroonians will manage Cameroon as their patriarchy instead of the foreign estate of some pilfering alien dominion.

Obasinjom Warrior With Poems After Detention (1991)

In *Obasinjom Warrior With Poems After Detention*, the poet continues in his tradition of lambasting the leadership of his country, Cameroon, for their failures. In the opening poem, "The Kaiser Lied" (8), the poet revisits the Lake Nyos cataclysm of August 21, 1986, in which over a thousand Cameroonians and their farm animals perished. Besong confirms himself as one of those who believed or, at the very least, suspected the Lake Nyos disaster was some kind of experiment that led to the death of innocent Cameroonians. Hence, he qualifies the scene a "nuclear gymnasium"—a place for rehearsals towards perfection. The poet then jibes at the Kaiser of the so-called New Deal now gone wrong—"wrong deal"—for lying to the world about Nyos. Besong calls him a "nation-wrecker" and urges people to take a peek at his "Swiss-bound, Baden-Baden" bank account. In the second section of the poem, Besong hammers at the Israelis role in the tide of events in Cameroon, pitting it against the massacres of Jews in the Nazi camp at

50

Auschwitz, which he thought would have dissuaded the Jews from anything reminiscent of the holocaust, yet here they are in Cameroon supporting the atrocious regime in place. In spite of the numerous teams of scientists from countries like France, Israel, and Nigeria, Cameroon's government is yet to publish the results of their findings as to what happened at Nyos. The result is that rumours, which, as experience has revealed, always turn out to be true in Cameroon, are now being spread and believed. As indicated in the footnotes,

> Foreign and local newspapers, recently alleged Israelis had carried out nuclear tests in Lake Nyos. The Israel Ambassador in Yaounde said, it was a 'diabolical attempt by enemies of the powerful state of Israel to disrupt the very cordial relations existing between the Jewish state and the New Deal Government of La République du Cameroun' Helas! (11)

The poet, like everyone else, believes the rumours. The first three stanzas present Washington DC as the site where the spices for the eventual cooking of "A pottage of entrails" (8) were arranged, for as Besong observes, it was in this area that the shameless egret (Cameroon's leader) rehearsed this brief "peacock act" (8) on his play on nuclear exhaustion (consequences). The result was that the gymnasium where the play was at last acted out, Nyos, was marked by a "pottage of entrails" (8) belonging to the slaughtered locals. And then typical of the quisling rulers we have, who would rather live as unclassified citizens in a Swiss volt than in their own country, the egret from his reservoir of lies, as lie-telling is his best survival technique, fed the world with lies. He tells lies to hide the terrible dealings of the so-called "New Deal" government which has become, as a result of its atrocities, like capital flight about which the president is lying to the press, a "Wrong Deal" for the people:

… Ah! Moronic
squanderer; you
fed

kangaroo gonads
to the world press corps

to camouflage the soporific
bankruptcy

of a traumatized
brotherhood-in-
sophistry, already
shrouded
in the obituarist lagoon
of Wrong Deal! (8)

Accordingly, the Israeli presence at Nyos after the incident and their gift in the form of aid meant for the victims, are considered by the poet as a pointer (since they must have arrived the scene to witness firsthand the degree of success of their test), and a Greek gift respectively. As if his adventure into the "nuclear gymnasium" is not tragic enough to the citizens of Cameroon, the egret, the poet laments, is a moronic squanderer who has succeeded in emerging with a brotherhood, which Besong christens the Wrong Deal, skilled in fallacious reasoning. The poet sees the egret as a sham of a leader, "a nation wrecker" as obvious from the figures in his Swiss bank account. The poet's anger continues to swelter as he condemns all those responsible for the massacre of innocent citizens as "A clan of minotaurs" (9). The poet hints again at the possible Israeli involvement in the Lake Nyos massacre when he alludes to the plight of Jews in Nazi extermination camps such as Auschwitz and Tremblinka, while also mentioning Simon Wiesenthal, the Nazi hunter's name:

At Auschwitz thro' tremblinka
A clan of minotaurs of Chaim
Hertzog
(*time again & again*) had,
doused

the pogrom charters
with the Yiddish
bitumen
of jew Wiesenthal- …. (9)

It is as if by confirming how the Jews "doused / the pogrom charters" (9) by bringing to justice the perpetrators of this evil against the Jews, thanks to Wiesenthal's findings, the poet is also making a promise that Cameroonians, someday, will also be able to bring to an end Biya's oppressive reign and like Simon Wiesenthal, Cameroonians will also hunt down the Jewish quisling "crack units" (9) now cooperating with and maintaining this dictator in office. The poet ultimately laments that although this leader is indeed a nation-wrecker, nobody could fathom that he was in search of "lethal artesians" (10), such treacherous gifts like that of Nagasaki, for his people? Yet, this gift was to hum towards Lake Nyos "gkpim!!" (10). Besong concretizes through this onomatopoeia, his conviction that some sort of a bomb was tested at Lake Nyos, hence this explosive sound "gkpim."

In section three of the poem, Besong reiterates his belief that the event at Nyos was no accident. Not only was "nuclear cargo" (a bomb) dropped there on the Sabbath, the Jewish day of rest, the motive was genocidal. And who would blame the poet for these convictions, mindful of the fact that no explanations have been given Cameroonians by the government as to what took the lives of their dear relatives and compatriots.

Led by a lying Kaiser, the people of Cameroon are at a loss for reliable leadership, hence after reiterating the failure of the Biya regime, the poet, in "You Must Come to Our Rally" (12), calls on the highest ranking Cameroonian in the Roman Catholic Church, His Eminence Christian Cardinal Wirghan Tumi, to come to our rally, the rallies of the dissatisfied which characterized the political atmosphere of the country in the early '90s. By summoning the Cardinal, Besong is urging religious groups to join in the struggle to free the nation from the grasp of an untrustworthy leadership instead of staying neutral in the face of the political, social, and economic decay of Cameroon under Biya, while preaching posthumous salvation to a hungry and disgruntled people.

In "Letter to Mungo Beti" i–v, an effort reminiscent of Dennis Brutus' *Letters to Martha* (1968), in which the South African poet documented his prison ordeals in that then notorious country, Besong churns forth poems in which he complains, laments, and insults because of the plight of his fellow compatriots in the hands of a kleptocratic government. In "Letter to Mungo Beti i" (14), the poet laments the personification of failure who was made president by the verdict of a tribunal. Besong's frustration emerges in the second and third stanzas as he insults:

the K-legged prodigal
and ex-
suffragan

in to the carrefour
a horsewhip for his obsequies
- to the gallows -
a garrotte
for his ligature
so-so. (14)

Besong ridicules the physique of the leader by describing the structure of his legs as "K" in shape. True to this leader's biography, a former seminarian, Besong describes him as an "ex-suffragan" (14). But contrary to all the religious doctrine he should have acquired in training, on becoming the leader of his people, he transformed himself into a wolf, their tormentor, with "a horsewhip for his obsequies" (14) instead of a staff for shepherding his flock. The poet further insults this sham of a leader for failing not only as a leader but also at his most favorite pastime, golfing. He is an intoxicated golfer, a squanderer of the nation's wealth who enjoys posing as an almoner and an intellectual. In the fourth stanza, his reign, which is characterized by the near total decay of the nation, a onetime social, political, and economic exemplar on the continent, is described by the poet as a "season of deranged vagaries" (14). The hollowness of his effort at documenting his political catastrophe of a doctrine in a volume, *Communal Liberalism*, is made obvious by the lines: "*Communal Liberalism* / & so on" (14). Not only the hollowness of this effort comes to light here, but also the fact that the poet refuses to credit this leader with the slightest academic integrity to write such a piece. The work is not only a false representation of the country's malaise, but written by someone else—"ghost crayoned" (14) like all his speeches. Of course, the effort is "pompously tambourined" (14) in a positive light by the government owned media since it is supposedly their master's effort at justifying his rigged position: "as amanuensis / of the intellectual / affray"

(14). The poet's final blows at this corruption of the idea of leadership lies in the fact that in spite of the "zonked golfer's" skill at make-believe, Besong shatters through these walls of appearances by not only calling him a tyrant but by accusing him of his effort to whitewash his disgraceful tenure in office by calling it "a new deal" (14) instead of "an abominable deal" (14). Besong goes on to celebrate a time after Biya, "the K-legged prodigal / and ex / suffragan" (14). Instead of a real funeral, his corpse will be dragged out in public and whipped for all his political blunders. Looking back, he will be remembered as a "zonked golfer" who from time to time faked love and concern for his people, "ostentatiously posed, as / almoner ..." (14). His was a completely misleading era which he hypocritically referred to as the "new deal" (14) era.

In "Letter to Mongo Beti ii" (15), Besong abandons the master himself, for the time being, to explore some of his assistants. In a poem loaded with sexual vulgarity, the poet sees the woman involved in this political propaganda as "whorls and whorls of prurience" (15), an image which conjures up layers and layers of disgusting human flesh (fat) and the sexual act. This travesty of a female wing of the ruling political party, to which this fat woman belongs, he condemns as a "debauched sorority" (15) and sees the women as "...copulating / adders / in that reptilian / slough" (15). The poet is possibly hinting at the idea that instead of a political party indulging in political ventures, this branch of women have transformed their political meetings into witches' Sabbaths with their leader as the devil himself who tops his paramour, the most notorious in this group of debauched, sisterhood—Francoise Hippopo (sic). By using reptilian images to present the activities of these women, Besong succeeds in communicating their wily and dangerous activities which in no way smack of *amor patriae,* the love for one's country. They are a bunch of devil's advocates steeped in sexual orgies, in the name of politicking, under their female leader Francoise Hippopo of the Wouri subsection of the pilfering political party now interring the nation in the economic graveyard. Besong's anger towards this woman can hardly be measured; he presents everything about her in a most disgusting light. Even her genitalia—and a woman's genitalia is held in awe in most of Africa because of the major role it plays in procreation—is presented in the most sickening manner. She:

pasteurized her water-
hole genitalia, cleanser?
pasteurized her mammoth-
genitalia. (15)

In this second section the poet shocks his reader with disgust, by splattering prurience all over the place as another characteristic of this regime with orgies enacted during drunken stupors. One of those involved is Francoise "Hippopo," a name which brings to mind a Douala based obese CPDM female Whig as she marched, drenched in perspiration, urging the nation to support a failed regime and political party. Not only are her genitalia obnoxiously described as a "water-hole" but also the idea of the woman being repulsively fat is communicated in the idea of "her mammoth genitalia" (15). Besong validates this woman's outrageous size when he calls her "Francoise Hippopo," after the revoltingly huge and dirty hippopotamus of the waters of Douala. He goes on to reveal that Francoise Hippopo is the party "accordionist"—the Orwellian Squealer and praise singer of the "Water" subsection of the ruling "kleptocratic party" (16)—Wouri subsection in other words, a name gotten from the River Wouri. Bate Besong is definitely not trying to be subtle here even if that's the impression one gets. In fact, by deliberately delaying and hovering around his victim's identity with the use of disgusting yet graphic innuendos that ultimately lead to her identification, Besong succeeds in sharpening and making more poignant the effects of his verbal projectiles at this overzealous traitor of a party accordionist. Accordingly, before one could identify his victim as that disgustingly fat woman, called Francoise, and possibly the spokesperson, if not self-declared, of the Wouri Subsection or else the noisiest woman in the subsection, one has waded through so much trashing of her person before finally arriving at the hippopotamus-like figure. This is Besong's intention, and he succeeds, for it is with a lot of effort that one wades through the surrounding disgust and prurience before finally arriving at this personified garbage heap of the Wouri Section of the thieving ruling political party. As if he has not insulted this traitor enough, he goes on to the ultimate—he insults her siblings by likening them to unneutered male horses:

may your siblings

neigh
like stallions of the wild;
in our quiet
Monrovia (16)

Besong's ultimate metaphor, in which he compares Cameroon to Monrovia, the capital of Liberia, is charged. This is significant when one recalls that Liberia at this time was on the verge of war, saturated with the buffoonery of a political parvenu in almost every way akin to Cameroon's even if he must be credited for fighting his way into office instead of pretending to be servile only to bear his fangs after inheriting office like Cameroon's Paul Biya did. By calling Cameroon, Monrovia, Besong was already sounding a warning note of an impending uprising against the political leaders of the day. Besong was right in his prognosis, for the country was tormented in the early nineties by uprisings which climaxed in a State of Emergency declared in then North West Province of the country.

In "Letter to Mongo Beti iii" (17), Besong, characteristically, laments the plight of a country in the hands of traitors. He paints, in the first stanza, a revolting picture of party thieves heading a nation, for which reason he calls them "kleptocratic," "cranks," "brigand-barons" (17). They are bastardized buccaneers who have hijacked the ship of state and like typical analogues of Ali Baba and the forty thieves are carting away the wealth of the nation. Yet, they misinform the world through a sycophantic national press of what is happening at home. The whole drama of piloting the ship of state to ruin and misinforming the world is to the poet "buffoonery" (17). In the fourth stanza, Besong laments this ruler's trip abroad to visit his wealth stolen from the nation and stacked away in a Swiss bank—"to pay homage to his Swiss- / Killimanjaro (sic) bank loot / from Baden- / Baden..." (17). When one realizes that Baden-Baden is a spa town, a bathing place, or *ville d'eau* in the state of Baden-Württemberg in southern Germany and in close proximity to France and Switzerland, one begins understanding why it is this leader's destination of choice: beyond all else, these are environments noted for offering hydrotherapy which is good for one's health. No doubt this god once told off his citizens whom, fed up with how long his unproductive tenure had lasted, celebrated the false news of his death, that he would live for twenty more years. As powerful as this idiot is, with regards to this declaration of his, I wondered why he just did not settle for eternity given all the wealth he has stolen from Cameroon along with his ability to easily access the life-giving waters of Baden-Baden. Alas, how many Cameroonians can afford such luxury, the result of so much stolen public funds even as the rest of the population rots in man-made misery engendered by bad governance. The amount stolen from the people can only be compared to nothing else other than Africa's highest mountain—Kilimanjaro. The voice over observes that this was the "aboriginal motion" (17), the first step towards the collapse of his reign, a leadership marked by fetishistic practices. Besong then accuses this leader of being drunk for his

> … aardvark –
> orifices became

> hostage
> to the ghastly
> geysers

> of gelatinous
> rum; (17)

In the seventh stanza, we are reminded of the reason why the government is called opportunistic. The leader was the spoilt brainchild of his predecessor, Toura. The poet cries out to Mungo Beti as he compares the head of state, whom he considers an opportunist and thief at the head of a cultic band, to Ali Baba and his forty hoodlums. The poet wonders then if there was ever "such / gallows-humour as Baba's nemesis" (17): that he handed over power to such a bootlicker who worked for him, only for him to turn around suddenly and persecute Baba to the point of maintaining him in exile even posthumously. What an irony indeed, what a macabre humor!

"Letter to Mungo Beti iv" (18), a much shorter piece, takes us back to the Lake Nyos disaster as the poet wonders who could have exacted such a revenge on his people and then go in for plastic surgery since the person was never caught or else registered for plastic surgery just to look good. Basing our arguments on facts from an earlier poem, "The Kaiser Lied" (8), it is possibly the money paid this manic leader for the nuclear tests in Lake Nyos that was used for plastic surgery at 33 Foche Avenue where he had to pay billions of Francs CFA for acetylene creams so he can look as young as he thinks he does at his age. His heritage, the poet destroys through the expression "gehenna heritage," an expression which smacks of a worthless legacy. This section again emphasizes the poet's anger and disillusionment towards Biya who, as a leader, has only hurt his people instead of serving the nation. The poet confirms him the devil himself and emphasizes that his "reedy voice / marks him out," (18) as such. If at all one doubted the individual thus insulted, the lines: "his reedy voice / marks him out" (18) are almost synonymous to the man's name—the tragic anti-hero in Cameroon's national drama with a reedy voice could not be better pitched; not even speech therapy has been of any significant help.

Besong is so preoccupied by the misdeeds of the regime in power. In "Letter to Mongo Beti" v (19), he cannot help wondering at some strange political dance-steps being taken by this unscrupulous regime. At a time when virtually all of Africa and the world—at least ostensibly—was against the deranged apartheid regime of South Africa, this "crank-brained extremist" was imagined by the poet to be audacious enough to see in de Klerk a befitting partner to the extent of zooming:

... off on a Solidarity
tour
with Comrade de Klerk

as honoured guest
of the South African
Broederbund? And, what if he did? ... (19)

What sarcasm by Besong! Biya is thus confirmed a "cruel joke" on the Cameroonian people in this section. After all, is it not said birds of the same feathers flock together? In any case, are the thousands of lives lost at Nyos not somewhat analogous to the thousands of apartheid asphyxiated black South African lives? After all, is it not the blacks who are "troublesome" in South Africa, and the Anglophones, especially those from the North West in the poet's homeland?

Besong then goes on to warn that although vice might now be in control, the hour of retribution must come: "Doomsday must freshen / the early morning / dew" (19). Once more, the poet compares the Cameroonian scene to the Liberian by calling our turbulent country euphemistically, yet ironically, "quiet Monrovia." He also points out that on one dawn to come, a cockerel will tell him of vultures gathered like hyenas around the decomposing corpse of another overthrown dictator like it happened to the Liberian, Doe. After this, calmness, as if to compensate the citizens for the atrocities of this regime, shall descend at noon over the national territory.

For the first time in this volume, Besong goes to his second home, Nigeria, in the poem "After an Impeachment" (21). The poet laments the unfortunate plight of the first governor in Nigerian history, Abdulkadir Balarabe Musa, to be impeached. This representative governor who stood for the common man as he struggled against a leadership suffused in old corrupt ways is praised by the poet who presents him as out of place, a "Flower glowing in a sullen tribe, lone pilgrim / His head was wreathed in true luster / Thus, he declined the syphilitic sperm, of a fortressed god" (21). A governor who would not soil himself, thus he declined the unhealthy gift of "a fortressed god" (21). This governor, to Besong, was a good example denied the opportunity to improve upon things as he, this meteor, is "muted" (21). He is flattered and falsely praised only to be falsely accused and tried by people the poet considers "dancers of the void" (21). So, although in the eyes of the ignorant, Governor Abdulkadir Balarabe Musa was humiliated, to those who know, he stood for change and remains a true hero defending the exploited masses.

In this dirge "Requiem for Abonikim Davina Deurwaarder-Loderusa (1952-1988)" (22), Besong makes it clear that he is lamenting the death of Deurwaarder-Loderusa, a woman he held in high esteem. Besong addresses her "Abonikim," a title given by the Bayangi to leading women who can fight a cause. The news of her death transmitted by telegrams resulted in the keening of dirges for this dowager. The poet did not find the mourning for this distinguished lady profound enough, befitting in other words, for he describes the singing of dirges as "guttural rehearsals of idiot moonsongs" (22). The poet's respect for this lady whom he reveres in the light of a goddess and whose ideas he considered sacraments, comes out in the fourth stanza where he apostrophizes lamentably: "O Abonikim Davina whose sacraments / were blasphemed ..." (22). This distinguished lady must have died in an accident for the poet presents her corpse all covered in blood "like truant centurion with blood-soaked revelations" (22); he is later on to add:

> smudged with haemorrhages
> of blood and brain (she who was
> ridden on hump –
> black sarcophagi), scattered... (22)

Davina's fatal accident is thus painted as ghastly.

In Section ii (23), the poet tells us the accident occurred "on a cold drab December eve" (23). The poet goes on to jibe at this "stone-aged Imam ayatollah" that is to blame for Davina's plight. It is he who, like a usurper, ambushed the matriarch's laughter and impaired her breathing in the midstream of her life. Through this poem, Besong immortalizes this dowager whom he holds in high esteem.

In Section i of "For Osagyefo Thomas Sankara" (24), Besong briefly rehearses, mentally, the putsch that cost the charismatic Captain Thomas Sankara, leader of Burkina Faso, his life. Because many hoped for a better future through him, Besong calls him the liberator, *Osagyefo*, a title used in describing another great African leader in whom many hoped—Kwame Nkrumah of Ghana. The poet attacks Sankara's then alter ego, Blaise Compaoré, for betraying his closest friend, thereby confirming himself a traitor. The poet sees this turncoat as a French stooge, and reminds him that France expects those they help to betray their nations, like Compaoré, to deliver the goods. Besong describes the attire of the "Mongrelized Iscariot" (24) like Jesus' Judas whom the former trusted so much, yet was betrayed by him. Indeed, Blaise Compaoré was to Sankara what Judas was to Jesus: confidants who trusted each other. Yet, this Iscariot with "morgue-like" eyes butchered into "grey hours of dawn" (24) to eliminate this personality who dwarfed him. Besong consequently invokes Mfam, the Bayangi god of vengeance to pay back this traitor.

In section ii (25), overpowered by feelings of loss and betrayal, the poet names the traitor—Blaise. Besong belittles Blaise in every way: he is a minion who has uprooted the great baobab tree under whose weight he can only crunch. His new position as president of Burkina Faso, after he stabbed his friend Sankara in the back, is compared to the blood-stained throne Macbeth in Shakespeare's *Macbeth* acquired after eliminating his host king, Duncan. Yes, Blaise Compaoré most treacherously had to let Sankara's blood flow for him to rule Burkina Faso. Blaise is dangerous, hence he is compared to a stalling crocodile. His bloody-crown is an uncomfortable heritage and so like the condemned biblical serpent, Blaise the crocodile, must crawl on the sandbank of state. Besong sees Compaoré, for murdering Sankara, as a nonentity when pitted against his victim; hence, Besong presents Compaoré as a mere object without brains, "carrion-brained mannequin," and a murderer of royalty, "liege-slaughterer" (25). Compaoré is a leader who promises his people nothing, that is why he is just a co-puppet under France where he owes his allegiance.

"After Mandela's Earth" (26), which is in three sections, laments the atmosphere of anomie that has been characteristic of many African countries. Besong paints a picture of a leader who enjoys himself with cake and tea while using the blood of citizens as a cleansing lotion for his fingers. He is like a mullah over all the land, whose hopeless reign only helps the citizens to die. This reign, like that in South Africa before Mandela's presidency, when blacks were discriminated against, discriminates against the minority Anglophone population. The Anglophone-Cameroonian compatriots are victims in their own country as even a liter of petrol is valued more than a liter of Anglophone blood (26). Hence, the predicament is an albatross about the neck of the Anglophone-Cameroonian, which they must carry "for centuries to come" since the poet does not seem to see a solution in sight.

Section ii (27) reveals the failure of Francophone dominance with opaque columns of dung rising up everywhere as they continue clinging to worthless counsels from advisers whose success story is the likes of the embarrassing Jean Bedel Bokassa of Central African Republic. It was he, while as leader of his country and a French puppet, who, in spite of the poverty in his Central African Republic nation, in a most expensive ceremony full of pomp and pageantry, declared himself an emperor in the twentieth century in the tradition of dead French emperors. There was also Houphoet-Boigny and his folly of a Yamoussoukro Basilica. This was a president who was so rich his citizens did not know he had such wealth until shortly before his death then he thought he could bribe God and so built, arguably, the best Catholic

Church structure in the world in a location surrounded by so much poverty and suffering. Pope John Paul II agreed to inaugurate the super structure only on condition that schools and other facilities to benefit the poor were built around the Basilica first.

Section iii (27) declares that with these characteristic blunders by Africa's leadership, not even a god might be able "to give judgment / in these matters" (28). As a last jibe at African leadership, the poet remembers the death of a school kid at the hands of a so-called officer of the law in the presence of the highest provincial authorities. What decadence and despair, the poet seems to be lamenting.

Besong's next poem "Eve of An Apocalypse" (29) is dedicated to the poet's friend, Nol Alembong, who is himself a poet and critic. In it, Besong presents members of Cameroon's National Assembly as some kind of priests whose sessions are meaningless as all they do is earn the money given them without having any work done.

In "Resurrection" (32), an ode, the poet does not only praise the patriot Samson Agbor Adeoye George as a person but goes on to compare the hanging of this patriot, in an effort to hide wrongdoings by those in positions of authority, to the crucifixion of Christ. Hence the poet sees the victim as a martyr. He declares proudly thus:

Samson Agbor Adeoye George
This is the threnody
I have woven for you; It is I, Bate Besong:
troubadour from a dehumanizing
regime. (33)

"State of Our Union" i and ii are addressed to Peter Essoka, an Anglophone-Cameroonian who was at the time a senior journalist and anchor person for the Cameroon government owned and managed radio and television corporation (CRTV). Peter Essoka's was usually the over voice translating into English each time the president of Cameroon addressed the nation. In this poem, which addresses the state of Cameroon's high jacked federation, the union of two states, East and West Cameroon, Besong exposes the embarrassing predicament of the union as the nation's national head is bent in shame, need, and disillusionment. In this poem, Besong does

63

not only accuse Peter Essoka of being the government's propagandist, he questions what this respected journalist thought he was doing playing pro-government propagandist even as the union stunk and still stinks. By comparing Essoka to Goebbels, one of Hitler's closest associates and propagandist, Besong makes his dissatisfaction towards Peter Essoka's lead role as the presidential voice-over obvious. In this poem full of agrarian images, Besong captures the plight of Cameroon today: a nation which because of its socio-political inefficiency, like a giant guinea-corn stalk, is unable to hold up its head. The nation's head is bent now like that of a criminal waiting to die by the guillotine. Besong's image is certainly revealing. By using the guillotine, a reputed French weapon of the Robespierrean manipulated French Revolution, is Besong insinuating, given the existing political link between France and Cameroon that the former is responsible for Cameroon's ultimate death, her collapse as a nation? The poet thinks of how the nation can be saved; he observes, however, that the road to redemption is full of tribulations. Conscious of our difficulties, the poet invokes the god Ekpiinon to help us during this hour of need (34).

In "State of Our Union" ii (35), Besong zeroes in on the president of the nation himself whom he qualifies as the "prime iguana" (35) before accusing him of mismanaging the nation into a state of decay, even as he decries and compares Biya's bla-bla of a "renouveau" (new deal) political doctrine to a passenger in a Cameroon Airline's plane, a symbol of the nation, "about to crash" (36). What premonition, mindful of the fact that the national air Travel Company, like much else in the nation under Biya, has crashed leaving Cameroon without a national airlines. In his fury, Besong sees the president as a "cruel" and "useless peacock" who is never in his depraved country; an absentee landlord so to say.

"Prison Blues" Section i (37), amounts to an effort at recapturing the poet's experience in detention. Like the grey walls of such cell blocks, even the pervading air is described as grey and punctuated only by the bloody torture as even the overseeing official is "in a suit of grey" (37). The poet sees the grey prison cells and their dampness as a cyclone barricading the voices of the detainees from getting across (37). The existing torture, the monstrosity of the tormentors, and consequential bloody nature of the cells, are facts communicated which qualify the detention unit as a veritable human abattoir operated by "cannibal militaire" (37). This official was so skilled at what he did to detainees such that one would have thought he pulled his beastly deeds from a torture manual. The result is that the poet saw these torturers as belonging to a special group of human beings "the beau monde / of that octopan / jubilee" (37). The monstrosities of these personages are such that Besong compares the prison officials to a "gargoyle of leviathan proportions" (37); hence, with his stripes on, or maybe his bellowing at detainees, Besong's "gulag" of a detention cell shook. Besong complains about the drowsy nature of the completely sealed cells which like catacombs bored the detainees, thus transforming them into victims of the biblical Lazarus' pestilential disease.

Section ii (38) begins with the poet decrying the fact that the leaders of the nation have not been messiahs for "Messiahs do not gather / conches of thorns / for a bacchae"; in other words, messiahs do not enjoy causing pain and discomfort—torture—while enjoying and celebrating it. Instead these leaders have been minions who fell short of what they were supposed to be doing. Accordingly, Besong considers the administrative machinery under Biya, the monsters, "cannibal *militaire*" (37) manning detention units especially, as filth, dung, quisling functionaries, deranged insomniacs. They are masters of the art of terror with thong-glued calendars or private entries that reveal the horrible deeds they have orchestrated, all leading to deaths from torture of confessed prodigals in jails. Besong laments further the plight of the detainees, victims of "'New' Deal demonolatory" (38), whereas the perpetrators of such slaughter houses are members who amount to nothing more than "the hydraulics of terror" (38), ghouls, with the love for cadavers. Hence their outstanding achievement—the torture of political detainees until death—has caused them to be associated with the biblical killing fields with numerous bones of their victims as their "thong-glued / calendars register / gaudier golgothas / for sanctuaries..." (38). In the last stanza of the section, Besong warns that the tide someday will turn and the mad perpetrators of such a system shall turn prodigals, begging for forgiveness from behind bars.

In Section iii (39), Besong reflects briefly on the political concerns of these detainees, which have transformed them into guinea-pigs of the regime's torture chambers-cum-laboratories managed by human beings turned monsters, cannibals, and lunatics by their hideous deeds to other human beings, to the point that "human gore" is their "porridge" (39). In this endroit, he considers himself above all else present—the iguanas for officials and the other detainees, for he sees himself as a "lonely eagle" (39) out of whom rebel convictions are to be flushed through the use of torture. He also thinks of the elimination of empty praise parades, typical of sycophants that shower praises on this failed leader. He talks about Baden-Baden where, while neglecting his native soil this unpatriotic leader has stashed away the nation's stolen wealth in secret bank accounts so high they can compare only to the highest mountain in Africa, Kilimanjaro and of a decree signed from Baden-Baden which is known to be Biya's "Beatship" permanent haunt. From here, the decree warranted all the torture experts of the regime,

> Djinns, lunatic-butchers
> toe-breakers, anthropophagi,
> Iguanas
> whose porridge
> is human gore
>
> vagabonds bereft
> of mind, zonked
>
> Scallywags in the employ of that carousing
> evolue of another
> Kangaroo Traoreian
> Swagger.   (39)

to extract by all means this rebel's radical faith from him.

Typical of his style, Besong's poetic consciousness suddenly jumps to Mali where General Moussa Traore, another *évoloué* [6] was wreaking havoc against his own people. Besong is possibly referring to the student leader, Abdoul Karim Camara a.k.a "Cabral," like Besong himself, who, arrested after a student uprising in 1980, died from torture at the hands of Traore's Gestapo when he declares:

> They were to wrung
> from him his rebel faith:
> a lonely eagle

chained behind bars. (39)

Section iv (40) is a quick description of one of the cells possibly, with iron grills that are used to hem in detainees. The conditions of the units are like barouches occupied by people that have been reduced to mere shadows of themselves by torture. Even then, torture continues causing tremors in the detention units in which prisoners now reduced to mere silhouettes are almost choking due to the asphyxiating quality of the cells.

In section v (41), Besong denies these monstrous leaders the chances of ever passing for messiahs of their peoples as he reaffirms the view that their terrible deeds are unbefitting of messiahs. According to Besong, the deeds of messiahs are transparent and beneficiary to society as they, for example, would "not gather conches of thorns for a bacchae." (41). He affirms that hollow deeds are by dwarfish dictators who need to blow up their shrunken images: only minions do the impossible, "gathering figs of thistles" (41) to give seeming value to their meaningless and equally worthless lives.

In Prison Blues vi (42), the poet explores the state of the mind in detention—a usually dangerous state for the human mind as the detention of most ideologues is intentionally designed to destroy their minds. As a result of detention, the jarring conflict possibly within one mind as it battles with itself over ideas, or that of two different minds which leads to disagreement, we end up holding in things instead of venting things of great significance, "cyclopean realities" (42). Because one keeps these things within oneself, one can be compared to an eagle chained behind bars in the usually conflicting if not idiotic group mentality, "the alloy / of caravan / imbecility…" (42). And so the persona observes that to contain the dangers to a mind in detention, such a mind, "A lonely eagle / chained behind bars" (42) has to create strange and sometimes even, foolish thought patterns (realities) to occupy and busy the mind which if unrestrained, can go round the bend. The poet sees himself as a "lone eagle chained behind bars" (42), caught in the folly of a political caravan reduced to nonsense by group stupidity – "caravan imbecility" (42).

In "Prison Blues vii" (43), one encounters the same pervading tone of ire and disgust. Besong thinks of leaders who torture dissenting citizens to death. Again, section vii is presented in three parts like speeches from three different birds: Ibis, Flamingo, and Eagle. There is not much association between the birds other than that the Ibis and the Flamingo are tall or long-legged birds while the eagle is noted for its power and high flying altitude. He laments the fact that because of tribalism such "Excellencies" (43), "Carcase-on-High" (43), are maintained in power even if by means of blood transfusions (international aid) as such leaders are usually physically as unhealthy as the socio-economic state they maintain in their countries. Accordingly, at a glance, this section reveals Ibis informing us how the physical health of such a head of state is maintained through blood transfusions which nurture this "debauched Carcase-on-High" (43). While his physical health is being taken care of through blood transfusions, his government is kept healthy, that is maintained in power by "Cannibal phylons" (43) the confusions he sets at large which culminates in tribes eating each other figuratively and literally through tribal rivalries generated by the philosophy of divide and rule. Flamingo then talks of the torture chambers, of slabs void of deodorants, where the harvests were the remains of tortured citizens, "…a scarlet / Harvest iodoformed / in terror" (43). It would seem that this extraordinary detainee becomes stronger as he evolves, developing from a wading Ibis through the wading yet taller Flamingo into the powerful and soaring Eagle ready to dive down with fatal blows for its targets. A Frankincense of a torturer scrubs the underground torture chamber—the crypt—freeing the cell of any evidence of the battered out gore of citizens who apologized for their deeds against the government but were bludgeoned to death still, hence the "prodigal gore" (43), remains of "clotted / marrow, / And bone" (43). The poem ends on the emphatic note reminiscent of a Catholic prayer that things have not changed in spite of the brouhaha of a new regime and a new approach to governance: "*As it was in the beginning….*" (43).

Once more, in *Obasinjom Warrior With Poems After Detention*, Besong explores the plight of mankind, especially in his native Cameroon, before looking at select individuals' personal experiences in jail. In this volume, he remains the conscience and voice of his abused and exploited society.

Disgrace: Autobiographical Narcissus and Emanya-nkpe Collected Poems (2007)

In his last collection of poems and the last book he published, *Disgrace: Autobiographical Narcissus and Emanya-nkpe Collected Poems (Disgrace)*, which was launched the eve of his death, one is immediately struck by Besong's rather gloomy title and so one cannot hesitate questioning if Besong was already giving up his fight with the nonsense concretized by Cameroon of his days and so was left with nothing but to reminisce and relish his own dreams which he could not realize for his country in the manner of Narcissus or what? But then, this suspicion is allayed when it is realized that Besong was only metamorphosing from the Obasinjom in to Emanya-nkpe as suggested by the title of the second section of this collection: The Obasinjom had completed its task of identifying the "witches and wizards" of this leadership coven of a nation, Cameroon, and it is now time for them to be dealt with accordingly. The relevance and authenticity of this interpretation is realized when Joyce Ashuntantang's comments on the Ekpe society are considered:

> Ekpe is a secret society (leopard Society [sic]) in the Ejagham and Bayang culture open only to men. Central to this society are two masquerades, the Ebongu and Emanyangkpe. While Ebongu is calm and two of them may appear together, Emanyangkpe is usually alone and always appears ferocious in its full-body netted costume. Emanyangkpe is a distraught masquerade which does not hesitate to use the cane which is always in his hand to whip those who are not on his side. (121)

The implication here then is that Besong is using the poems in this collection in the fashion of a whip and in the hands of his new spiritual form— Emanya-nkpe. In this volume then, Besong is the meeting point of two powerful cleansing spirits: the old Obasinjom which continues to identify the corrupt (witches) of the nation, and Emanya-nkpe which punishes them by exposing (whipping) them virtually. Consequently Beban Sammy Chumbow observes of Besong's matter and manner in the "Foreword" to this volume:

> ...this collection of poems is yet another bombshell. Indeed, the poems in this book individually and collectively, are loaded with tons of emotions, crafted in a rich array of stylistic devices heavily charged with enough semantic venom to have the impact of a plastic bomb
>
> The first part of the sixteen autobiographical poems aptly titled *Disgrace* and borne out of the poet's experiences with university life and the university system, constitutes a series of tabloids in which BB

lambasts, castigates and stigmatizes all and sundry responsible for the sorry state of the university and the university system from 'autocratic' leaders, through 'collaborators,' 'post mortem intellectuals' and 'comatose professors' to 'dead lecturers' who 'organize the ignorance of the Faculty and pervert and muzzle discourse.' (viii)

It is 2007, and the world of Besong's concern, Cameroon especially, has not changed under the same disillusioning leadership Besong celebrated at its dawn. There was nothing to celebrate or help alleviate the brazenness and flavor of insolence characteristic of Besong's tone and diction in the earlier decades; hence the narcissistic bent in his title. Besong has, all his life, stared at the Cameroonian nation, a true reflection of himself with all the travails and sadness like the mythical Narcissus, to no avail. In spite of all he has done conscientizing the people in an effort to improve upon the tormented national portrait and essence which is a reflection of his, it is all in vain. Besong then, in desperation, prophetically announces his impending death and posthumous transformation into a narcissus.

Disgrace is in two parts. The first part is titled "Disgrace: Autobiographical Narcissus," and the second part "Emanya-nkpe Collected Poems." It is remarkable that Besong opens the first part with an interesting quotation with a biblical tenor and supposedly from "The Letter of Jeremiah, 47." But there seems to be no such biblical verse, and Innocent Futcha confirms this for he observes: "This seeming quote from the Bible is nowhere to be found in the book of Jeremiah" ("Jeremiah in Cameroon"). This notwithstanding, the quotation is a summation of Besong's train of thought in this first section of the volume: "These people leave nothing but deceit and disgrace as an inheritance for future generations" (2). What a shame! What disillusionment! It is as if Besong's frustration and existential angst have peaked and plateaued to no avail as there seems to be nothing rewarding he can show after all these years of battling the forces of evil surrounding him. By creating such a verse with an overwhelming biblical accent, Besong makes his role as a Cameroonian scholar, poet and playwright sacred. Of Jeremiah the Bible reveals:

The prophet's own inner conflicts were as dramatic as the events in which he played a part. Of an affectionate and gentle disposition, he was

70

nevertheless called 'to uproot and to knock down, to destroy and to overthrow', and disaster was the keynote of his message. This man of peace was for ever at war, with his own people, with kings, priests, false prophets, the nation itself, 'a man of strife and of dissension for the whole country'. He was tortured by a duty he could not refuse. ("Introduction to the Prophets 1171")

In this light, Besong sees himself in the guise of a Jeremiah, a prophet in other words, on a mission from God to fight with and purge his society of the ills tormenting it; hence, the seemingly distressing life he had since he was always at war with himself or with society.

In the first poem "The Foolishness of Trusting in Tribal Gods" (3), it is obvious Besong is ill at ease with an authority figure whom he qualifies as a tribal god. This person he considers a god, must have been from the same locality where this institution this god is heading is located, and so the idea of trusting in tribal gods: a god who belongs to the tribe so to say. One could have thought this powerful figure is the head of state, but then one is redirected when one learns that the poet's daughters, instead, have suffered as a result of his activities: "My daughters have endured the suffering / that should have been mine / the pain that I should have borne..." (3). If it were the government targeting Besong this way, then his entire family and not just his daughters would have been victimized. One cannot help thinking then that the poet is referring to the University of Buea hierarchy where Besong was a professor and possibly his daughters, students within the same institution. The poet laments the fact that this authority figure has increased his pain and frustration instead of bringing him healing from the wounds and pain he had been experiencing from the onset when he was underemployed and rejected by the university system and later on, after he earned his Ph.D.

In Section ii (4) of the poem, Besong laments the consequences of sycophancy as he points out the damaging effects it has had on the subordinates of this administrator turned tribal god. Even the god's subordinates are themselves autocrats who have been reduced into deaf, blind, and unthinking morons who judge by appearance even as all they seem well equipped to do is "roar, over allocation money" (4). The tendencies of these individuals the poet describes as evil are compared to the waves of the

71

restless sea as every activity of theirs, like the waves of the sea, brings in only "filth and muck" (4).

In section iii (4), in a rather sarcastic manner, the poet makes it obvious that he had never expected much from this tribal god of a leader and so this god should not bother or permit herself to feel any pain since it is only a fact that she had never been the one expected to bring about any change for good. The evil nature of this tribal god is such that she would "…cook a young he-goat / or heifer / in its mother's milk / so you and regime collaborators will / receive the Legion of Honour / from the local party Corruptibility" (4). Nothing brings out the evil in the setting like the fact that this god is willing to sacrifice even the young and innocent for her own pleasure and success. One cannot help believing the poet is referring to the Vice Chancellor of the University of Buea at the time, a woman who seems to have established a reputation as an authoritarian hence in spite of the masculine noun "god" I continue using the feminine pronoun "she." Besong might have been too blunt had he written of tribal goddesses. Piet Konings, in the same light, writes about this woman's handling of a phase of the University of Buea Students' strike in 2005:

> Dr. Njeuma, who in the meantime had returned to Cameroon, bluntly refused to enter into dialogue with the UBSU leaders. She declined to recognize the newly revived UBSU….
>
> In reaction to the VC's authoritarian behavior and continued police violence, the UBSU leadership added some new demands calling for the immediate replacement and transfer of the long-serving VC…. (116)

It becomes obvious then that VC Njeuma is one of the tribal gods Besong is referring to; consequently, in his notes Besong writes as if to emphasize the identity of the god he is referring to: "*Mbamba* Rebecca N. a mediocre instructor, in that house of fear and mass betrayals, would, (sic) be transformed into a veritable werewolf and archetypal administration informer" (117). Does the "N" after *Mbamba* Rebecca's name relate in any way to the "N" after Vice Chancellor Dorothy Njeuma's last name? This is possibly the reason why *Mbamba* Rebecca degenerated into an informant of the administration. Whatever the case, in spite of this god's contentment in her despotic ways, the poet warns: "When the clouds are full, / It rains" (5), before going on to show his determination to fight this evil when he urges the god to "Bring the best arguments you have" (5).

In Section iv (5), the poet continues his regret that when he looks into those sycophants gamboling around this god, none of them is such that could bring about positive change in society; accordingly, he points out that nothing awaits this god but trouble and terrifying darkness along the corrupt path into which she is being driven.

In "Post-mortem Intellectual" (6), the poet seems to be addressing another individual this time, one who had given him hope that he would fight and bring about change only for him to be disillusioned. He points out that from the culprit's present itinerary, one cannot tell how busy he had been, by day and by night, doing all to fight against those in power who have transformed the nation into game to be hunted and eaten. His present ways, of course, are contrary to what was expected of this intellectual mindful of the frescoes he had engraved earlier on. It was believed that he would, in this light, continue to soar in the manner of Nelson Mandela because of his devotion to the cause of the oppressed and exploited lot of society:

> We thought you would always soar into the sky like a
> Mandelan meteor, exalt, your
> luminosity unto the Spartans risking their
> lives on a daily basis to give voice
> to those on the margin. (6)

Alas, Besong is disappointed with the culprit's new trend. As a result, the poet reiterates the guiding principles of those struggling if they must succeed in the end. To him:

> Bloodfounts of injustice can be vanquished only by the
> Lantern of fearlessness and torrential down-
> pour of outspokenness. (6)

The poet then goes on to lament the fact that this once upon a time heroic intellectual that was considered the voice of the voiceless in society has allowed himself to become ineffective by succumbing to blackmail.

73

In "Collaborator" (7), the poet's anger at someone considered a traitor is sustained by such outrageously vitriolic language hardly before used by Besong in his poems. Until this poem, only his plays carried such shockingly repulsive diction as a way of establishing his point. Of such virtually taboo language Kingsley Widmer writes:

'Forbidden' language, used more or less seriously, serves not only to shock but to re-emphasize natural functions and exalt 'common' awareness. Done with skill, curses can provide defiant prayers, obscenity a poetry of outrage. Indeed, a literary rebel whose language does not achieve some such sort of violation in itself is neither very poetic nor very rebellious. (5)

In this poem, like in all his works, Besong then is the true literary rebel as his disgust at this traitor is spelled out in a most caustic and equally shocking manner. He confirms that the lady is bedecked in silver and gold, dressed in her "Rdpc" party uniform tailored in the fashion of a "kabba ngondo," [7] even then she is nothing, just a worthless part of the synagogue belonging to "that tribe-crazed god;" possibly the head of state who is indeed tribe-crazed in the sense that he has surrounded himself with his tribesmen to whom he has given high offices in government, while pitting those of other rivaling tribes at each other's throats. Besong then comes up with a unique existentialist perspective on life by declaring that no one should ask why people are the way they are for everything has its purpose, before going on to affirm:

You cannot offer mercy or give help to widows and
orphans.
you cannot restore sight to the blind or
save anyone in distress. (7)

Then he accuses the traitor of enjoying her benefits in life alone, typical of those belonging to a political party that has almost transformed itself into a sect, hence her worthless curriculum vitae which is embroidered by "incantations" in the likes of "*le Président de la république par interim*," (7) honors from a worthless political leader instead of titles of academic papers and achievements. The outcome is her woeful ineptitude as a scholar but a distinguished bootlicker for political minions like this tribe-crazed god of a party chief. To Besong, who is completely disillusioned with this collaborator, she is nothing; she is repulsive and "no more than dung" (7) left without any honor like the stooge that she is, living in constant disgrace: "A stooge has no honour. He lives / in constant disgrace" (8).

In "The Mouth of Liars will be Shut" i (9), Besong is as mordant as ever, with his rage directed towards a female character who did not only rejoice at the poet's woes for certain, but was prejudiced in her dealings with people. Consequently, the poet guarantees her that her evil deeds will destroy her and no presidential decree will be able to rescue her from such destined destruction conjured into her fate by her own atrocities. Stanza two further assures the guilty female that her belief in and use of fortune tellers and the practice of necromancy in an effort to control the events of her life will only bring her sorrow. The poet alerts the woman to the fact that she is doomed and she brought this fate upon herself because the evil she has done unto others will be visited upon her and her children and grandchildren even to the fourth generation:

You are doomed,
and you have brought this upon yourself.
What you have done to others will be done to your
children, and
grand-children to the third and fourth
generation. (9)

What harsh words, reminiscent of the self-inflicted curse of the Scribes and the Pharisees when for no just cause they anxiously pursued the crucifixion of Our Lord Jesus Christ. However, beyond just stating facts about this feminine gorgon and her atrocities, Besong's words segue into a prayer, if not a curse against his enemy, after the manner of the Psalmist. From these lines, one gets the picture of an administrator who is without pity in her conviction of serving a corrupt government because of how it benefits her, so much so that she will not hesitate doing anything to rid herself of anyone or anything that is in the path of her ambitions. The final damnation of the woman concerned is the knowledge given her that death awaits her, but not before she has gone mental and stripped naked in public view. Hence, people would see her humbled and shamed after all her wicked deeds.

In section ii (9), Besong's indignation, which is even more astringent and volcanic, is directed towards those who practice weird cabalistic rites just to remain in office. They have become so powerful such that they have hijacked the wealth of the nation here symbolized by "the Bakassi oil wells" (9) and made it party property; the party of flames and this is none other than the Cameroon People's Democratic Movement (CPDM) with the burning flame as the core of its party logo. The monstrosity of the party along with its infernal activities is captured in these lines:

> Party of infernal Ophidians
> Galagoes, Prostitutes, business-
> Men of the Gog and
> Magog world. (9)

These party personages are compared to hellish creatures, "infernal ophidians" (9), their evil nature is such that it is now obvious in their appearances as is the case with the hellish monsters, forces of evil, "Men of the Gog and Magog world," (9) determined to do war against that which is just. This is a bunch that does impossible things, besides the disrespect it shows the diplomatic services in the nation. The lead offender continues to harass all those in the system, distorting their dreams and plans by a policy of divide and rule, "divide we ride" (10). Then the poet goes on to show how by vile means practiced by those of this party and her government, things thought impossible are made to happen: like people going against their own convictions, with victims like the terrified "trade unionists" (the leader of SYNES) and the "ambushed and tattooed" "Maxist whore" (10). It is all about how the powerful, who are corrupt, can do that which would be considered impossible by normal human beings just because they are powerful and want to remain in power.

In Section iii (10), the poet continues the barrage of attacks on this leader whose officer seemed to have ordered an end to the "F-AFFAIR" by an over display of force, rather than diplomacy, on campus. The image of threshing "Osama bin Laden mountains of campus / insurrection" (10) and destroying Aymal al Zahwari is intended to expose the waste of valuable assets in a meaningless witch hunt on campus. This was a particularly effective image at the time because so much had been put into the search for Bin Laden by the US government, including the heavy bombardment of mountains considered possible hideouts, without results. Even then, this leader's deeds are such that interestingly and typical of the system in place, she is honored instead despite being a swindler.

In Section iv (11), the poet continues his attack on this leader for appointing a "moron" to lead a column of destructive forces whose only line of attack was by writing graffiti backed by cultic forces. To the poet, these characters are nothing other than jackasses who waste time blabbering about nonsense after intoxicating themselves with powerful locally brewed alcoholic portions: *"See how they chatter after jugs of akpateshie / and matango"* (11). He then ridicules this culprit's reliance on fortune-tellers and gossips who reassure her that nothing can go wrong with her.

Section v (11) warns her that when the tide will turn, she would have learned to be afraid of high places in society. Things would be so bad she would not be able to savor the pleasures of the political party patronizing her. She would end up humiliated, "stripped naked" (12) as everything about her would be crashing, from her symbols of recognition by her political party, which party is giving her all the horns to treat others the way she is doing, to her questionable wealth believed to be plantation workers' money she has stolen. All will come crashing, unable to buoy her in her position of power and influence hitherto sustained by corrupt practices. She will end up a total wreck.

The next poem, "The Playwright & the Campus Giants" (13) is, as usual, overflowing with Besong's vituperation. The title in itself is very revealing; these are giants only on campus and hardly anywhere else. Then the poet goes on to tell what manner of human beings scholars are: they are wise and always fair and the nature of their discourse brilliant. Then, assuming the royal "we" (13), the poet points out that his likes are never bothered by academic dwarfs masquerading as scholars, even with their involvement in demonic and fraudulent activities:

We are not worried
on account of the bureaucratic
obfuscators; sorcerers of

Staff Development Grants; necromancers
of a thousand Mission Warrants
who gloat over the erasure of
memory. (13)

Again, the distinguished and true academic is not bothered by those who use false scales to value faculty, possibly for their promotion, those who plot against and hate him. He is confident that they are hollow and they would weigh nothing if put on a scale; they would be "lighter than the ostrich's feather" (13).

In Section ii (13), the poet points out that he does not regret the death of those who scheme and plot to destroy others. He reassures others that falsehood may thrive for long, even on this campus, the history of which has been written in blood, but in the end it will fail, and in the process bringing down with it the perpetrators like some Vice-Chancellors and Registrars who have fallen and are unable to rise. Section iii (14) reveals a poet acknowledging the rather challenging nature of his life so far, even as he affirms his lot as that reserved for those who fearlessly profess the truth:

Test and trials come to us all in life,
Playwrights are those who suffer
persecution
for their bold testimony
a pearl receives its luster from
the grating bits of sand. (14)

In a rather ironic yet mordant manner, the poet's persona, the playwright, damns this heavily present "You," possibly then Vice Chancellor of his university, in the last couple of poems, not only for her dubious ways of dealing with things even as trite as "petrol bonds" but because she is "heavy-footed" (14). He is disgusted by the fact that this individual, rather opaque in her dealings, was convinced that forever she would be in the good books of an equally corrupt government which will go on maintaining her in office by one decree after another because of her terrible deeds in service to the government which includes betraying her colleagues in exchange for a worthless medal of recognition like Meka, Ferdinand Oyono's main character in *The Old Man and the Medal*. It is for this reason that the playwright sees her as a traitor who would soon die, having degenerated to the level of a mule to be controlled by political baits "bit and bridle" (15). He assures her that spineless administrators like her would soon die out, but playwrights and scholars will possess the hitherto tumultuous campus "and enjoy intellectual prosperity / & peace" (15).

In "The Professor" (16), the poet marvels at the fact that a politically biased scholar and servant of an unpopular regime is the one serving in the professorial chair of an academic institution. The impact of this is only felt when it is understood that being politically biased to a party in Africa is not the same as elsewhere mindful of the hatred, viciousness, and vindictiveness that those in the ruling party display towards those who belong to the opposition. At once, because the government is theirs, they assume the nation and all its resources are also theirs and so they see the opposition as enemies trying to deprive them of their livelihood, kill them in other words, since the opposition is out to get them out of power, which power they abuse to the fullest. With this, one can now understand the poet's troubled disposition towards this politically biased and pro-government party official serving in a professorial position. Such an individual immediately begins hunting down colleagues, who usually are of the opposition and against the government and the ruling party, without any qualms, convinced he is doing the right thing since he is simply protecting himself by safeguarding his office. The poet points out that whereas this individual-in-point's smooth talk may buy over the uninformed, the truth is that in his heart there is hatred and his flattering words are loaded with deadly deceit. Convinced of the wicked and devious ways of this chair person, the protagonist can only wish that his fame be short-lived. Without any obvious evidence that the poet is referring to his female chancellor with whom he has been fighting in earlier poems, I will use the male pronoun for this professor since Besong could easily be referring to another professor who came in after her, or who is the chair of a department this time. This is especially the case when it is recalled that Besong had denounced her as a failed scholar with mainly political instead of academic accolades in her résumé. One thing is certain, Besong's fight is still with a political puppet heading a university or some kind of a unit for he writes:

Of what use is a politically
partisan mameluke
in a professorial chair?

Of what use is an
Establishment mole
With an academic's scepter? (emphasis mine 16)

Academic scepters are traditionally carried at the head of academic
processions and signify the authority of the faculty of the university
associated with it. Hence the idea of some top official and supposedly
academic.

Section ii (16) reveals further how this Professor wields all under his
spell: by "...organizing the ignorance / Of the Faculty" (16), and by
preventing effective discourse from taking place to the point of being
determined to choke the revitalizing spirit on campus. Like a true mameluke,
he stabs with his academic scimitar and pierces with his administrative bows
even as the professor brags about his or her determination to stifle the
research zeal on campus by withholding fellowships, and if need be, sending
the subversive scholars to prison. Having established the manner of person
and scholar Professor is, the poet is left with no other choice than to vomit
all manner of bad wishes on the Professor:

Professor,
May your name, now,
Like a broken-down fence, never
Be forgotten

May you go down
Alive, into the
Sanctuary of the dead.

May your jacaranda and nym
Your sun and moon
Always stand still
In your carrion sky. (17)

"Dinning with the Devil" (18) reveals the treatment meted out to a traitor of the people by the People's Army—a mob. He had been suspected of being a traitor and established as an irritating politician spreading unfortunate tribal sentiments and was about to be fired from the party. However, they made the mistake of just brushing him aside as not of any threat to the people until he betrayed himself and his name was published on "the casualty list of social miscreants; clones who rig and usurp the people's votes" (18). As a result, right in front of television cameras, "The mob placed a used tyre around his neck, and set / him ablaze" (19).

In "Elegy for Two Students Assassinated on Campus" i (20), the poet decries the fact that although theoretically the University of Buea congregation condemns violence on unarmed students, many members of the university administration condone violence and are willing to kill for an office. Yet, on convocation day, these hypocrites are the ones who are about trying to convince others of their love for peace and order—civil disobedience—in the manner of Mahatma Gandhi, Martin Luther King, and Madiba Nelson Mandela. That these things are being done by so called academics shocks the poet as he declares, how academics have now, regrettably, earned a terrible "recognition as ogres and mutants of terror" (20). The poet goes on to warn and observe emphatically in the following stanzas respectively:

When the fire of martyrdom is
set ablaze
it can smoulder for centuries.
A plague gave this hatred
an excuse
& the hatred gave the fear
of the plague
a focus (Poet's emphasis 21)

In Section ii (21), the poet grieves over the fact that women who should otherwise be noble leaders, have transformed themselves into "matriarchs of terror" (21), altering a university campus into a playground for phylons to perpetrate "racism and cultural contempt" (21) against those struggling for freedom. Alas, he points out that when the students shall know the facts and become aware of their rights, it will be the end of this reigning totalitarian at the head of an academic institution. He echoes with certainty his conviction about her impending fate: *"Politbureau matriarchs will not always have the last laugh!"* (poet's emphasis 21).

In "Appointments in UB" (22), the poet is again at war with the practices on campus. And so in Section i (22), he talks of university personalities who have degenerated into mere numbers in a francophone suffocating environment, a "Gaullist galley" (22) as such, with reversed values. He reiterates the fact that he is talking of yesterday's undesirable lecturers still suffering from the scars of the occult warfare they practice against each other on a campus built by stifling the voices of dissent, a campus where totalitarianism is in control considering that "the sword and / the bullet" (22) are of incredibly powerful influence even as the memories of those slain on campus are being deeply hurt and wiped out by the buffoonery that amounted to the Abouem à Tchoyi Commission and its findings to cite an example.[8]

In Section ii (22), the poet continues to mourn for student martyrs whose premature death and burial was as a result of a tricky Wonganga village mentality displayed by "the zoologist-assassin / with her predatory / stupidity" (23); again an attack on then Vice Chancellor at the time, Dr. Dorothy Njeuma. As a result, the poet hopes all can now arise against the university's most astringent leader who treated her subordinates like animals—the zoologists assassin with her predatory stupidity. To the poet she is an *"unparalleled monster, la terreur"* (23).

In Section iii (23), as is the case with virtually all the preceding poems in this volume, the world is Besong's university campus at Buea. Accordingly, with the same pervading spirit of bitterness and dissatisfaction at the goings-on on campus, the poet contrasts the disposition of today's trade union leaders which is unlike those of the past whose lives were governed by materialism, along with a slave consciousness that has been fashioned by idiots, unprincipled members of society like those peopling Wole Soyinka's tragic satire *Mad Men and Specialists* (1971). It is no wonder the campus air is already polluted by excess phlegm generated by the pervading ignominy spawned by the attitude of the mad men and specialist parading campus corridors. Hence, the poet affirms that he is writing against freakish leaders parading themselves as messiahs, so that his (poet's) likes may rise against them and their foul and greedy ways. He is writing against yesterday's campus philosophers who are now obsolete because of their heinous ways and as a result are limited to their ostracized offices that are now reduced to cells, virtually, with tormented memories and material belongings which can bring them no joy as they cannot hold conversations with these lifeless things. Hence the ephemeralness of material possessions for which many are willing not only to kill but also to destroy their own integrity. Besong hopes his words would function as obituaries sealing the fate of such nescient academicians whose presence on campus transformed what was supposed to be a warm academic environment with academic gladiators engaging in worthwhile dialectical exchanges into a "morbid refrigerator" (24); these nescient academicians are therefore compared to "Dead cormorants off / A kapok tree." (24).

In "Why We Laugh at Politicians and Give them Names" (25), Besong is warning against betrayal. He points out that in a uselessly unproductive democracy like Cameroon's "White Collar Delinquent Democracy" (25), in which power is monopolized by those who got it the wrong way, to begin with, and use the state apparatus the wrong way, a system whereby election results are influenced by the French, "won / under the *ogogoro* of / Monsieur Chirac's distillery" (25), many Southern Cameroonians have been misled and are trying to do the impossible. This tendency is represented by the idea of trying to "count the raindrops or / the sand along / Victoria beach" (25). They refuse to change. For that reason, the poet warns that worthless armies along with self-appointed military brass will soon realize their own valuelessness as "everything made by racketeers of power / will decay and perish, along / with the thieves who made it" (25). He points out that those who build a nation and cause it to progress are transparent people for they "do not follow the example of the *kokoro* insect / feeding fat / under the leaf of / the vegetable" (25-26). The poet goes on to warn that there are certain wrongs that can be forgiven and mended, but to betray one's confidence is a hopeless situation; just as thieves must suffer disgrace so too traitors— mutants—will be severely condemned (26). The poet then goes on to present certain inconsistencies in the tide of events and possibly the attendant emptiness of certain politically motivated deeds that are predisposed. For example, he ridicules the idea of Re-unification which he ties to the death of The Lord Mayor of the Ewondos:

> The Lord Mayor of the Ewondos died, and
> Re-unification shone like a
> precious stone, like a jasper, clear as crystal. (26)

Besong then goes on to point out that "Injustice, arrogance and wealth cause federations / to fall from / power" (26), but then "others rise to take / their place" (26). Lastly he points out that if the Sultan of "Go-if-you-don't like it-here" (26) is despised while he is on the throne then how much more will the corpse of Ahmadou Ahidjo be humiliated because of the idea of re-unification.[9] In a rather prophetic voice, Besong then urges people not to ask questions about why things are the way they are, claiming that these questions will be answered at the right time, a rather passive stance for a writer as aggressive as Besong is in approach.

In "Confidence Placed in the Party Comes to Nothing" (27), the poet presents the predicament of a party devotee who used to be powerful in party circles such that whenever she went into places, distinguished guests and members of the party revered her. As a result, she went about affairs after the manner of a Secretary General of the Party Praesidium, fortified in her conviction and disposition by futurologists and others "in the firmament of power" (26) until she heard the bad news of having been relieved of her post during the 1: 00 clock news over the radio. Now, with her pride and power deflated, she is like a "badly hurriedly buried corpse; whose ambulant legs stick out from the Faculty cemetery…" (27). Summarily, this is a poem about a party devotee who put her trust in the political party to which she belonged, and it failed her when it took her off her position leaving her shocked, disturbed, and a laughable figure to those she oppressed once upon a time as a party stalwart; hence, the idea of the "badly hurriedly buried corpse" (27).

"Camouflage" (28) amounts to a word of advice about appearance and reality. The poet talks first of how the ruling political party transforms morons into undeserved royalty while abandoning patriotic and better qualified citizens who will not echo the party chorus. The effect on these unworthy princes is that they lose control over themselves as

Their minds now work like a
cartwheel going
round and round
circles. (28)

As such, when worthless governors whom the poet compares to armed
robbers hiding behind dark glasses shout out seemingly patriotic slogans
without the love for their country at heart, the poet consoles abused citizens
by urging them not to worry, for it is out of their own excesses as they
pretend to love the country that their demise will arise:

Don't worry
Gluttony has been the death of those
who make good appear evil, who

find fault with the
noblest actions

and plough
the ground to
sow seeds of
injustice. (28)

In the same vein, like the Psalmist to society with regards to the rich, the
poet urges that one should not be bothered by the success of a festering
carrion (25), for one does "not know what disaster awaits him" (29). The
poet goes on to use another portrait of disaster, that of Jean Bedel Bokassa,
the worthless, narcissistic clown of a twentieth century emperor of Central
African Republic, to rub in his point further. Such vermin portraying
themselves as people of substance cannot help their nature which ultimately
brings them destruction. Hence he points out that even when one suffers
humiliation, one should be patient for

Great things often have small
and humble beginnings; but they

survive, grow steadily, and
flower. (29)

In "The Mimic Academic Passes On" (30), Besong praises young student radicals who stood up against a system, within the university campus at Buea, which they could not condone. Besong is obviously proud to see the students are taking after him for he points out that they are the "eagles" of his "Critical Theory seminar class" (30). The professor representing the administration is described by Besong as a "bogeyman" (30) whose duplicity is such that he can only speak "through his throat," meaning inaudibly since he is not telling the truth. He is damned as being a friend to the leader of every Rapid Deployment Force so he can summon them on campus at will it would seem. Beyond his ideas, Besong risks committing *ad hominem* as he attacks even the professor's person as ugly, just like his ideas or ways of going about things. Besong is disgusted by the fact that these individuals are where they ought not to be—university administrative officers—as they are hand-picked puppets. The ugliness of the campus bogeyman is what endeared him to his boss, or else, I dare suggest, his better half, "the liege-hippopo" (30) did. The former is more likely as he and his likes are portrayed as "regime informants" (30), with ridiculously worthless positions in most cases:

Heads of Division of
Sports and Orchestra, Etat-
Major in otiose guffaw
Faculty officer in charge of Cafeteria
and other lean and withered wolves
of Inquisition who speak
only through

ORDERS FROM ABOVE
at Faculty Board Rooms. (30)

When supposed academics and role models at dialectics, like the manipulators these portrayed by the poet have degenerated into, just accept and pass on orders to their colleagues like waiters taking and repeating orders in a restaurant kitchen, it is certainly as disturbing as it is disgusting.

In Section ii (30), this particular campus bogeyman of a professor is still being jibed at: he is a "Clay-Pot Professor" because Besong does not hold him in high esteem. Besong considers him porous and without substance, hence he sees him as a professor who sows mediocrity in the minds of undergraduate students while assassinating young radicals, students of Amilcar Cabral's revolutionary ideology who, from an objective stance, revolted against all the politicking and mess going on on campus. A rather negative personage for an intellectual as not only does he tell lies, he destroys the potentially rewarding efforts of his colleagues also when they do a better job as professors: planting vineyards instead of straw like he does given his paucity:

> Whenever his peers sow
> the fields, and
> plant vineyards, which may
> yield fruits
> of increase; he will burst their
> ankles with fetters; the campus straw-man will lay their
> tendons with iron and hot
> thunderbolts. (31)

Section iii (31) continues to lambast this same professor by presenting him as being physically inept, for he reels and staggers all the time "like a / drunken whore" (31). He is equally intellectually retarded, for as much as he idolizes wealth and materialism, his ability to do effective research is slow and moronic like a beast of burden grazing:

> He has changed his research zeal into
> the similitude of an ox that
> eateth grass
> His idols are silver and gold; the work of
> men's hands. (31)

This explains why it is a worthless group of blind admirers, "A circus of sycophants" (31) who gave any meaning and security to his feeble scholarship by according him tenure. This "mimic academic speaks only / through his throat / to the gondola" (32), a boatload of lost souls answering to the supreme dictatorship of their female leader on campus—*iya mbamba*—even with all the occult practices thriving even during seminars. The poet denounces these as pointers to a new world that is uncertain.

In "Shame" (33), the poet heaps shame on the last vestiges of the geriatric politics of the Cameroon National Assembly. It is not surprising then that the poem begins almost with some kind of stage direction as if it is to be performed; "as in a dirge" (33). How else could the poet's mournful note be adequately portrayed? Not only has the nonsense that the National Assembly is been revealed but also the hopelessness of the entire regime in place. Hence the poet compares the handing over of the state to the present leader, by Ahmadou Ahidjo, as the placing of a carnation "on the coco-nut head of the Father of the Nation" (33). A disparaging remark which is in every way patronizing and condescending, especially the tone, as it reduces the head of state to a child, a truant who can be unflappably ridiculed thus: "with his coconut head" (33). A step further and the same nation-gift to the new president, since he did not campaign and win an election, is compared to "a gold ring affixed to a bush-pig's snout" (33) just like the worthlessness of the Foumban referendum is becoming obvious with the "lamp flickering out in the charnel" (33), with all the perpetrators—the founding fathers of the nation—dying out, even as everyone from Ahidjo to Biya was and is manipulating the terms on the whim.

The poet then goes on to talk about the likes of Gerard Emmanuel Ondo Ndong, former General Manager of the Special Council Support Fund (FEICOM), who was sentenced to prison for fifty years for stealing billions of CFA from FEICOM, which money he was supposed to use to render financial assistance to local councils. Accordingly, Besong points out that many such as Ndong are there who end up ruining their careers whereas unknown benefactors reap what is theirs. He ridicules these pilferers of public funds by comparing them to dogs that are doomed, like hunting dogs that fail to hear the hunter's whistle and so lose their way in the forest. These rogue-administrators, because of their avarice, fail to hear or identify warning signals as they thrive in their fraudulent activities until it is too late and they are nabbed and slammed in jail. The poet confirms that we have seen so much of this and heard of more striking examples even, of people who are too busy making money, pursuing honor and prestige, all ephemeral values with equally short-lived satisfaction. He points out that leaders like these fail to realize that they would be judged on the basis of the crowns accorded them by the suffering masses and not by the empty symbols of wealth they struggled to acquire while in power and holding the populace hostage at gun point. And then he moralizes in an uncharacteristic manner: "Statesmen who look straight ahead with honest / conviction; never hang / their heads in shame" (34). Besong points out that "A city is happy when honest people have good fortune, / and they are joyful" (34) when government delegates enjoying castles, in other words the wealth of the *"ennemies dans la maison"* [10] die.

Still damning the corrupt leaders of the nation, even within the National Assembly, Besong goes on to warn that only diplomats without a vision would think that success lies in looting state coffers and storing the money in *"Ghana-must-go-bags"* [11] in their homes while basking in the luxury of parliamentary immunity, the kind voted in dishonestly by dishonest electoral serving bodies like that under Francois Xavier Mbouyoum's—National Electoral Observatory (NEO) body. Besong goes on to warn that it is when things go wrong, like the discovery of the sycophancy and conceit displayed by hypocrites at the foot of disgraced autocrats, or the indifference displayed by an organization like the IMF (International Monetary Fund) when tribal tendencies come into play with funds that our hopes, our future can be considered wasted—slaughtered. For that reason, the poet hints that it is not by hiding behind the shield of party discipline that a smart person becomes hated by his own people because a lone voice can still achieve success if the owner has the people at heart. The poet goes on to decry the mishandling of Cameroon's independence as a lost opportunity to put in perspective the dreams of our national patriots like Um Nyobe Reuben, an act which would have endeared him in the hearts of his compatriots as a distinguished nation builder after the tradition of Toussaint L'Ouverture (sic) who, by his military genius and political acumen, transformed an entire society of slaves into the independent black state of Haiti. He would have been a uniting force dear to the people of the nation from the Mentchoum Falls, through Boumnyebel,

Barombi, to the hills of Mayo-Louti, and as a result, he would have been flooded by wealth from these different parts of the nation:

Your barns would have been filled with citrus fruit,
vegetal ark, sweetcorn, green beans and
pepper sauce; you would have
had much honeycomb and cacao to be able to surmount
the algebra of
monopoly capitalism, masquerading;

as the democratic
hyacinth to the prodigal ambition of
aimless drift. (36)

Now, however, all the fantastic things that would have emerged from this must be missed out on.

In "Year of Restoration" (37), one can only relate the restoration to Cameroon's economic growth mindful of the year this particular poem was written. According to the International Monetary Fund (IMF) Country Report number 07/129 of March 2007, between the year 2005 and 2006 the government of Cameroon in an attempt to correct earlier fiscal slippages, tried restoring conditions for macroeconomic stability and improved governance; a move which overall, helped Cameroon to earn additional debt relief under the Multilateral Debt Relief Initiative (MDRI). But before this could happen, Besong laments the fact that a contemporary of his could only learn, after hitting rock bottom in his fall from "grass to disgrace," that anyone joining democracy's morning star, Paul Biya for sure, to eat from politically immature, hence morning star's "cooking jar" (37) is not a person to be emulated. Besong laments the fact that this contemporary's fall is so tragic that even his remains cannot be found. He observes that his friend should not have tried serving under such a regime when he writes:

you should not have aspired to
celebrate the champagne party
of whale sharks and implacable foes

of our common solidarity; brutes
yelping
with party voices. (37)

For this mistake, this contemporary now has to pay for his misdeeds against the land, the law, and God.

In "Scholar" (38), Bate Besong paints the portrait of who a scholar is, according to him. A scholar is like a tree that grows by a stream and so flourishes. He is famous according to the fights he has waged against decadent and decaying societies, and sure-footed like a deer, a personification of knowledge, who makes bookwork his chariot, his means of transporting himself in the form of ideas while getting his knowledge from "the séances of old Wagadougou" (38) and through his quest for knowledge will free an ideological prisoner by his finding on the world-wide-web. A true scholar is usually tried, tested, and refined like gold through a furnace. By day or by night the scholar delights himself with academic relics that position him such that he can learn of great figures like Okomfo Anokye and from great scholars and their writings like Cheikh Anta Diop. He then re-echoes his view in a manner reminiscent of Psalm 1 that scholars, honest men and women in other words, must position themselves such that they are prolific in terms of academic writings so that their leaves do not wither and fall off the tree of the web:

Scholars are trees that grow
beside a stream
that bear fruit at the right time

and whose leaves do not
Dry on the world-wide-web. (39)

In "Just Above Cameroon" (43), which opens Section II of the volume titled "Emanya-nkpe," Besong is celebrating Alexandre Biyidi-Awala a.k.a. Mongo Beti for his life's struggles, especially for his writing the work *Les Deux Mères de Guillaume Ismael Dzewatama, future camionneur* in which he recounts the kismets of a number of revolutionaries like himself who fought against and defeated a French-backed regime in their newly independent country. In this poem, the poet points out that Biyidi's past is made up of beauty and strength. He urges any inquirer to stop and look back at what Beti has undergone and figure out how many can risk the bold and daring path he trod? What will be found are unending stories about dungeons, with the cackling of hyenas as they feast on cadavers from the regime's "corpsemine" (43), that is the regime's torture chambers that spew forth corpses like a production line its products. All that which will show up would be strong memories of puppets in places where they ought not to be, and the display of rigged majority winning elections they ought not to win in a culture that uses terror to oppress and profit. In Beti's history will be found examples of how decrees were defied, the confusion caused by unwholesome business partners and "the pyramids of a Mameluke helms dog," (43). He points out to the inquirer that even though Akometam, a location in the Center part of Cameroon and possibly Beti's village, is blooming with flowers, one will find an ominous atmosphere "screaming with bones which fold and die; / to the paralyses of a fugitive's sigh…" (44). This is possibly referring to the deaths of fugitives themselves, or the relatives of those who were depending on all who became fugitives during the Ahidjo regime and so ran away leaving behind destitute relatives who degenerated into mere bones who bent over in pain and died in the absence of their loved ones and their support.

Besong then puts himself at par with freedom fighters like Beti as he wonders if he should feel guilty, if he had taken a wrong turn in his own struggles, for he too has, by his works, crushed into silence the brazen theft by those whose hands are soiled with the blood of our heroes and ill-gotten wealth, but he had, at times, unlike a true revolutionary, "(chewed / the curd of complacency…) / to lose sight from pain / from the obsequies over the wall / of state torture…" (44). This is the case because he too has gone back into history and called forth the cadaverous past of long ago, sometimes even celebrating some of its deeds, "glorified ostrich mask" (44) while taking upon himself the responsibility of setting right blunders of the narcissistic leader qua muse responsible for these errors like the Obasinjom masquerade he has come to symbolize:

… and poured
the rubble
of its narcissistic muse

on my masquerader head …
have built. (44)

At other times he has vented his anger at the situation by creating obscure poetry, "poetries' canaans / in obscurities…" (44), which led "to the labyrinth of my [his] own inertia" (44) a line with varied potentials as it could be referring to Besong's stagnation for a while in terms of professional growth because of his stance against the powers that be, or else his stagnation as a poet whose obscurity is alienating mindful of the fact that he is said to be the voice of the masses. It is possible that Besong could have bought into Hugo Friedrich's opinion of obscurity which had segued into an aesthetic principle (Moore 77). Nevertheless, Ngugi who has often argued that "The greatest use for literature is to effect change and to do this, it must be addressed to the masses," (qtd. in Alemji), [12] would have frowned at Besong for the latter's matter, manner, and objective conflict, turning him in to a paradox since one cannot understand how he would be claiming to speak for, and sometimes to, the suffering lot of society when they cannot, but for the intervention of the appraising critic, understand him. Interestingly, "the inclination has persisted to ascribe poetic obscurity, if not to intellectual arrogance, at least to insufficient concern for the common understanding" (Moore 74) Karl Shapiro is even more damning in his convictions about obscure artists: "Complexity and obscurity in art or poetry are always signs of the sick, enraged, frustrated artist, the nihilist, the destroyer of whatever is living in man and in nature" (qtd in Moore75). It is in this light that I have always considered Besong's style his own self-made literary noose since not many people are likely to read any of Bate Besong's works a second time for the pleasure of it—maybe his plays, but certainly not his poems. Besong finally confirms that he too, like Beti, has documented the ugliness of a century's decade which he decides to describe as "dark" and he claims to have done this to the best of his ability but this effort is hidden in a "curfewed song" (45)—a song that is not easily accessible—unlike Beti who brightens the sky, the horizon with his brilliant contributions. He confirms that Beti is leaving behind a lot as he "speaks to history" of that which was the bane of the exile.

In "Twenty Years After the Coup d'Etat" (46), it is obvious Besong is taking stock of the tide of events, the ills he and his contemporaries have been fighting against. He writes about the coup, which to him seemed to have been a treacherous act, that after extinguishing the tides of treachery that was raging in the nation and cuffed the wrist of those who favored the coup even while pacifying those hurt by the events that accompanied the coup, he cannot help but remember the savage massacres that characterized the coup attempt and followed in its wake. Because of all this, he points out that the opportunity for statesmen to learn, especially from foreign voices, has been missed out on. He deplores the government's loss of focus after this attack which ushered in the reckless indoctrination by the leaders of the party, culminating in a dictatorial system that led to the loss of voters who could no longer stand the imposing and equally autocratic ways of the party barons without whose imprimatur everything came to a standstill.

> ...Yet
> In spite of the fervent disguises:
> The blinding apophthegms, in the doctrinal
> Gleam of the party praetors, or so lately
> In this demoniac
> Obscuring:
>
> Of the electoral code and seething hurts,
> Beneath;
> An increment of thickening parapets
> Of 'new deal' imprimatur
> Weaning an electoral society
> Daily; (46-47)

Besong goes on to point out that he and his likes still benefit from the deadly philosophies of the rebels of the April 6th coup attempt as a curative source for the nation's ill-health typified by the draining of her wealth and resources, "national apoplexy" (47). Alas, Besong predicts that should things not improve, then there is no other choice other than a full-blown war:

> But already, the iron swallows gathering

On the cliff
Are sharpening their frightful talons

And the first bangs of mortars
Will tomorrow be forming
Hideous patches

On the grass
In the mornings. (47)

"Beware Frog Brother" (48) is a bitter poem in which Besong castigates Mbella Sonne Dipoko, a distinguished Cameroonian novelist and poet the generation before Besong's, for what many of his followers and compatriots considered a betrayal on the part of Dipoko. As a writer, an internationally acclaimed one for that matter, Dipoko was believed to be fighting for the oppressed, be it politically, racially, or religiously. Accordingly, it was scandalous when the revered poet, novelist, and playwright returned to his native Cameroon after about a quarter of a century in the West to join a political party that was oppressing his people; hence Besong's anger. Besong begins even in the dedication by calling him "ajasco gerontocrat" (48), a laughable womanizing and aging politician in other words. This is the case given that the original "Papa Ajasco" is a comic character who is a womanizer with fantastic and equally ridiculous ideas in one of Nigeria's comic magazines and later television series, *Ikebe Super,* by Wale Adenuga. Besong's anger is scathing indeed, but knowing Besong, he was as passionate at whatever he did. He must have felt personally betrayed by Dipoko's strides later on in the day. In Section i (48), he points out that Dipoko had failed to decipher the truth about the structure and agenda of the ruling party, Cameroon People's Democratic Movement (CPDM). This is a fact Dipoko was later to confess to when he failed to bring about the change he had hoped to bring from within instead of crying foul from without as he himself had explained his decision. Hence his confession in a 2006 poem titled "Hawking Slogans": "… the sadness I sometimes feel / Because I abandoned the front of smoking guns / For the comfort of selling slogans." (Tande, "In Memoriam: Mbella Sonne Dipoko").

In his anger, Besong goes as far as attacking Dipoko's dressing which like the "frozen consistency" (49) of the party he could not change:

of its frozen
consistency towards your
psychopath revelry, which

like your plague-
ridden every-ready marabout
black mamba wrapper-
wrapper

You had neither skill nor will
to mend. (48)

Besong remained convinced of Dipoko's involvement with the mystical which he urges the writer-turned-politician to abandon, and in spite of his rejection of religion pray intensely, even before branding him "Debauched / Prophet of Ya Mboka" (48), the Afrocentric spiritual movement, *Esimo Ya Mboka*, Dipoko had started and whose High Priest he was until his demise on December 5, 2009.

In Section ii (48), Besong presents Dipoko contradicting himself by joining the CPDM as equivalent to "unsaying all that [he] had said" (48). The result was that Dipoko found himself on prime-time-television all the time trying to make himself relevant by activities that were of no consequence even as he tried to account for what is considered his eleventh-province [13] dubiety since one was never too sure where Dipoko was from until the very end of his life. It is for this reason Besong titles his poem "Beware Frog Brother" instead, as if to insist that Dipoko is not a genuine Anglophone. He seemed satisfied to be considered of Douala since he was born there, and even Francophone since his French was impeccable. At the end however, Dipoko seemed to have reconciled himself with his true identify – a man from Tiko in the English speaking part of Cameroon. A move reminiscent of Rocafil Jazz band's famous Prince Nico Mbarga's soul searching song "Home be Home," in which the musician reassures all that one's home is one's home, that one could tour the world from north to south, from East to west, the last place one will always return to is one's homeland; so did Dipoko: he returned to Tiko after decades roaming the world. Besong's bitterness heightens when he raises the idea that his culprit had been accused of exposing his pubic hair "to a minor of the opposite sex" (49) before going on to censure him as one who could not be trusted even before denouncing his collection of poems, *Black and White in Love,* which he claimed "could hardly survive inspection / through the lorgnette / of the revolutionary sublime" (49) given that it is more about his days as an orgiastic vagabond globetrotting with a sex mate in tow. Of himself Dipoko once declared:

> I became for many years, what you might call a traveling lover, a dreamer searching for God between the women's thighs – those days when I was at the height of my intimate powers. You had to see me! I was like an angel stuffing recoilless erections into just where they are most needed – into the fleshy folds of winter! But I did it with rosy summers too. (Tande "In Memoriam: Mbella Sonne Dipoko")

For all this, Besong is convinced Dipoko was out for selfish interests in his political venture even if his tenure in office as Mayor of Tiko can prove Besong wrong.

In Section iii (49), Besong, in a figurative manner, promises the end to Dipoko's activities, "Your pick-axes and mattocks will soon be blunt" (49), as a result of his activities which seem to show no respect for his own personal habitat, since Besong accuses him of roosting in the same place where he drops his crackpot droppings; a presentation much akin to Achebes bringing home ant-infested fagots (*Arrow of God* 67). He accuses him of feting with corrupt personages with whom they execute their deeds in the likes of buccaneers. In the end, Besong declares his pity for the poet whose worth is already waning at "near 70" (50) before pointing out that whereas some writers make history, others like Dipoko, mar it. This is quite a disturbing yet seemingly authentic observation which reminds me of an earlier regret with a similar sentiment that I shared about Dipoko when he wrote his poem "Ntarikon Blues" in the heat of Cameroon's political reawakening in the mid 90's. The era was the peak of a tide of political upheavals provoked by Ni John Fru Ndi's political activities and aspirations under the auspices of the Social Democratic Front political party with its headquarters then at

Ntarikon where Fru Ndi, the chairman of the party, used to reside. I wrote in reaction to Dipoko's rather insulting poem:

> That Dipoko is an accomplished writer is true, but this is one poem that should never have flowed from that pen of yours. I would rather you called the 'Ntarikon tiger' and told him off verbally than tarnish thus your literary integrity as this poem amounts to nonsense after the tradition of Lapiro's career blunder. Dipoko should know that without this 'tiger' all the 'dogs gamboling in Cameroon's political arena today would have been nowhere. ("Dipoko's 'Ntarikon Blues'")

Besong then goes on to alert that judgment must not be hastily arrived at considering all the wonderful praises that according to him had been heaped on Dipoko before he betrayed his ranks by dining with the enemy.

Besong points out that in another country, the likes of Dipoko who was almost sphinxlike would have left office or whatever position of worth they held in disgrace for the commoners to elect their new leader in the manner of Oedipus, himself so mysterious, who had to leave in shame for the Thebans to look for a new leader. Besong emphasizes his target by concluding that the new leader to be elected is their Sango; a term of endearment that some used when addressing Mbella Sonne Dipoko. Besong warns him in the end: "Beware, Frog Brother" (50). It is as if he, Besong, can still not trust Dipoko and so refuses even to acknowledge his Anglophone roots by considering him a "Frog Brother" after all. [14]

In "Star gazer" (51), the persona is daydreaming, and tells of how he was awoken by a cockerel "from the window / of our quiet / Monrovia." With dreaming or daydreaming, virtually anything is possible, hence this persona paints a picture of being in his own country which is like a bedroom with a window through which a cockerel from the outside, which happens in this daydream to be the country Liberia with the capital city being Monrovia, calls out and wakes him up to a disturbing scene with a mummery of vultures gathered like hyenas around another civilian's corpse who happens to be Doe, the late Liberian military leader turned civilian. One can only wonder what it is this persona is dreaming about. Is he being made to see the future of the leader of the poet's own country currently under a civilian's whims or is he being made to see the mess things can become with people like Doe at the helm of nations? "Star gazer" is a poem that can be interpreted in so many ways and it would be in line still. At the very least, it is a presentation of the disturbing manner in which dictators end up leaving office.

"Election results" (52), is itself a kind of warning against one nursing any hopes during election time as the results usually amount to nonsense. The results, commonly rigged, amount to an insult on the collective will and intellect of society as evidenced by the chaos that leads to election results as presented here by Besong. If the elections were well organized, with a sincere will to have the winner be that chosen by the people, then we would not have aggressive marauders destroying and casting out an abundance of party waste on the otherwise organized public opinion which is here presented as a "hedgerow of collective pain" (52), pain not only at the way things are in the country, but also pain caused by the manner in which the results of the elections turn out.

In "Horoscope" (53), a short poem rich in images, Besong says a lot with a few words. From the word horoscope and the events he is describing, it dawns on one that Besong is recounting one of those useless days set aside in Cameroon, in this case May 20th, to celebrate, supposedly, the birth of the Cameroon nation; a rather paradoxical date since one cannot tell the nation being celebrated: the Federal Republic of Cameroon, the United Republic of Cameroon, or todays' Republic of Cameroon. Accordingly, Besong sees the activities marking this celebration as a circus come to town and the officials involved as horoscopic jokers, in other words pranksters revealing of the times mindful of the Greek horoskopoi and its meaning "markers of the hours." Yes, these buffoons led by a provincial governor, the tank commander for the military leader, and other political party stalwarts are compared to pierrots, characters in French pantomime, because of the way they are dressed and following along the lines of party nonsense like children, yet all of them are old leaders of party caravans, "geriatric caravaneers" (53). Besong even suggests the presence of catamites in this political caravan, thereby hinting at some of the obnoxious practices rumoured as accompanying the acquisition and maintenance of political offices nowadays. From this time, all of a sudden, and from nowhere, a kid is found holding a major political office that leaves all wondering how he got there. The whole picture is disgusting and reeking of filth and the offering of sexual favors in exchange for offices and administrative positions. For this reason, Besong bashes the system as loaded with "whorl and whorls / of prurience unmoor / even the visionary eye" (53). His eyes, those of a visionary, are offended by layers of indecency he could see in this party bazaar of a celebration which is a pointer of the trends of the hour, hence the idea of the horoscope.

"Mamfe, this Time, Tomorrow" (54), is a poem reverberating at two different levels; hence, the combination of agrarian and human images. Besong seems to open the poem mourning the agrarian loss of Mamfe's vegetation in the guise of the extraction of the territory's forest, for which reason he writes: "Timber of willows, of flesh-leaven / Mourn at harvest of death- / throes" (54). Herein, comes a level of ambiguity: who or what is being harvested, and whose death-throes is the poet referring to? Then it seems more like Besong is referring to the death of Mamfe's timber out of which forest emerge Moon-skulled vampires, bats flying out of their habitat, tearing at the petal-thrones of these gigantic trees. It is true these vampires could also be symbolic of those benefitting from these deals leading to the exploitation of Mamfe's forests as they "exude silvery castanets, prime chronicles of Deceit" (54), the noisy promises they make to the naïve and uninformed locals about their wonderful plans for the region which is why their wood is being carted away. Hence, Besong sees the young shoots sprouting from the decay of the old roots as "sewage-tubers" (54) infected by the tumor of their plight as plants about to be recklessly harvested someday. Remarkable, however, is the fact that this is where Besong's agrarian image segues into the human perspective. As these stalks are described as "Nude stalks / of pain" (54) at once evoking a male phallic symbol that, like a penis, letters through peeing and orgasmic ejaculations during "vigil nights of drinks; of brothels" (54). Hence the idea of "A ring of bowed apparitions" (54), drunks, their silhouettes coming across as if they are apparitions and their murmur in "drugged slums" (54), slums overwhelmed by nocturnal picaros drugged by excess alcohol help offer the poet clarity even as he laments the things done to Mamfe's maiden's skull. Of course, with all these activities and the attendant consequences, the poet was already feeling some spiritual filth in his own life or society as a whole, for which reasons he chose to seek some "spirituous unguent" (54) that should have brought him some relief. It is remarkable that the unguent has been "Cleansed by planetary tassels" (54) which here symbolize diverse worldly experiences which, like the tallit on the corners of a Jew's prayer shawl, continue to remind the wearer of the need to follow God's commandments instead of one's own desires which are usually in conflict with what God wants of us. Had Besong seen too much filth and even the approaching end such that he needed to enshrine his purging voice, hence "voice pools"? (54). Besong then claims the poem is by Mfam, a view which results in this perception of himself as a spiritual being out to purge society of her ills mindful of the role of Mfam in Mamfe society which is somewhat regulatory. He calls Mfam a "fiery Artisan" (54-55), a veritable alter ego of Besong and vice versa as their goal is eradicating tyrants after the tradition of Liberia's Doe. This is part of the wishes, requests, and complains from society, so numerous they are fibrous "fibre from Eyang-Atem-Ako" (55), trapped in the throats of "Sub-men" (55), cowards who, unlike Besong, could not voice their grievances for fear of dictators who end up grieving and questioning "Why this was so?" (55).

In a conclusive stanza Besong combines both his agrarian and human images to emerge with a perfect picture of what Mamfe would be like by this time tomorrow: there would be those whose voices are in their protestations and lamentations choral altos high because of the number of wine-skins they would have emptied and so become bold enough to speak up as they mourn the collapse of Mamfe's integrity, or is it Besong's, which shredded would "lay in ague" (55) tormented by some strange malady. One can only hope this sorrowing concretized in the call "Come home, my darling" (55) would not be too late for Mamfe by this time tomorrow. One cannot help observing that Besong died shortly after publishing the volume containing this poem, leaving one convinced of his experiencing that pervading nudge of his impending demise described by Modupe Olaogun as the "premonitory hint" (126) in Christopher Okigbo's "Path of Thunder."

One is left shuddering as the weight of this, seemingly personal poem, settles in on one's psyche leaving one wondering if Besong saw himself as a sacrifice for his people. According to W. K. Wimsatt Jr. and Monroe C. Beardsley,

The meaning of a poem may certainly be a personal one, in the sense that a poem expresses a personality or state of soul rather than a physical object like an apple. But even a short lyric poem is dramatic, the response of a speaker (no matter how abstractly conceived) to a situation (no matter how universalized) (249)

It is common knowledge that Besong's opacity in technique remains his greatest Achilles' heel and he himself seems to have come to terms with that by the end of his life since he was now willing to include some notes at the end of *Disgrace* which explain some of his very personal and private allusions and symbols. This notwithstanding, I continue to wonder if Besong was not intentionally trying to introduce theatrical and prosaic techniques in the writing of poetry: the absurdist and stream of consciousness approach in the presentation of poetic messages. This is the case for his finished products are definitely powerful feelings, but their conception and recollection are certainly far removed from the Wordsworthian hypothesis of "overflow and tranquility" as it is obvious Besong labored to create poetic mazes that even the initiated would toil to navigate meaningfully. He barely fell short of Okigbo's supposed boast that he writes his poems for other poets. J.O.J. Nwachukwu-Agbada writes of two of Besong's greatest influences:

> In 1962, and at different interviews with Lewis Nkosi, both Christopher Okigbo and Wole Soyinka showed by their utterances that they gave little place to audience consideration in their writings. Okigbo is known to have said: 'Somehow I believe I am writing for other poets all over the world to read and see whether they can share in my experience....Nowadays everything is done for the study and on few occasions it steals out, I think it is to please, but not a large public' (*African Writers Talking*, p. 135). Soyinka said a very similar thing then: 'I don't think I need bother my head... at all about the audience, whether Nigerian or the European. (165 – 66).

It is poets like Besong who caused Shelley to describe the poet as "a nightingale, singing in solitude" (Jack 2); yet as Ian Jack points out, "the essay which contains that phrase ends with the proud claim that 'Poets are the unacknowledged legislators of the world'" (2). Jack goes on to reveal, in this same vein, that "...we have only to look at Shelley's letters to find that he was always deeply concerned about the potential audience for his poems" (2). Besong was beginning to be concerned in like manner, hence the inclusion of explanatory notes at the end of his book *Disgrace*. In Besong, like it is with the fleeting human mind, his concerns rush from one thing to another from stanza to stanza and sometimes with hardly any related concerns within the same poem other than the fact that he is decrying some ill in society. That is the case in this poem "Mamfe, this Time, Tomorrow" (54).

"Malediction" (58), in keeping with the definition of the word, is a short poem that has to do with calling down a curse on an unidentified personality's siblings whom the poet wishes should neigh like horses instead of the human beings that they are. Monrovia here can only be referring to a once upon a time battlefield which has returned to calm. To Besong, this can be the campus of the University of Buea which was virtually a battlefield with second grade politicians masquerading as academics while disrupting an otherwise ideal academic setup, or, at large, the Cameroon nation with her woes at the dawn of a new era after decades under a failed despot.

The poem "Ntarikon, Massacre, 1990" (59) is a poem of gore about the killings that took place in Bamenda, Cameroon, during the launching of the Social Democratic Front political party which remained the sole reliable opposition party for a long time until people started losing faith in it since the founding Chairman, it was said, would not hear of another chairman other than himself, a tendency interpreted as much akin to that of the incumbent dictator. Besong mourns for those who were murdered: those who gave up their future for a better Cameroon as their "tomorrows" became "shards of broken glass" (59) instead of the Promised Land of a nation for which they had hoped.

"Another Country Where Poets Lie" (60), a title possibly triggered by Mbella Sonne Dipoko's confession to Dibussi Tande in an interview that broached on his controversial political choices just before the end of his life, is a poem in which the poet points out the ridiculous activities that take place behind the scene before a visit from the unpopular head of state. In this interview, Dipoko hinted at the idea that he must have lied or contradicted himself by his political choice for a party when he asked: "Who hasn't cut corners? Who hasn't told a lie? Who hasn't sinned…? And I am not myself sinless…" (Tande "In Memoriam: Mbella Sonne Dipoko"). In this poem, just before the president's visit, he must have sent a memo to the branch president of his political party (Cameroon People's Democratic Movement), possibly a political maverick, to find out how he was preparing in the face of the president's impending visit. This is the case because before such visits, the press and all high ranking members of government would go about singing and chanting all kinds of mantras about the president and his wonderful deeds and love for the nation; hence, one of his ridiculous titles as "father of the nation" and so on. The CPDM party leaders involved were convinced by forwarding the president's memo to the editor of *The Post* newspaper, Francis K. Wache, he would fall into their trap by rushing to publish the upcoming visit of the head of state as worthwhile news. Not Wache; himself a poet, Wache lied to the powers that be about his inability to print, an effort by which he would have been assisting in preaching the government's propaganda in favor of a worthless leader, by claiming that the administrative machinery, the president's beast, had seized his computers during their characteristic raids of such private and neutral press houses. This state of things, according to Wache, meant he could not do their bidding. Like Dipoko, Wache had lied, hence the idea of another country where poets lie.

In "I Dance to Your Scented Guts" (113), Bate Besong begins by wishing for certain conditions as *sine qua non* for victory. Accordingly, he points out that when we destroy the fear in us and stop hoping "for a miracle from a flagstone" (113), and when we lament the condition of our earth, and when foolish and moronic leaders are transformed into better beings and citizens through the communal process of purification, the stars, symbols of victory, will come out. The poet's wish evolves from the general into a particular as he zooms in on one portrait he conjures into existence to represent the human effort and ultimate victory: that of Dipoko with his "vermillion mane of hair" (113). That's why he dances to his guts which are now scented because of his recent romance with the unpopular regime in place at the time. His anger, at this former idol of his, climaxes in the next poem "Sell-out."

In "Sell-out" (114), Besong is venting his anger towards Mbella Sonne Dipoko, a writer and critic who had spent decades in France, during which years he toured Europe and North Africa while establishing himself as a major African writer and critic of the ongoing ills of the hour. Only for Dipoko to return to his native Cameroon later on in life, 1985, and instead of joining the masses to continue the struggle against an incumbent despotic regime, Dipoko shocked his peers by aligning with the corrupt regime in place through acquiring membership of the obnoxious party in power. In his defense, in an interview granted to Dibussi Tande, he pointed out:

Who hasn't cut corners? Who hasn't told a lie? Who hasn't sinned...? And I am not myself sinless, even though lots of people have always considered me as a kind of picaresque priest because I stand by my people and I shall always stand by them until my dying day. In fact, I was standing by my people when recently I ran for Parliament as an alternate member of the ruling party which I was sure I could better influence from within than from without. Better to preach the necessity for a change of direction in the councils of government, and impose that change on it, than to pelt the palaces of power with sterile stones as our Opposition chaps are doing... I prefer to preach the need for change not from outside the ranks of government, but from within, that in (sic) the ruling circles and to those people who actually have the power to bring about change peacefully. (qtd. in "In Memoriam: Mbella Sonne Dipoko").

What an incredible display of ignorance with regards to the trends of politics and power, especially in Africa where autocrats wield absolute power. Dipoko was to get first hand lesson in the saying that power corrupts and absolute power corrupts absolutely. It is unbelievable that a man of his caliber would have convinced himself that these are the likes of leaders who would bring about change peacefully?

Dipoko joined the ruling CPDM party and even became the Mayor of Tiko, thus his portrait as a sell out to a passionately devoted critic like Besong. Dipoko, as a writer, was supposed and expected by the public to a stance against the corrupt government in power. By joining the corrupt regime and thereby abandoning the masses and their struggle, Dipoko became a sellout. On second thoughts, however, Dipoko had, his entire life before returning to Cameroon, remained passive towards the ruling class in Cameroon, never saying anything against them as all he wrote about was the beauty of life in our beautiful coastal villages along with our beautiful women. At his most vociferous Dipoko lashed out against racism and European double standards and not about African politics and power grabbing politicians even though he claims in his 2006 poem ("Hawking slogans"):

...the sadness I sometimes feel
Because I abandoned the front of smoking guns
For the comfort of selling slogans
In the public place,
I who used to think like Jomo Kenyatta did
Before age and the comforts of high office softened him
Into embracing the British he had so valiantly fought... (Tande "In Memoriam: Mbella Sonne Dipoko")

The populace stands to blame then for immediately assuming that because Dipoko was a writer against western hypocrisy, racism, and negritude, therefore his was the voice of the oppressed within African autocracies; it was not the case. He himself observed once:

But to tell the truth, during all those years that I was abroad, I never joined any political organization that fought Ahmadou Ahidjo. I never in public criticized him. For, in my head, I was a soldier, a born member of the Cameroonian armed forces. And the armed forces, spiritualized, made incorruptible, patriotic, are the finest thing in any country. They are the backbone of a nation's destiny. So how can one who is born to exercise traditional command take to criticizing the government whose auxiliary he is born to be? That is why I never became a politician in exile.

I was content with being just a poor poet, just a roaming writer, comfortable in the luxury of memory in which the most palpable pain can be massaged artistically into the sweetest messianic songs.

The other reason why I would not criticize the El Hadj's regime was because I felt that it really is not courage when one can only shout invectives from the safe distance of exile. (Tande, "The Luxury of Memory")

What nonsense! I cannot help but convince myself that with such reactions from Dipoko, he must have been completely out of touch with reality while in France. I will never be able to tell why now that he is gone, and so I chose to remember his great works than the unfortunate verbal revelations he went on spewing forth after his return to Cameroon. I refuse seeing this once upon a time hero of mine in another light.

Besong's *Disgrace*, the last work he published, is very easily his opus magnum because, besides its length, it amounts to an ensemble of his thematic concerns and his stylistic approach; that is, the manner in which he delivers his message to society. In *Disgrace*, Besong's note is in a most premonitory manner final as he paints a clear portrait of the kind of scholar and critic he had been before this volume in the portrait of the Hebrew prophet of the bible, Jeremiah. Like Jeremiah who, with God's support, was determined to free Israel from an "impending cataclysm," Besong had all his life been determined to free the oppressed from the selfish claws of the purloining powerful and the Anglophone-Cameroonian from domineering Francophone regimes at home, hence the apocalyptic tone of his works, especially in this volume. Like his biblical alter ego Jeremiah, Besong in *Disgrace*, like never before, is obsessed with the level of degeneracy that has overwhelmed his society, even the world of academe which is powered by professors cum administrators who take their rise from the shrines of fortune tellers, with God seemingly dead in this world of the absurd; therefore, his poems warn about tribal gods and cabalistic ventures that leave these characters defiled. Besong's message is clear: the need for scholar administrators to be scholar administrators resolute in serving the masses instead of voodoo practitioners determined to go to any length just to stay in offices and positions of power which they defile by misusing them to abuse the suffering lot of mankind. His style remains the same: modernist, enriched by alienating personal and classical, otherwise foreign images and symbols. Besong's meshed and jumbled up syntax, his far-fetched metaphors, and alienating and equally perplexing diction did not alleviate things. The end result it that, as a poet, he left a lot to question as one cannot help wondering what his intentions were: to communicate or to create puzzles since his poems come through like splurges of ink across a canvas from the brush of a possessed artist, gasping and belching forth fractured ideas and messages from time to time such that a critic has to go to work to make the necessary connections for the ordinary reader, if he or she is still patient enough to get the entire picture. Small wonder then, towards the end Besong concluded his last volume *Disgrace* with some notes that helped the reader to situate, in a way, some of his otherwise bizarre verbalizations.

As indicated then, Besong's poetry jars, echoes, stutters, with an all too intimidating diction and an imagery that summons his critics to work at instead of being spontaneously drawn in to a piece they enjoy. As Dan Izevbaye confirms of elusive and difficult poetry while commenting on Christopher Okigbo, "It demands of the reader an unusual range of knowledge, whether it be of the archeological excavations of Egypt, or the uncovering of Gilgamesh tablets, or African oral traditions" (124). The poet, Besong, is, without doubt, a victim of the thematic and stylistic values of his influences, primarily Okigbo, Wole Soyinka, and at a secondary level, Eliot and Pound. W. H. Stevenson confirms in the "Foreword" of *Polyphemus Detainee and Other Skulls*, "Newly found influences are being absorbed, new themes explored." The poet himself had this to say in the acknowledgement:

> In creating *Polyphemus Detainee and Other Skulls*, especially the collection **Throes** and also in **Looms**, I have obtained a lot of clarity and a creative commitment in 'Wole Soyinka's two major poetical scrolls: **Idanre and other Poems** and **A Shuttle In The Crypt**. In **Masks** there is a strong imagistic communication with T. S. Eliot. (sic)

The difficulty of Besong's works then is a consequence of the degree of his alienation from his society through his dependence on influences who are themselves difficult, along with the employment of foreign beliefs, concepts, and imagery; this is not necessarily a vice given that every culture has and continues to borrow. On the other hand, Besong privatizes his art through the use of concepts and mythical ingredients from his own native and personal world view that are no longer very current nor were some ever public fodder. Because of this, a work of his is likely to take repeated notching and hammering even with possible contradictions and counter contradictions to slowly unravel Besong to his readers as was the case with those who influenced him.

Overall, Besong, as a poet, is a possessed craftsman at work chiseling here, drilling there, planning here, and brushing there in his creative stupor. To this poet, shoved into a creative trance by his craft and muse, his message is a gem and so he expects his reader to be a determined and equally skilled literary miner who must also rise into Besong's clouds or drop into the shafts of his creative tunnels and then begin digging, drilling, transporting, burnishing in order to emerge with the gem which may then reward his effort with a story, a message, a lesson or an idea. But this is the bane of his art as not everyone can be a miner in this case and so emerges the discord between objective and technique. If Besong is the defender of the suffering masses as his messages and literary works depict him, then his style, usually loaded with encumbering symbols, images, and myths, alienates his charges as they are all too often dazzled by his mental and emotional flights than enlightened by its all too often angry yet brilliantly profound messages. His poems sometimes stutter raucously like a jarring collection of discordant musical notes; the usually mystical symbols and images strewn about without respect for regularized stanzaic patterns or regular poetic lines and the likes, startle, leaving the reader in a near state of shock and denial if not outright rejection. Of Besong's difficulty as a poet George Ngwane writes:

> At first reading the lines make no sense because the conflict is enacted through language itself and through those symbols which are the very embodiment of the drama of external conflict now internalized and transfigured into a private vision. In consequence the language becomes recondite and difficult to decode. (*Symbol* 22)

He adds with regards to Besong's over inventive and so more often than not elusive diction and symbols; "You must be current with historical events, and abreast of socio-political trends. His symbols are deeply rooted in social changes. His clustered images range from distant civilization ... through local metaphors ... to sexual overtones..." (*Symbol* 22 – 23). In Besong's poems, because of his tortuous vocabulary and private symbols and images, as often as they fail to communicate even after sometimes excruciating attempts at deciphering his message, the truth remains that they are formidable poems thematically but stylistically overtaxed by the poet for one to be able to say with certainty, at all times, what they are all about. It is not surprising then that whereas Peter Vakunta bemoans that Besong "is ... a man who can turn writing into an opaque nightmare by dint of outlandish lexical choices, ..." George Ngwane, on his part, advises: "His poems are best understood when you read the lines in segments instead of a whole for his flow of ideas seems to be in episodes than in a continuum. Although his use of digressions do not provide coherence in ideas, they provide unity in purpose" (*Symbol* 22). For a spokesman of the underprivileged and exploited, as observed above, this conflict between purpose and method is certainly baffling. Naturally then, from time to time even professional critics may not agree entirely on every aspect of his poems. These, however, would be the nitty-gritty of his style as the main concern and messages are rather more conveniently acquired, comparatively speaking, in a broader picture. Whatever the case, Besong's overall poetic aesthetics reveals a poet in keeping with Percy Bysshe Shelley's observation that the poet is the legislator of his world even if unacknowledged (Elimimian 112) or as Daniel P. Kunene puts it, "…the synthesizer and conduit of the concerns of the society for which he claims to speak" (37).

Just Above Cameroon: Selected Poems 1980 – 1994 (1998)

In "Druidical Rites" (34), the only never before published poem in this collection of selected poems, Besong takes a break from his characteristic concerns with the ordinary such as bad governance, irresponsible leadership and the likes, to soar into another realm of the soul's existence altogether. At the beginning of the poem, the persona points out that the night is over, leaving one wondering if indeed he is referring to the fact that it is a new day, or if he is being metaphorical and referring to the end of the troubles that had transformed life for him into a one long night. The later interpretation seems to carry the day as the persona laments the deadening activities that had characterized the period before which he referred to as "night." There had been "so much crush of stamens / In the brain." The fact that the period that has just gone past was stifling in every way comes across when one remembers that "stamens" are the reproductive organs of a flower, but this time they are lodged in the brain, hence the complete death or, at the very least, the stifling of creativity. As a result, the creative genius in this persona moved on to the next level (plane) of the existence of the human soul, hence the idea of "sought, / A dwelling shroud in the next plane" (34). Is the persona astral travelling? Is he being conscious of the re-incarnation of his soul? These are all potential explanations given the fact that the persona

110

laments a repeat of his troubling encounters he had experienced before: "I have passed this way, gathering / In, the angsts" (34).

In the next stanza the persona seems to be facing the new realm of his existence, and he is also convinced that he has been this way before and it was a lonely experience but that was in keeping with his mission: "To fill my hunger of its: monkish plenitude.." (34). The persona was in this realm, after the manner of a solitary monk in quest of superior knowledge, a superior state of existence, "monkish plenitude" (34). It was also a period of gestation before the soul's return to earth or reality, hence the persona's soul was "Moving across, across laden clouds, in the void…" (34) of this other realm, the realm where the soul spends time developing, a realm where he had, before, heard the cawing sounds of the waters. After the convictions of reincarnation, the soul must develop here to a certain level before making it back to earth, hence the idea of "gestations" (34).

In this new realm, the soul had sought to hide its weakness by displaying itself in a most distorted manner—looming—supporting itself between irrelevant prophesies on the one hand and trivialities on the other, aware of its inadequacies which needed to be purged during this period of gestation in this new realm. The debased state of the troubled human soul and as such its inability to fit into this new dimension or state of existence seems to dawn on the persona as he laments before pointing out the uncomfortable and unsuccessful life style he had lived plunging in and out of mundane pads, hence he considers himself as manqué:

O so much debasement of the angst-soul!
To march the alien eclipse of the mind,
I had marched: to quickening plunges, in
Mundane pads, manqué. (34)

The persona goes onto observe emphatically that he had returned here over and over, into a cosmos free of earth's whiles but with mysterious characters "masked sphinxes" (34) around him.

At last, when, as the phases quickened into minutes, it was his time to be freed from this abode, weaned like a breastfeeding child from its mother's milk to something more advanced, impurities fell off of him, he generated a tornado, and like a hooded shuttle with sparks all around him headed back to base—earth. Interestingly, the persona laments the fact that it will soon be dawn and the nocturnal round of their *esoteria*, their secret activity reserved only for the initiated, will come to an end.

There is no doubt that Besong's poem, "Druidical Rites" (34) is predominantly supernatural in its concerns. This is obvious when one recalls that a druid is a member of the priestly class among the Celtic who appear in Irish and Welsh sagas and even Christian legends as wizards performing magical rites. Accordingly, one immediately thinks of the persona being a part of some supernatural activity or rite carried out nocturnally as a means of perfecting the self through repeated visits to a superior plane before returning to earth, hence the idea of "Druidical Rites" (34).

6

Drama

After treating Besong's poems, even if he had been known first as a poet before a playwright, one can claim now to see why his friend and somehow mentor at the Cameroon Protestant College in Bali advised him to direct his energy towards theatre. As a poet, not anyone will pick up Besong's work and go past a couple of lines without a special reason because of the obviously obscure nature of his work, a generally acknowledged fact. Understanding Besong's poetry is a chore in its own right and it calls for an appropriately equipped mind, culturally and literally, to undertake the appreciative task. In other words, Besong is not the traditional poet whose lines enchant at once due to the intricate yet bewitching simplicity and accommodating sensorial appropriateness of the diction and the splendour of an orderly syntactic structure, or the rhythmic and rhyming musical overtones of his devices and an overall soothing style; no! He is instead of a certain order reserved for the initiated who must be willing to dig and drill deep into the crust of a brilliant but complicatedly oriented psyche while putting to test other drilling tools and theories in an effort to see if this or that diamond-headed bit will hit any substance of value. Shadrach A. Ambanasom confirms this by commenting on Besong's poetry thus: "He is a poet with an elliptical poetic imagination; his poetry is often erratic in its movement. There is no rigid respect for chronology in the expression of his thought and idea, nor an attempt to stick to syntactic logic in the structure of his sentences" ("Too Difficult" 45). Such a soul headed towards Besong's poetry therefore, must think, or else be convinced that this raging spirit of a literary secret society conjured into existence on his own terms, has something to say. In keeping with this conviction, Martin Jumbam declares:

> I am one of those reasonably well-educated Anglophones who never understood, nor greatly admired BB's literary endeavours. When Douglas Achingale told us the other day of a young university student who asked BB to go back to school and learn to write simply, I nodded in approval. I abhor literary obscurantism, which seems to have been BB's literary

headgear. The few things I read, or tried to read from him—be they articles in papers or some of his books—sounded either too opaque or too pompous for my liking; and I always ended up tossing them aside.

This is the manner of artist whose plays one is about embarking on and it does not take long to realize that that mystifying quality of his at the level of style, in his poetry, has been adequately transferred onto his approach to theatre. Alas, beyond diction and speeches theatre is endowed with other voices generated by stage props, attendant symbols and similar literary tools. Even then, Besong, just as in the case of his poems, had precursors in the way he wrote his plays, the only difference, as already stated, being that whereas a poet's imagery could be so private as to render his poems virtually reticent, a play is a lot more structured and in several ways more restricting than a poem. In this light, a play's category, unlike a poem's, is more likely to help in cracking through the walls of opacity than in the case of a poem. Furthermore, language on stage can be buttressed by action and so will generate more meaning where a poem would have failed to communicate, along with the scope it accords the playwright, hence the importance of metatheatre in theatre of the absurd, Besong's favourite approach. In keeping with Besong and his style, Martin Esslin has observed about The Theatre of the Absurd:

> The Theatre of the Absurd, on the one hand, tends toward a radical devaluation of language, toward a poetry that is to emerge from the concrete and objectified images of the stage itself. The element of language still plays an important part in this conception, but what *happens* on stage transcends, and often contradicts the words spoken by the characters. (Esslin's emphasis, *Theatre* 7)

Esslin was later to add elsewhere:

> The Theatre of the Absurd has opened up a new possibility for poetry on the stage. Having renounced the function of telling a story, of exploring character, of discussing ideas, of solving problems, it has been able to concentrate on the presentation of what is essentially *a sense of being*, an

institution of the tragicomic absurdity and mystery of human existence (*Reflections* 9).

An appealing creative recipe for a playwright like Besong, it would seem, given his tendency to be so wrapped up in the art of marshalling across his sadness, fears, joy, worries, hopes, dreams—his concern for the human species so to say—so much so that he becomes convoluted if not mysterious instead.

Consequently, Besong's approach to theatre is more within the tradition of the absurd with its disturbingly illogical disposition than the traditional. Of the difference between traditional theatre and theatre of the absurd Martin Esslin, the dramatist and critic who first introduced the term which he gave as the title of his book points out:

> If a good play must have a cleverly constructed story, these have   no story or plot to speak of; if a good play is judged by subtlety of characterization and motivation, these are often without recognizable characters and present the audience with almost mechanical puppets; if a good play has to have a fully explained theme, which is neatly exposed and finally solved, these often have neither a beginning nor an end; if a good play is to hold the mirror up to nature and portray the manners and mannerism of the age in finely observed sketches, these seem often to be reflections of dreams and nightmares; if a good play relies on witty repartee and pointed dialogue, these often consist of incoherent babblings. (Esslin, *Theatre* 3-4*).

Equipped thus with an understanding of the seemingly absurd in theatre of the absurd, one can be certain then that approaching, experiencing, and appraising Besong's plays would amount to a far more relaxing ride than his poems, the heat that causes his poetic balloons to rise in challenge, like many within absurdist theatre, having thus been exposed in its aberrant technique.

The Most Cruel Death of the Talkative Zombie (1986)

As a playwright, Besong's works amount to avant-garde drama within the realms of Anglophone-Cameroon literature, as much about his plays violate established traditional theatrical norms. According to Antonin Artaud about avant-garde drama:

> The function … is twofold: it must by being consistently uninhibited, protest against the artificial hierarchy of values imposed by culture, and it must, by a 'drama of cruelty,' demonstrate the true reality of the human soul and the relentless conditions under which it lives.
>
> The manner in which this violent attack on the everyday is to be accomplished involves a fantastic, larger than life callousness that enables the characters to disregard the amenities of social behavior, and a rejection of speech as a means of communication. (Wellwarth 18)

Accordingly, one can hardly talk of a plot in *The Most Cruel Death of The Talkative Zombie* (*Zombie*) with the idea of a neatly mapped out logical tide of events displaying levels of exposition, complication, crisis, and the dénouement. Any idea of structure lies in the fact that the play, beyond the prologue "From Genesis to Revelation" (1-5), is in three parts: Part I "Once in a Fit of Fear Badjidka Had Called Me" (6-29), Part II "*Il N'ya Pas De Dieu Ici*" (30-62), and Part III "The Most Cruel Death of the Talkative Zombie III" (63-80). Steeped in the tradition of theatre of the absurd, *Zombie* centres on the sayings and deeds of two characters mainly—Toura and Badjidka—as they mime, clown, fight, sing, embrace, and curse. Thus *Zombie*, as a whole, is made up of bits and pieces of dialogue and actions which make sense when seen in the light of Cameroon's political growth along with attendant existentialist apprehensions. Accordingly, Toura comes across as a facsimile of Ahmadou Ahidjo, the leader of the Francophone East Cameroon, while Badjidka represents John Ngu Foncha and Solomon Tandeng Muna, leaders of the Anglophone West Cameroon, who were, more often than not, seemingly servile in their relationship with Ahidjo as opposed to the rebellious Bobe Ngom Jua.

Without a typical plot as such, what one encounters, as if through a kaleidoscope, are the changing attitudes of the two central characters—Badjidka and Toura—as they interact. In the process, they bring out overwhelming revelations about the nation, their political doctrines, practices and malpractices towards their political opponents, backed by a malicious secret service and egoistic foreign powers out to protect their alien interests. At the head of the secret forces of oppression is Commandante Yaro Bakary

Amichivé, a name that brings to mind the name of the real head of Cameroon's Gestapo under Ahmadou Ahidjo and Paul Biya—Jean Fochivé—at this point in the nation's history. Amichivé, this incarnation of evil, relishes and thrives on torture and the murder of supposed subversive elements. He is a character whose thirst for human blood transforms him into a monster so brutal even the head of state himself is troubled by his overzealousness. According to Amichivé, "We will bomb a whole province in search of one man to extract his confession!" (37). His deeds alone conjure into existence a pervading macabre and grotesque atmosphere that tells the world the circumstances under which some human beings survive while others thrive. Amichivé is the beast that remains of a human being when justice is absent, the conscience dead and greed left to reign. It is in this light that one sees *Zombie* as a play set during the politically unstable period immediately after independence, when crude methods were used to bring about the kind of uneasy peace, nurtured by fear, which reigned then. It is therefore Toura's and Badjidka's ramblings and their deeds which amount to a trend in *Zombie* as these characters just speak and react in the manner of spontaneous thought patterns which do not follow any sequence. This notwithstanding, through the exploitation of metadrama, Besong makes his characters communicate poignant issues he wants to remind his audience of or familiarize them with. So the audience learns from Toura himself that national heroes like Um Nyobe were neutralized by the French colonialists, while the dreaded Yaro Amichivé confesses his own wickedness by admitting that he is the incarnation of the devil. From Badjidka, the audience is bluntly told that they have been manipulated this far by the tyrants because they are spineless fraidy-cats who cannot stand up for their rights.

The absence of a plot *per se*, notwithstanding, it is obvious that there are problems responsible for the jitteriness of Toura and Badjidka who end up, through their japery and slapstick, exposing the corrupt and dictatorial practices of the leading tyrants. It is, first of all, obvious that Toura is trying to assert himself on Badjidka (and he succeeds ultimately) and at the same time combating opponents. For these reasons, we often meet these two agreeing, disagreeing, laughing, dancing and so on. The goal, Toura's especially, is to subdue all opponents and this is the core of every word or deed of his and so the play remains virtually the same from the beginning to the end, with the same longings and protestations being made known as there are no obvious conflicts which could have caused the play to evolve through the logic of cause and effect.

In keeping with his avant-gardist approach to drama, the list of Besong's dramatis personae is scanty, with Toura and Badjidka doing most of the talking. Not only are the main actors two in number, they are miserable lepers with their disease mutilated bodies dangling on crutches as they spend time begging professionally. Their sickening appearances are heightened by the fact that they are troglodytes. As characters, Toura and Badjidka are lithe as their personalities change depending on the situation at hand. Toura, for example, is at one time dictatorial and assertive towards Badjidka and at another time submissive and friendly. This adaptable nature of theirs is best communicated even by the playwright's stage directions: *"THEY FIGHT. RECONCILE. THEY FRATERNISE. THEY CONFER: IN DUMB-SHOW"* (62). It is, in any case, these major characters whose dialogues and actions amount to the play *Zombie*. Minor characters like Commandante Yaro Bakary Amichivé , Voices, Stooges, and Gorilles are there as foils mainly to confirm the all too familiar monstrosity of the regime in place, headed by Toura and Badjidka whom the former is doing all to subdue.

This duo's language is sometimes uncouth and foul as they both curse and occasionally sing trite songs like hoboes in an effort to fill their tormented days with assorted rant and relieving yet revealing shenanigans. Besides English, the characters employ French and Hausa to drive home certain points. Even Latin is made use of: *"Ite Missa est ..."* (65). Befittingly, these rustics' language is uncouth yet realistic as their style drops to that of slangs and other informal expressions. Consider Badjidka's diction in the following dialogue:

TOURA: (*his turn now to throw accusation*). Badjidk after this
   small gift you were all teeth and obsequouisness.

BADJIDKA: It was an honour to serve under an ex
   -Commis de Poste whose virgin mother's ding-dong
   was brutally dug into by Mr. Holy Spirit himself. (61)

Or consider the triteness of one of their songs:

119

Tumbu Tumb
Bos Kalaba
Titi Mbala poom
Mbala mbala kai kai
kai
Titi titi mbus.

Tumbu Tumbu
Bos Commandate (sic)
Titi Badjidka poom
Mbala mbala kai kai
kai
Toura mbus (49)

The songs in themselves may not say much, but their triteness reveals the low esteem in which these characters are held by the playwright, and given that they are effectively types, communicates the playwright's disgust for their likes in real life. Beyond their seeming pedestrian quality, the titles of Besong's songs are revealing of the totalitarian regime they depict: "Ballad of a Party Cadre" (9), Ballad of the Civilian Junta (51), and "Song of the Great Fatherland" (60) are examples. That Toura and Badjidka are lepers shows them as physically inadequate human beings; by extension, they are politically inadequate and misfits in their leadership roles. Yet Besong exploits their inadequacies as shown already by making them confess and expose themselves like idiots, or by involving them in mime and parody through which they expose and ridicule themselves and the system in place. Toura and Badjidka as voices, for example, show the role of fear in the established system:

TOURA: (*recovering*) Who is that?

BADJIDKA: Don't you remember my voice, you asthmatic ruffian?

TOURA: (*smugly*) Political speeches without sincerity.
SILENCE. TENSION. CONFRONTAtION. THE

LEPERS EXCHANGE GLANCES.

BADJIDKA: (*prodding*) Thus it means you are reconsidering?

TOURA: (*vehemently*) It means nothing! I am reconsidering
nothing!

BADJIDKA: But Tcholliré! The evil rooms of Tcholliré...
Do you know what you're denying?

TOURA: Leave me alone! Leave me in peace! I've said
more than I should. Admitted more than I had a right
to.

BADJIDKA: (*to the audience*) Fear was a weapon we used
with extraordinary skill. I speak professional-ly. (13-14).

Besong, in time and space, sets his play shortly after independence in the
emerging Cameroon federation. This is obvious as we realize that Toura and
Badjidka have just taken over from colonialists to whom they are still
answerable about their plans for their country as revealed by Toura's speech
during the congress:

TOURA: **TAKES EYES OFF PRESIDENTIAL
LECTERN. SURVEYS HIS COWED AUDIENCE.
METHUSELAH BADJIDKA IS LOUDLY, SNORING.
TOURA BANGS BOTH FISTS ON THE** *TABLE
STARTLING* **HIS SNORING AIDES ETC.** *AS HE
STARES* **GREEDILY AT THEM AS ONE MAN ALL
RISE AND CHEER: CHEERS RESOUNDING LIKE
A MIGHTY PEAL OF THUNDER.**

Fraternal Comrades, in this connection, we should
enhance the role of our Great World-Wide Party,

which like the Maginot line, is consolidating its
position against any divisive activities and any threats
to our national patrimony and leadership.

Long Live the Vision Given to me by our Allies. Long
Live my patriarchs: The Saints from Jerusalem's Third
Cycle!

Long Live my External collaborators ... tireless
defenders of our bastion of Touralogy. I now declare
the meeting suspended till this mid-night when you'll
resume your rewarding work on the invaluability of the
covenant of Babacracy: Touralogy. (22)

One can tell that Cameroon is the geographical setting because of the
occasionally bilingual nature of Toura and Badjidka's dialogue and the
derogatory reference to the minority Anglophone population. Toura, for
example, questions Badjidka when he swears that Anglophones desired
power: "Had you Anglo-fools a pseudo-independence? Where is your
currency? A flag, A national anthem?" (15). All this goes to emphasize the
Anglophone/Francophone conflict in Cameroon, with the Francophone
appearing or claiming to be superior to the former, which is Besong's main
thematic concern. It is this predicament which is highlighted by the dialogues
and actions which take place between Toura and Badjidka. At a subsidiary
level, the nature of Toura's totalitarian regime remotely controlled by the
French, is another of Besong's concerns. The instrument of fear is Toura's
bloodthirsty cur, Yaro Amichivé, of the country's secret service which thrives
on torture. Hence, in Amichivé's wake, according to the stage directions,
soldiers are running about killing, brutalizing, and razing houses to the
ground and in the process trampling on children and women even as
explosions are heard in the background (53). Amichivé is piling up his own
Robespierrean red mass, but this is no revolution à la France to trim imperial
excesses; instead, it is the suppression of the voice of society, the voice of the
exploited proletariat. Shadrach A. Ambanasom's analogy of Amichivé and
Mary Shelley's Frankenstein is apt, (*Education* 82) for, like Frankenstein,
Amichivé is a controversial figure whose strong belief in his crude methods

of extracting information—torture—has transformed him into its devotee such that even his own mentor is no longer safe. As the playwright himself tells of Amichivé:

> ... Colonel
> — Escandron Amichive is the most powerful
> man in the country — Uncrowned fuehrer of
> The Chapels, even the Father of the Nation
> thinks twice before issuing decrees unfavou-
> rable to him.... (33)

Besides these themes being stated by the principal characters, even if only fragmentally, they are also implied by their actions. The topicality of Besong's themes notwithstanding, much of what obtains in this formless play like the dictatorship by Toura and the use of torture by Amichivé and his "gorilles" are universal malpractices. In the light of the play's title, Amichivé is certainly the talkative *Zombie* who dies in a cruel manner in need of blood transfusion.

Through a rich exploitation of the recipe of theatre of the absurd, mime, humour, parody, and the use of songs and confessions, Besong is able to communicate his message to the world. In keeping with J. B. Steane's convictions about a work of art, Besong's *Zombie* cannot be seen as "an object created in isolation" (10) for from the characters' deeds, their words, their song, their dreams and activities, and particularly the historical echoes vibrating around nomenclatural absurdities passing for names, a wide variety of which brings to mind historical figures in Cameroon, *Zombie* is a work that mirrors the spirit of the era that gave it birth. While attacking the pilfering bourgeoisie of his hour, Besong deals with the oppressed with velvet gloves; they are the exploited underdogs of his society taken advantage of by those who should better their lot instead, and in the process they are tortured almost to death in large numbers, a practice that cultivates fear deep into the abused psyche of the downtrodden.

In a nutshell, Besong presents a picture highlighting the predicament in his country, Cameroon: the obnoxious atrocities of an undemocratic regime; this is all not without an overriding verbal message from the playwright. Besong's idea is, to my mind, to affect his audience mentally through the disgusting scenario presented rather than through straightforward messages.

The point is simple: all is not well, but the playwright leaves the audience to see for themselves. Possibly, Besong is also warning killers like Amichivé to realize that there is an end to everything as Amichivé himself dies shamefully in the end. The perpetrators of evil seem to be Besong's target and his subtle message to them communicated through Amichivé's fate.

Besong's *Zombie* is a play in the tradition of theatre of the absurd for it violates, to a large extent, dramatic conventions with two main characters in the manner of personae. In its avant-garde tradition, it does not depend on dramatic conventions much but on Besong's use of stage directions which are sometimes very elaborate. The events in the play occur without any logical sequence, with the past occasionally brought to the present through flashbacks. Consequently, one is left with an overwhelming feeling of confusion and disorder in the way events occur, yet it is obvious that this is the atmosphere Besong sets out to portray as he brings together strange forces with strange ideas in a seemingly motiveless interaction, as chaos and fear are the end-products in a bid to maintain mediocrity in power.

Beasts of No Nation (1990)

The plight of the suffering masses and the dung-heap that socio-political malpractices have transformed Ednouay into is the focus of Bate Besong's *Beasts of No Nation (Beasts)*; a title which brings to mind a musical collection by Fela Anikulapo Kuti, the late Nigerian firebrand musician, rebel, and king of Afro-Beat and thereby the international nature of Besong's concern in *Beasts* even if Cameroon is of primary concern. Yet who are those suffering, and where is this municipality called Ednouay, are some of the pertinent questions to be answered if Besong's second play must be fully grasped and with the intended impact.

Unlike *Zombie*, there is some sort of a plot and more of a structure in *Beasts*. Foremost is the presence of the Night-soil-men who, along with Cripple and Blindman are the doomed carriers of the fetid waste of Ednouay city council. They are basking in the stench of their predicament even as the opening stage directions reveal:

*The stench from the lavatory
stands in the theatre like the
pangs of SAP (Structural*

Adjustment Programme).
One of the night-soil-men
sits on an empty bucket.
He is asleep besides his
Night-soil equipment. (85)

It is remarkable that they are asking for their professional identity cards, the only means at their disposal for showing they belong to some kind of union—the transporters of waste or better still faecal matter. In contrast and direct conflict with the Night-soil-men is the powerful Supreme Maximum Mayor of Ednouay Municipal Council, Comrade Dealsham Aadingingin with the ability to play the city's anthem backwards (82) who is denying the Night-soil-men their rights to an identity card; this is the conflict which propels the play. The Night-soil-men are demanding recognition through owning professional identity cards, but Narrator whom they are addressing, and true to the cumbersome nature of governance typical of the play's geo-historical context, asks them to go through Chef Gaston Lazare Otshama. From here on, *Beasts* moves in leaping stages identified by sub-titles. The opening part is titled "Parabasis" (85) followed by "Beasts of No Nation" (103), then there is "Aadingingin and the Night-soil-men" (118) and "Aadingingin and the Night-soil-men - Aftermath" (126). Like in *Zombie*, Besong is still much an experimentalist who is little concerned with generic conventionalities as one can hardly talk of the exposition, complication, crisis level, falling action and a conclusion in this order. Besong's exposition and the level of complication are tightly together at the opening of the play, which then maintains that tension characteristic of a crisis situation, to the very end, without the crisis being resolved. Pathetic Night-soil-men are attempting to bring meaning into their lives as they grope in vain for recognition in a stifling and unrewarding abyss of a society through the acquisition of professional identity cards.

When *Beast* opens, the very complex character—Narrator—is encountered in a manner reminiscent of the Greek chorus before his revealing exchanges with the Night-soil-men who come in asking for their freedom while complaining bitterly about the stench from their place of work—the lavatory. Besong subtitles this section of his play "Parabasis" yet if there is anything comic here, it is the grimness of the smelling landscape and the absurd yet profoundly revealing interaction between Narrator and the Night-soil-men. Even then, this humour is stillborn as one's laughter at the disgust and incredulity of the situation is immediately asphyxiated by the recognition of the reality of the pervading gloominess. Again, we are still at the beginning of the play, whereas in the earliest forms of comedy "Parabasis" usually led to the end of the play. Accordingly, there is the possibility, considering the definition of parabasis and its role in earlier comedies that Besong started his play from the end, went through the middle and then to the beginning. Besong's exposition is at once loaded with complications immediately assuming crisis level; hence, the established existence of an *agon*. The Night-soil-men's demand for their freedom bounces off a display of absurd governmental bottlenecks as Narrator advises them, condescendingly, to respect protocol and channel their grievances correctly:

> Don't complain to me. Complain
> to Chef Gaston. Complain to Chef
> Lazare Gaston Otshama. Make
> your complaint through proper
> channels. (88).

It becomes more obvious then that Besong's "Parabasis" is indeed the end of his play coming first. The Night-soil-men are fed up with their experiences with the government and the system in place portrayed in what can be conveniently referred to as Section III, "Aadingingin & the Night-soil-men," the true beginning of the play. They are confirmed as Night-soil-men and accordingly beasts without a nation in Part II, "Beasts of No Nation." It is for this reason that they begin clamouring for recognition in Part I, "Parabasis," which is in fact the end of the play. In other words then, Part III, the true beginning of the play establishes the Night-soil-men as Night-soil-men, Part II confirms them beasts without a nation, as a result, and the supposed Part III, "Parabasis," leads to their protestations culminating in the uprising which concludes the play. *Beasts*, then is a play standing on its head like the nation of which it is a microcosmic representation—Cameroon—with misplaced, if not reversed, priorities. Yes, it has taken Anglophone-Cameroonians so long to begin agitating for recognition in this so-called fatherland of theirs where they have been abused and exploited as

126

concretized by the accusations levelled against Cripple in the mime:

CRIPPLE: You say I am an excessive
Champagne drinker.
You say I own five jaguars
And fifteen benzes
And that I have built
In spite of S.A.P.
Ten storey houses
Under five months
Rented out to Government
Which, brings in a neat pile
Of C.F.A. 5 million a month...(118)

Such exploitation suffered by the Anglophones led them to realize in Part II "Beasts of No Nation" that this reunification with the Council of Ednouay was not really a homecoming but a declaration of their position as national bastards hence their inability to own even identity cards. The Anglos now realize they had a burden, a "cross":

All: Anglo carry your cross alone
Anglo Turanchi. Shege! (125)

Thus, on their behalf, Narrator points out:

Even a fool when he holdeth his
peace is counted wise. Since the
blind lead the blind, both shall fall
in a ditch. Let me see, ... What is
it we were talking about (sic). *I have
waited tiredly for the thaw of the
spring. Instead, I've been given a
homecoming of canisters and
launchers, of truncheons and
silence.* And I have given you an

127

example, and recalled the time
when the burden would have
rolled away…. (emphasis mine 89)

Accordingly, the Anglos in *Beasts* want recognition by being issued their professional identity cards just like their real life counterparts.

The second part of the play titled "Beast of No Nation" is a burlesque with the Blindman acting Aadingingin, and the Cripple playing Otshama as the two engage in very revealing dialogue which intensifies and makes lambent expositions by Narrator and the Night-soil-men in the section titled "Parabasis." The Cripple, as Otshama, reveals the importance of the Night-soil-men's professional identity cards as without these cards "they won't be able to march …" (111) nor could they be considered integrated. The consequences would be the writing of petitions. But according to Aadingingin (Blindman), "Anglos will always write petitions. It is in their make-up" (112). To further compound the difficulties in the path of the Night-soil-men's demand, Aadingingin (Blindman) while chuckling as if to say he is having fun at the expense of the Anglos orders Otshama (Cripple) to

(*chuckling*) Tell them to put in an
application, and attach on it: fiscal
stamps to the tune of one million
c.f.a. per application (112).

The third part of the play "Aadingingin and the Night-soil-men," opens with the Cripple, the Blindman and Night-soil-men in another ludicrous imitation of the treasonable habits of the municipalities' thieving and unpatriotic aristocracy. The "aftermath" under the section "Aadingingin and the Night-soil-men" (126) then opens with the Night-soil-men at work. It is the most disgusting scene of the play as the fetid nature of the Night-soil-men's job is overpoweringly experienced. The initial half of the aftermath paints a clear picture of the corruption characterizing Ednouay and the collapse of the laws that uphold communal life in a modern set-up. The very next scene in this part shows Aadingingin and Otshama in a conversation during which Otshama shows himself to be a master sycophant reminiscent of some African bootlickers. In a shameful declaration, Otshama tells his "Eminence" in a bid not to display his inability to handle the Night-soil-men and their demands that the Night-soil-men "... sincerely regret their past actions and now want their bygones to be bygones, except this little matter of their identification papers" (141).

This kind of blatant misrepresentation of facts before authority is not only shameful but misleading, yet how much similarity exists between this display and that which is obtained in regimes headed by dictators which, needless to say, abound in Africa. It is in this scene also that Besong exposes mismanagement in a bid to jibe at the misappropriation of government funds, another flavour in the broth of governance in Africa. Aadingingin shamelessly displays the financial disaster he is as Mayor of Ednouay council in the allocation of his budget:

> ...You know the Crisis
> budget I have to work with. [..] A
> mere c.f.a. 500 million. Now, I
> have already spent 350 million for
> toilet tissue. [..] c.f.a. 100 million
> for izal, disinfectants .... (140)

This is the situation made worse by the demands of the Night-soil-men. Unsurprisingly, Aadingingin instructs Otshama to execute them before coaxing his hangman-to-be with a brown envelope full of scarce c.f.a. notes. Before Otshama could leave the presence of his "Eminence," (141) the emptiness of his loyalty and all his lies are exposed by the sudden arrival of the rebellious Night-soil-men. The inefficiency of his administration strikes Aadingingin in the face as he realizes that the hour of truth has come when his misdeeds would be revealed, and so he tries to destroy available incriminating evidence. The play is brought to an end with Aadingingin displaying a misconception from which administrative failures like himself suffer: they always think the rebellious masses want their heads instead of positive change from the administration. Here Aadingingin questions: "You bastards! Bastards I say! What is it you want from me eh? Others have eaten and do not lose a second's sleep?" (142-143).

Shortly after this, he kills Otshama with just a shot, the Night-soil-men escape, he then retrieves his bulky envelope, desecrates the corpse of his closest disciple, Gaston Lazare Otshama, by kicking it before going on, like Goneril in Shakespeare's *King Lear*, to declare his dictatorial status:

> My Word is Double Law.
> I am the law. (143)

One cannot help recalling a similar French declaration of centuries before by Louis XIV: "*L'État c'est moi.*" The thought of the French Revolution which resulted from the squandermania that accompanied such arrogant and insulting declarations make it obvious that Aadingingin has an Ednouay Revolution brewing as he has dealt only with his sycophant, while the Night-soil-men regroup in preparation for another definitive encounter with him. This potential uprising is what we encounter in Parabasis with the Night-soil-men asking boldly for freedom, thereby confirming the cyclical nature of Besong's plot as is the case with Samuel Becket's Endgame. Thanks to the conflicting interest of the domineering twosome represented by the Night-soil-men on the one hand and Aadingingin on the other, Besong's *Beasts* with its amusement at the surface level as well as its subterranean messages turns out to be tartly impressive. Its impressiveness lies in the disgusting intensity of the overriding stench coming from the smell of shit suffocating the atmosphere; a most effective representation of the genuine predicament of the Anglophones in a nation they consider their own, and rightfully so, but where they do not feel welcome.

Beasts is set in a fictitious African municipality, part of an entire nation suffering from social, political, and economic degeneration. Narrator and the night-soil men paint the picture of decay in the section "Parabasis." Narrator condemns the entire generation as wasted while the Night-soil-men cry for freedom in a stench filled environment. This totally nauseating setting conjures, with precision, Besong's disgust not only towards Ednuoay municipality, but the nation as a whole. Through his characters, the playwright strives to jug the minds of the citizens out of their characteristic moronic stupor as Narrator cautions:

> Out of your own mouth will I
> judge you. Woe unto them that are

at ease in Ednouay. Multitudes in
the Valley of Darkness. You'll
continue to walk in perpetual
darkness. You'll never see the
great light. Where are the fruits as
evidence of your salvation? (91)

The corruption in Ednuoay is heightened such that Narrator sees in the
municipality an equivalent of the biblical Sodom and Gomorrah for he
observes:

If I find in Ednuoay
Two righteous Directors,
Then I will spare
All the place for
Their sake. But
They have left undone
Those things which they ought
To have done
And they have done
Those things which they ought not
To have done (94-95)

Completely convinced that the "frog" occupants of Ednuoay cannot manage
the finances, Narrator and the Night-soil-men, in a song, full of mockery,
taunt the frogs

So my dear frog-
Brother wack
And burn
This damnbrubah Ednuoay
Dear frog-
Brother wack
And burn
This damnbrubah Ednouay

For seeka goat
Di chop
For place weh
Dey be tie him (101)

The group further compares the "frogs'" handling of money to the locust's handling of green leaves:

When you eat money
The way locusts
Eat tonnes of green,
When frogs eat money
The way Locusts
Eat tonnes of green. (102)

The section "Parabasis" is in this way very revealing. The "anglos" are the Night-soil-men and, like Narrator, the eye-openers of society; whereas, the "frogs" do one thing best: "eat money the way locusts eat tonnes of green," (13). The "Parabasis" equally sums up the state of things in Ednuoay: like a lavatory, it is a municipality which reeks and stinks not only of shit and filth, but also of corruption.

The question of the traditional plot as such is certainly not Besong's preoccupation, but there is a structure unlike before: there is a crisis situation—corruption—from which the events in the play unfold. Besong is out to highlight the corruption in a society where anyone can steal any amount of tax-payers' money simply because the truant has an "umbrella" in Ednouay who would shield the crime. It is in keeping with such corruption that a delegation to Seoul Olympics, supposedly to represent the nation, is made up of only five athletes—the main participants—and fifty officials (104). In the face of such unpatriotic activities, the citizens remain uninformed because according to the Voice of Aadingingin:

The truth will be kept
Away from you
Our lies will be told
Boldly and persistently

For you can be made
To believe anything. (104)

Although focus is on the economic diarrhoea of the nation triggered by the "frog" bacteria of financial misappropriation, Besong is more concerned with the Anglophone's predicament in this nation; a nation tormented by all the ills a country can face, a situation made worse by the gullibility of law enforcement officers to whom "Taking bribes is all they know" (105). For fighting to free themselves from "horizontal colonialism," the Anglophones are branded "traitors and slaves" (105). The playwright's sympathy is for his people—the Anglophones—who work for the Francophones to feed fat. After all, is it not in this inferno triggered by the so-called economic crisis that Mercedes 500s and Japanese Pajeros are driven by Francophones in the main? Although Besong's sympathy is with the "Anglo," he also jibes at some of their own weaknesses, such as the backsliding of Anglophones by their fellow Anglophones who are fond of petitioning. As a result, Blindman points out: "... Anglos will always write petitions. It is in their make-up" (112). Besong's play is also focused on this society which, like a fountain, spews out corruption and debauchery of every category, for the playwright goes on swinging from one ill to the next: misappropriation of government funds, lies-telling by the government, and swindling from state ventures and parastatals to cite a few examples. The government's use of expensive taxation as a way of frustrating requests peculiar to Anglophones is also hinted at. The demand for professional cards by the Night-soil-men, and it is their right, is virtually frustrated by the exacting procedure introduced by the government (Blindman): "Tell them to put in an application, and attach on it: fiscal stamps to the tune of one million c.f.a. per application" (112). This second part of the play "Beasts of No Nation" is indeed a repertoire of the evil machinations frothing in the municipality of Ednouay.

The section on Aadingingin and the Night-soil-men is a repetition of the Anglophone's albatross in this nation of Agidigidi as they complain bitterly against the exaggerated wealth of their oppressors. To emphasize the ephemeralness of earthly wealth, the Second Night-soil-man mocks:

When I die,
Bury me with my

133

Skyscraper
And twenty billion c.f.a.
In my golden Coffin. (120-121)

Narrator then jibes at the consciences of the oppressed:

> ... my co-workers
> in the field of shitology don't have
> their independence and freedom. It
> appears that you'll soon have to
> decide to fight or run. A hero goes
> to war to die. (129)

Besong's work, as already indicated, amounts to a catalogue of the ills of Ednouay: from corruption, the misappropriation of government funds, through flattery, to the murdering of any one who dares to oppose or falters in his official duties for which they are answerable to Aadingingin alone. Besong's anger is choking and so his pen pukes filth, that grime, smut, which is the plight of the Anglo Night-soil-men in Ednouay. *Beasts* is definitely Besong's "filthiest" play, yet this is the filth that is Ednouay. Financially, morally, politically and otherwise, the Ednouay municipality is a garbage heap, its administrators-cum-manipulators bloated flies.

Still along thematic lines, the demand for professional identity cards by the Night-soil-men is a metaphor charged with the identity crisis facing Anglophones in a nation they call theirs, as they have been refused integration which they could only get through their acquisition of an identity clearly spelt out in the symbolic identity cards they are demanding. This, beyond *Beasts*, is indeed the plight of the Anglophone-Cameroonian in today's *La République du Cameroun*. It is in this light that Anglophone-Cameroonians are presented as the working hands fuelling, by their labour, the socio-political well-being of *La République du Cameroun* while remaining, themselves, "beasts of no nation." As Southern Cameroonians, the Anglophones had a young nation striving towards maturity under the auspices of the United Nations with Britain as the administering authority. The Anglophones, accordingly, had an identity. This identity was acknowledged even when Southern Cameroonians were only partners with

La République du Cameroun in the Federal and later on United Republic of Cameroon structure. But Bate Besong, in *Beasts*, is stating categorically that as Southern Cameroonians in a nation today bearing only the name of a former partner-state in the Federation—*La République*—Southern Cameroonians have thus been reduced to beasts without a nation. Furthermore, *La République* is today thriving because of the odd jobs done by "anglo Night-soil-men" who are at the same time threatened and tortured by the types of Aadingingin.

Besong's characters in *Beast* are types, "recognizable portraiture" (49) in the words of Annemarie Heywood, representing the levels of patriotism and egoism, the exploited and the exploiters. One, then, can hardly talk of an individual as the protagonist and another as the antagonist outright as the plot is based on group rather than individual roles and conflicts—the Night-soil-men on the one hand and the municipal authorities on the other. In the light of today's Cameroon which Besong is out to portray with particular emphasis on the Anglophone, it is obvious that the Night-soil-men represent Anglophones and the municipal authorities, Francophones. This fact is exposed when the Blindman and the Cripple are playing Aadingingin and Otshama respectively, and the Blindman refers to the Night-soil-men demanding professional identity cards as "Anglos." This declaration exposes Comrade Dealsham Aadingingin and Gaston Lazare Otshama as personifications of the economically suffocating municipal government of Ednouay. Aadingingin is a flat character whose reasoning and personality are dominated by the Machiavellian political instinct as all he spits out has to do with doing all it takes even if it means brutalizing as a way of maintaining those under him in their position. Otshama, meanwhile, is Aadingingin's bootlicking and sycophantic aid, a wilderness of deceit as all he does is echo Aadingingin's disastrous socio-political image as successful. He is a former Night-soil-man now in a better position because of the arrival of the "Anglo." Otshama lies, coaxes, persuades, and flatters as means of bloating his master's shrunken confidence, thereby maintaining himself in office. But like his type, he dies miserably as the truth dawns on Aadingingin who shows the worthlessness of fellows like the astute Otshama by killing him first instead of one of the Night-soil-men.

The Night-soil-men are faceless people identified only by their servile profession which services they render to a municipality which does not

135

acknowledge them as citizens but wants them as work hands. For this reason, the municipality is sluggish about giving them identity cards as this would mean their integration and attendant promotion from the status of slavish alien labourers to citizens. This notwithstanding, the Night-soil-men are a conscious group aware of their rights and the value of their indispensable services to the council of Ednouay, a leverage for the demanding of their rights symbolized by the professional identity cards they want.

The Blindman and the Cripple, far from being mere pawns like Samuel Beckett's Vladimir and Estragon in *Waiting for Godot*, are themselves physically challenged human beings who amount to the garbled socio-political atmosphere that characterizes Ednouay: filth, greed, unaccountability, torture, misappropriation, to cite a few. They are symbols of the warped image Ednouay cuts. Beyond this, they are rustic characters much akin to Thomas Hardy's in *The Mayor of Casterbridge* as through their mock-character and role portrayal of Aadingingin and Otshama, they bring to light a lot about these persons and their ways, especially towards the "anglo Night-soil-men".

Narrator, on his part, is a very complex character playing the guiding and informative role reminiscent of the chorus in Grecian plays, while at other times he shows himself good and at another bad in the manner of Wole Soyinka's Eshuro in *A Dance of the Forest*. Narrator is, therefore, unpredictable. Sometimes he sounds like an "anglo" himself:

Open rebuke is better
Than secret love
Be not made a beggar
By banqueting
On borrowing.
We brought nothing
Into Ednouay.
And it is certain we can
Carry nothing out
(*in a pontifical tone*)
I have fought a good fight,
I have finished my course,
I have kept my Anglo-faith.

He that hath ears to hear,
Let him hear! (95)

And at yet another time, his condescending airs mark him out for a
sympathizer of the municipality's oppressive leadership role:

Comes the hour of the curfew.
                    ... Realize that
Ednouay loves you deeply and
Calls you to become her night-soil
carrier. Realize that you have
offended Ednouay with your life
by refusing to carry nightsoil
yesterday ... (97).

He is the typical sly who is, all notwithstanding, doing all he can to better
himself first. Narrator is indeed complex, even to the point of sounding wise
at one moment through the use of apt proverbs: "A beggar can never be
bankrupt" (127), or "It is a bad workman that quarrels with his tools" (127),
at another moment ridiculous as he professes the philosophy of a cheat
(109), and at yet another moment he passes for an ideal patriot. He is an
actor per se but a most controversial one as his ideas are a bundle of
contradictions. It is this, possibly, that has led Shadrach A. Ambanasom into
considering his slogan "A hero goes to war to die," empty (*Education* 99). On
the contrary, this is to my mind a pep slogan even if used by the hypocritical
Narrator sarcastically. To him, he might just be making noise, but to the
Night-soil-men, with their genuine struggle, the meaning of struggling comes
across to them in this line. This is particularly the case when he calls the
"Anglo's" demand "a fundamental delusion" (129) before declaring:

...If you don't have and
what will you say you have?... If
you don't have that you don't
have anything ... my co-workers
in the field of shitology don't have
their independence and freedom. It

137

appears that you'll soon have to
decide to fight or run. A hero goes
to war to die (129).

Again, even if Narrator spoke tongue in cheek here, his concluding slogan
cannot be described as "empty" as his advice that the "Anglos" may have to
fight or run in the face of their problems, is true. If they fight they are being
heroes, and in fighting some will, certainly, die. How true and loaded then
rather than empty is Narrator's slogan.

Besong's style in *Beasts* is characteristically fresh with characters being
themselves at one time and at another, playing roles. While, like in *Zombie*
where songs are a core stylistic element in the play, Besong, in *Beasts,* also
uses Pidgin, a corruption of Pidgin, and Latinate words and expressions. His
songs, even if they do, are not employed for the purpose of entertainment or
an interlude but to emphasize or deride a targeted philosophy. This is the
case with Song of the Prodigal (100-101), and that of the Night-soil-men
(101). Besong employs parody to the same end as through this technique he
is able to ridicule the unpatriotic leadership of the Ednouay municipality. The
seriousness and purposefulness of Besong's technique notwithstanding,
George Anastaplo says of art, while confining himself to verbal arts mainly:
"By and large, art both instructs and entertains us. It instructs us partly by
entertaining us; it entertains us partly by instructing us. We are likely to learn
from that which amuses us; we are likely to enjoy that which seems to teach
us something" (1).

Besong's figurativeness in *Beasts* is also given a boost: his characters do
not occasionally allude to the bible but sound very biblical themselves. It is
Narrator who declares:

> ... He
> changes the sinner into the saint
> (*pause*). Zaccheus, come down.
> Hurry, because I must stay at your
> house today (94).

He later declares again:

...The wind bloweth where
it listeth, and thou hearest the
sound thereof, but canst not tell
whence it cometh, and wither it
goeth (97).

Irony, sarcasm, satire, hyperbole, and an influential oral presence in the form
of songs and proverbs are features of Besong's stylistic arsenal that convey
an overpowering experience of nausea produced by the stinking atmosphere
of filth and shit. This atmosphere conjured by the metaphor of shit, displays
the playwright's disgust at the administrative set-up in the Ednouay
municipality, a municipality which resembles that of many Cameroonian
cities as subtly suggested by Besong.

The terminology "Anglo" is very Cameroonian and Ednouay is without
doubt an anagram from "Yaounde." Cognizant of the many other similarities
between events and happenings cited in Ednouay in line with those taking
place in Cameroon, such as citizens "banking" money in their ceilings, the
taking of more officials than athletes to Seoul for the Olympic competition,
and the "Anglo" identity crisis, one can conveniently see Besong's Ednouay
as a microcosm of the Cameroonian nation and in reality as Cameroon's
capital city, Yaounde. *Beasts* is, accordingly, a provocatively and equally
revealing play with its pungent smell of shit, Besong's concretizing image for
the decadent nature of the Cameroonian society, politically, morally and
otherwise. For this, Ada Ugah considers the play "Anglophone Cameroon's
most pungent indictment of francophone oligarchic rule in that part of
central Africa". Although the pervading experience is that of the reign of
mediocrity powered by injustice, Besong is beginning to hope for a better
future. Unlike in *Zombie*, Besong, in *Beasts*, leaves room for "people power,"
through the already sizzling potential of a revolution by the Night-soil-men,
to bring about change even if they have failed this time. The present
revolution as depicted fails, but that there could have been such an effort is
pointer to a potential regrouping and the repeat of this effort at liberation
contrary to Hilarious N. Ambe's frustrating and stagnating interpretation that

*This defeat of the liberation endeavour is the warning signal of doom and darkness
emphasised in the central organising metaphor of shit and stench.* This warning

139

signal is that class exploiters, those with excessive power and connections, such as Aadingingin, would always usurp the final decisions about any persons or group of persons' future if the struggle of the masses is not collectively organised and coordinated. (emphasis mine 194).

What Ambe fails to point out is how else this rebellion could have been "collectively organised and coordinated" (194) realizing that Besong is already doing what the educated class is supposed to be doing regarding his aesthetics which Ambe himself acknowledges when he observes: "For Besong partly believes, as does Osofisan too, that the educated and intellectual class could, more than any other class, assist in salvaging society" (194)

Requiem for the Last Kaiser (1991)

Requiem For The Last Kaiser (*Requiem*), like Besong's earlier plays, is also highly experimental in style. Without "Acts" and logical scenes as major parts of the play, *Requiem* is realized through Fragments and Movements with an Act Drop dividing the play into two unequal parts. *Requiem*, accordingly, opens with the "Initiations," followed by two "Fragments of a Scene," and then an "Act Drop," a "Fragment of a Scene," and two other "Movements."

Requiem is set in a fictitious African capital city tottering on the verge of total decay, a state of profligacy triggered into existence by the political inadequacies of brownnosers and unpatriotic parvenus passing for leaders. Nothing, Besong is saying, can survive in such an atmosphere of chaos as there is no system in place; this is the pith of the play. The struggle is between those interested in sucking dry the nation's financial lifeblood—legalized pilferers of the nation's wealth—as opposed to the progressives who want to save the deteriorating socio-economic health of the nation.

"Initiations" (1), the opening section of the play, set in a rich Iduote Marble Palace in the capital city, unfortunately, reveals a funerary atmosphere with the voice of His Majesty Baal Akhikikrikii Njunghu coming from a coffin. It is immediately important to note that the name of the Marble Palace "Iduote" is an anagram of Etoudi, the neighbourhood lodging Cameroon's presidential palace. His Majesty's words from the coffin amount to a spelling of the tragic *status quo* in this nation of Agidigidi. There is, first of all, a display of total lack of understanding between Baal Njunghu Akhikikrikii and his citizens for as one finds out later on, his people do not understand him the way he wants us to believe they do. Again, one realises that Akhikikrikii is a dictator who rules by decrees, which he uses to get his people where he wants them and not where they would like to be. True to his dictatorial nature, he stupidly declares:

> ...By decree number one million and ninety-ten...ninety-ten (*pause*). I'll get them where I want ... (a *spitting noise*) Take these journalists off and torture them... I am the Consciousness, the Tempo and Heart-Throb of Iduote ... The He-Alone and Guide. (*Short pause*). I am the One-Man-Band... (1)

A leader could never be better ridiculed than His Majesty is in this opening utterance of his. This opening speech sets the pace as a lampoon and justifies the playwright's continuous bitterness. When a country depends thus on the whims of one such idiot, the "divine" ruler of the people whose sole concern is his own welfare and nothing else, the plight of such a nation and the citizens can only be imagined. Little wonder in the following "Fragment of a Scene" (2), Woman is seen indoctrinating Student against the ills that characterize Agidigidi under the reign of Akhikikrikii and his likes, demonic leaders who have transformed themselves into "horizontal colonizers," colonizing their own kind. These are the enemies of the people as they have transformed the nation into a wasteland and the youths, the hope of every nation's tomorrow, into final idiots confirmed by alcohol (5). Not even the church with its sedating dogma on subservience is spared by Woman. Any whim contrary to that of the suffering masses must not be tolerated, hence Woman vows: "Struggle must be our life" (6). Beyond her vow is the playwright's wish for society which Woman again puts forward: "The people shall govern" (6). In a revealing metaphor, she sums up the youth's mission to the nation, since the elders, even the police and the army, have failed:

> What does a dentist do with a bad tooth? (*pause*). Note:
> it will take a hammer and chisel to knock off Agidigidi's
> bad leadership teeth (2).

The youth in Woman's dream is the dentist to free the national mouth of Akhikikrikii's bad tooth governance. Woman's voice is, therefore, the voice of hope, justice, and impending victory for the suffering masses.

In the following "Fragment of a Scene" (9), Woman has an opportunity to expose her feelings towards what she considers the Church's hypocrisy as she jibes at Holy Prophet A. A. Atangana's tendency of deifying a regime which is unrepresentative of its peoples. The Holy prophet Atangana, instead of joining the masses to fight for justice, sees the consequences of a conscienceless leadership as signs of the end of the world. He is accordingly dismissed by Woman:

> (contemptuously). Stuff your hypocritical Good evenings ... So long as you church Monarchs anoint and bless the elephantine plunder in Agidigidi; I'll have none of your white-washed theology. (9)

Atangana, besides his god, worships the nation's corrupt leader whom he refers to in absentia as "The Guide and Paraclete His Most Holy Excellency Njunghu Akhikikrikii wa Njunghu" (11). Besong, by bringing in Atangana as a character, is no doubt questioning the church's stance in politics and her role in a nation tormented by mismanagement and dictatorship in the guise of democracy. The fate of the church is sealed by Woman's lament: "Down with the fat thieves of the church! Down with the robbers in paradise" (14). In a flashback within this same "Fragment," power and politics are further presented as a cult with subordinates as priests worshipping their political leader. Abessollo also emerges in this flashback as the security boss of the regime. His techniques as security boss clearly come out when he threatens Woman against her patriotic struggles to oust the repressive regime:

> You may speechify and plot against us; I know that you'll lead them only to more suffering because of your sinister ambition ... And quote me if you so desire; We'll give you surgery without anaesthesia. And I'll hold the knife. 17-18).

These threats notwithstanding, Woman declares their insurgence "a popular uprising and not a coup" (19).

In the final "Fragment" (22) the misleading role of the West in Africa's

142

political scenario is highlighted as Ambassador and Swiss Banker flatter Akhikikrikii only to insult and ridicule him as soon as he turns his back to them. Ambassador, for example, tells Njunghu: "It has been a privilege meeting such a distinguished genius of politics" (22), only for Swiss Banker to insult him out of earshot a few minutes later on: "An impenetrable negro beast! Who will hammer his iron jaws open? ... A drugged fool!" (23). How ridiculous is their selfish counsel to Akhikikrikii when Swiss Banker decries thus the demands of the citizenry: "A national conference has no place in emerging nations. Tried leaders always avoid that leprosy" (24). Ambassador, true to their kind, only concords: "A national conference is an enemy to be killed on sight!" (25). Besong here is ridiculing the idea of Western spokesmen praising local economies to the delight of dictators of such ailing regimes while the indigenes are chaffing; a display which betrays the nonsense diplomacy and politics in Africa all amount to in relation to the West.

Besong has a way of sampling opinions about the tide of events. In the "First Movement" which follows, the forces of change are encountered. These are the qualified academics wallowing in a state of despair to which they have been relegated by a system which rewards mediocrity; there is Akonchong, Gambari, Poet as Mandela, Workers, and the voice of Woman. In this movement, in a parody by these academics, the regime is satirised while its diehard supporters like Abessollo struggle to defend it. Scene two of this "First Movement" reveals the forces of change, this time including the leader of the market women and Woman at work against the forces of regression which are defending Akhikikrikii's highhandedness. Beyond this, the academics in a mock-play expose and jibe at the regime. The result is a kind of eye-opening display with consequences detrimental to the regime, hence Abessollo's appearance with a gun in a sterile threat against the forces of change.

In the "Second Movement" which is the last section of the play, the tide turns against Akhikikrikii in favour of the forces of change that all the way had been against the regime in power. The scene is revealing as the forces of change, now including re-educated infantrymen, have surrounded the Marble Palace. Even at such a point in the history of Akhikikrikii's rule, Harl Ngongo still uses flattery in dealing with his leader. It is at this point that Ngongo the frog-mouthed "laureate" abandons his old ways by confessing his guilt and lamenting the plight of the people. Truth also dawns on Abessollo who, with the army having gone berserk, is left with no other choice than to abandon Akhikikrikii who is yet to realize the hopelessness of his lot without the army. It is in this light that Abessollo sums up the struggle that has characterized their lives as "... a battle of the entire nation against the dark forces of tyranny, tribalism and greed ..." (69) which, ironically, they incarnated. When justice finally catches up with Akhikikrikii as he faces his own downfall, his confession is a revealing warning to spineless unpatriotic leaders:

Under my administration I was never the corrupt one,
it was the French and the corrupt civil servants I
appointed into government who embezzled Sonara
money, not me. My hands are clean. These opposition
men. They are not fair to themselves! (71)

But these are words that are too late as they have been forced out of him by events than a genuine feeling for the plight of the oppressed proletariat. The result is that Akhikikrikii kills himself to make way, inadvertently, for the forces of change that are here incarnated by Workers, Poet, Woman etc., to force their way into the Marble Palace.

Talking of plot in *Requiem* would sound like an off-beat in musical time signatures as Besong's play is made up of fragmented routine scenes strung together mainly by the over-riding doctrine the play is preaching—the need to become conscious of the ills of the regime in power and so bring about change. This is the essential problem, the pivot on which *Requiem* twirls, but the "Fragments," "Movements," and scenes do not make an obviously logical whole with action leading to action, scene to scene and so on. This rather seemingly senseless amorphous quality of the play, far from being the result of the playwright's inability to structure his piece, is a stylistic flourish by an avant-garde exploited in a bid to concretely realize the chaos characteristic of the world distorted by Akhikikrikii's despotism. In this way Besong's theatre speaks to the spiritual quintessence of his audience while challenging them to confront their predicament in life and to perceive with laughter its entrenched farcicality which is the nauseousness of persecution, repression, corruption and the decadent worldview of a doomed leadership.

As events unfold, Akhikikrikii sees himself as the beginning and the end of the regime with its seat in the Iduote Marble Palace. It is in this light that he terrorises in the name of governance, reducing every official of his to a fawning toady; not even foreigners dealing with his government are free as they all must flatter him and air their true feelings only in Akhikikrikii's back. But things start going wrong when other progressive elements like the unemployed academics and Woman begin making their presence felt when they educate the masses and even the army in the line of their oppressed lot. The turning tide climaxes with the rebellion of the army and the desertion of Akhikikrikii by his loyal subordinates like Abessollo and Ngongo. Akhikikrikii's suicide seems to be the only way out for an unrepentant despot of his calibre. The funerary atmosphere with which the play opens pervades the play all through until the end, when Akhikikrikii makes appropriate use of the coffin from which his voice resounds.

Besong's characters are a collection of heroes and anti-heroes of both sexes. His Majesty Baal Njunghu Akhikikrikii is an apt personality representative of despotic wags who have not only betrayed individual African nations but have reduced this otherwise admirable continent into a laughing stock. In every way a wreck, Akhikikrikii aggravates the obnoxiousness of his blunders by being unable to identify his limits even as a despot. He is a minion without a sense of purpose beyond seeing himself as a god who distinguishes himself in the ranks of notoriety with blunder following blunder in the challenging exercise of leadership which he finds certainly overwhelming. Even when deserted by those on whom his travesty of a regime rested—the military, Abessollo and Ngongo—this incarnation of failure and incompetence blames others for his errors and like the cowards such maniacs are, seeks refuge in suicide rather than face the wrath of a citizenry he and his cohorts, indigenous and foreign alike, have abused and milked dry.

Holy Prophet A. A. Atangana is a spineless pastor trusting in materialism while banishing spiritualism from his "holy" presence. Instead of worshipping God, and like the good shepherd he ought to be taking care of his starving flock, Atangana transforms politics into a religion with Akhikikrikii as the god, much in the manner of Joseph Conrad's Kurtz, to be worshipped by his exploited and starving disciples. As a spiritual leader, Atangana is a failure. Besong uses this character to conscientize a church

145

slumbering in the face of bad governance which has given birth to a suffering population. Besong is in this light against religion being used as a political opiate for transforming the exploited into a lethargic lot in the name of humble "Christians."

While Françoise Hippopo couched as Madam Patriot is a nonentity, an opportunist making use of a corrupt system for personal gains as her creed is shamefully "Envelopes are juicier ..." (25) Ngongo is a similar miscreant; a writer who betrayed his noble craft by becoming a palace griot for personal gains. When the mess he has made of himself dawns on him, he bemoans:

As a writer, I destroyed my formula for national
salvation. Truth ... I burnt it on the mediocrity pyre of
state banquets ... Blood money in some far away
European commercial trap ... to become an important
robber, into ashes I burnt away my creative soul ...
Now, what can I call my own? (65).

Even then, Ngongo is a better state-tool than Françoise Hippopo as he realizes his mistake and repents. The similarity between these characters and others in the Biya regime of Cameroon today is alarming and certainly the source of Besong's inspiration.

Student represents the youths of today and the leaders of tomorrow, a fact which dictators like Akhikikrikii know but care less about. It is for this reason that with the present tide of despair brought about by a useless leadership, Woman decides to invest her hope in the youths and so spends her time indoctrinating Student against the unpatriotic, pilfering, and dictatorial regime in place and headed by the political disaster, Akhikikrikii. With Student, there is hope that all is not lost. Woman, this matriarchal figure, although betrayed by Françoise Hippopo, is the only sane human bridge between the present and the future through the services she renders her people by educating Student against today's kleptocratic bourgeoisie. She is the one who makes clear the plight of the oppressed and downtrodden lot of the wretched of Agidigidi while mapping out a plan of action which she infuses with a sense of patriotism. She, for example, refuses to see an uprising by the masses as a "coup" (19), as put by Akhikikrikii's hangman Abessollo, but as a "popular uprising" (19). Beyond Student as a political pupil of hers, Woman re-educates the brainwashed zombies in uniform, the last straw that breaks Akhikikrikii's dictatorship. In an address to penitent soldiers she observes:

> (*addressing group of penitent soldiers*). You cast your
> manhood, your pearls before robbers. You have lived
> off the backs of your own people - crumb-boys to those
> who turned their own fatherland into a successful neo-
> colony... By standing aloof from the struggle, you
> squelch the seed of the struggle. (56)

It is obviously due to this effort that the army later on goes berserk, as pointed out by Abessollo, leaving those in power helpless. Hence, the strategic role played by Woman in *Requiem*, comes to light. In the words of Eunice Ngongkum, Woman "... has the onerous task of conscientising all sensitive minds not only to an awareness of the situation but also to revolutionary action." (12) Beyond those with sensitive minds, Woman's words, her effort towards conscientizing, affect all and sundry, even diehard supporters of Akhikikrikii like Abessollo who end up victorious after seeing the wisdom in Woman's doctrine as representative of the collective will of the people. Besong's accordance to Woman of such a significant role in the preparation for, and realization of an uprising by the downtrodden does not augur well for the male gender, the hitherto so-called leaders of the world. To Besong, men seem to be failing in this leadership role where Woman has succeeded. It is not impossible that Besong is urging men to make way for women where they cannot achieve. After all, it is Woman who has brought an end to Akhikikrikii's reign of terror.

Ambassador Cracker Crookster and Swiss Banker, representatives of the West, signify continuous influential Western presence even after colonialism, hence the neo-colonial era. These social, economic, and political exploiters, masquerading as representatives of friendly nations, care less about their host country, Agidigidi. Their duty is to advise, even if wrongly, on how unpopular regimes can stay in power despite the wishes of the nationals. They are hypocrites who flatter and fake subservience in the face of Akhikikrikii only to insult him in the very next breath. These are confusionists with next to nothing at stake in view of the problems their unpatriotic counselling can bring about as all they do is flatter dictators and so pave the way for the continuous syphoning of a people's wealth by their home-countries. Else how can one account for words like those by Ambassador to an incarnation of political failure like Akhikikrikii:

(beaming approval) We see in you, Sir, a creative
symbol of the goal of our two but indivisible people.
As the consciousness of your nation we salute your very
great African culture.... (61)

Harl Ngongo is the "laureate" of Iduote. To serve in this capacity under an unpopular regime is tantamount to a betrayal of this profession as Ngongo cannot serve thus and yet be the conscience of society, as expected of writers, since it would mean biting the finger that feeds him. It is for this reason that as a writer, Ngongo has fallen from the pedestal of writing intended for the communicating of the plight of the masses, to writing propaganda speeches for an illiterate dictator who talks of "decree number one million and ninety-ten" (1). Ngongo is, therefore, twice a traitor for betraying the pen foremost, and then his oppressed compatriots. Realising himself when he observes "We the writers of Agidigidi crucified Truth. We nurtured the tumour that has eaten us" (65), Ngongo repents and joins the ranks to which he rightfully belongs with these words:

That long voice of protest pierces me *(sighs)*. I had
never been true to my inner self... only by destroying
this fascism and establishing on its ruins a new society
can the people save themselves from the horrors of
neo-colonial tyrannical terror ... (66)

État-Major Andze Abessollo holds that office which is a *sine qua non* for the survival of dictatorial regimes: he is Akhikikrikii's security boss, an office which entails, and most significantly too, the job of torture. Influenced by the financial crumbs from Akhikikrikii's table, he is blindly devoted to Akhikikrikii's unpopular regime. His devotion to the regime comes out in this answer he gives Woman when she addresses penitent soldiers:

148

(speaking into loudhailer from off) Mere alarmist!
Utter falsehood and slander ... Your (sic) are
only heading towards disaster ... I must warn you
of this illegal gathering. We will destroy whatever
stands on the path of the speech-making event...
(still off). We do not take prisoners! (56)

Abessollo further confirms his career as hangman for the regime when he
warns the rebellious Student:

(giving him a long puzzled stare). We will pour cement
clog into your asshole! We'll block your nostrils with
boiling tar! We'll feed you with your own testicles! (57)

Minority Nnyanyen is the Minister of State Oil who does nothing but
gambol around Akhikikrikii ready to answer to his calls and insults. That he is
just a puppet of a minister becomes obvious when hardly anything economic
is mentioned by him. He reminds us of some oil Ministers of Cameroon who
know nothing about the activities of Cameroon's sole refinery and so hate
questions from journalists tending towards oil money and attendant activities.
Minority Nnyanyen is supposed to stand for the minority in Agidigidi, but in
him we see a slow-witted coward subservient to a fault as all he does is fawn
when insulted by his god, Akhikikrikii, as seen in this exchange:

AKHIKIKRIKII: Where is the anini chap responsible for
  Minorities? *(growling as Minority Nnyanyen advances
  timorously to the end of the table; his sweat-damp report in his
  hands: The Guide seizes it. After looking briefly at it favours
  Minority with a cold, vicious stare)*. Imbecile of the most
  inferior calibre. Traitor of traitors. Jackal who licks his
  own mother's dunghill anus! Less then an atom of
  Bothadog! (sic)

MINORITY: Yes, you're your Anointed Majesty. *(said in a
  fawning manner)*. (23)

149

Dr. Akonchong and Mallam Gambari are unemployed academics reduced to vegetable vendors as a means of survival while nitwits reign over them. Their plight makes them conscious of the ills of a regime with misplaced priorities. They, along with Woman, conscientize the people, making them aware of the evils of the regime. They are, therefore, the forces of change together with Workers and Student and ultimately the repentant soldiers. The significant role played by this group in changing the socio-political tide of events in Agidigidi has been effectively represented by Shadrach A. Ambanasom: "The Woman and Dr Akonchong roughly represent theory; the student, soldiers and other workers, the potential for action. The ones represent reflections, the others praxis" (*Education* 92).

Besong's characters in *Requiem* come from the lowest to the highest ranks of Agidigidi amounting to a jumbled heap of personalities. They are members of a society without any sense of decorum and guided by an unprofessed law of the survival of the fittest as even the army is used by an unqualified and inexperienced leadership to stay in power. Whereas the major characters act out a tragedy of mismanagement in a dictatorship without justice and therefore the absence of charity towards the citizenry, the minor characters grunt for long under this bureaucratic yoke before bringing about an uprising triggered by Woman and the unemployed academics.

Consistent with the characters, the dialogue in *Requiem* does not only fluctuate between high and low style but obtains in many different languages. Although the characters converse in English, they occasionally switch into French, Afrikaans, Ewondo and Hausa even if it is only to interject, insult, or round up an expressed view. Besong's absurdist dialogue is always interspersed with many pauses, ellipses, and silences. Beyond these, it is often hesitant, spasmic, incoherent, and banal while verbalizing the self-evident when it is not outright meaningless nonsense. In the same vein, Besong paints diverse character portraits. To cite an example, the absurdist quality of his language along with the illiterate, corrupt and dictatorial qualities of Akhikikrikii come out when he speaks thus:

(*with maniacal hysteria*). Etat-Major Abessollo!! Mahok!
De Major! If the mountain does not rise up to meet
Baba Toura, why my dim-witted venal Ministers must go
to the mountain… De Major! Take my lick-spitting

nose-wiping Ministers to the mountain! A scorched-
earth policy, I say! My poisoned arrows! *Haba*! Marshall
General Abessollo...Promoted... Just like that...Kill
them all for me! Field Marshall! *Eee...grrrrrh*! *eei-*
ggrrrrrh! Mahok! *Haba*! Sonara money abui. Amot,
money abui! Sonara nkap abui. Essamba! Essamba!
Essamba! (69).

The messianic role of Woman, her awareness of the existing ills in society,
and the need for change come out whenever she dialogues with any other
character, even enemies like Abessollo and Atangana. When Atangana asks
her what her problem is, her answer is revealing:

The real problem is between the two irreconcilable
camps; the allies and customers of Imperialism: those
who sign unequal treaties and agreements whereby their
colonial puppet-masters enjoy special privileges. (*pause*).
See? the proprietors of corporate stores of political
intrigue and ambition; who to nourish their gargantuan
greed barter the patriotic minded progressive forces
prepared to stand up against them ... (9)

Lastly, Abessollo's tactics of torture and intimidation are better displayed in
his words to Gambari and Akonchong:

(*in a fury*) We are not going to allow you prowl our streets ... We are not
gunning for anyone yet. But just you wait. (*looks him up and down*) We'll cut
your ball (sic) off before you have a chance... (39)

Whereas filth pervades the atmosphere in *Beasts*, anger is what one
encounters all the time in the metaphorical and occasionally biblical language
of *Requiem* as the characters keep on cursing.

Besong's geographical setting in *Requiem* is a fictitious African state, the
state of Agidigidi, but more specifically the capital city Iduote. Iduote, as
already indicated, is Etoudi reversed; the neighbourhood where Cameroon's
presidential marble palace is located. One cannot help thinking that Agidigidi

is Cameroon and Iduote, Yaounde. This line of thought is further confirmed given some of the national languages of Agidigidi used by the characters— Hausa and Ewondo. These are Cameroonian languages, and so is Sonara the sole oil refinery in Cameroon. Such similarities abound not only in geographical and cultural features but also in terms of personalities. Consider Françoise Hippopo, possibly the same "accordionist" personality of Besong's kleptocratic Wouri party in his poem "Letter to Mongo Beti (ii)" in *Obasinjom Warrior With Poems After Detention*.

Temporally, Besong's setting is the present as through *Requiem* he dramatizes the socio-political odyssey of Cameroon in particular and Africa at large. This setting, therefore, assists the playwright in painting portraits that his readers can readily identify. It is not for nothing that Baal curses briefly in Hausa before expressing himself fluently in Ewondo. Besong, no doubt, is out to exploit sound effect in the names Baal and Paul; Baal certainly rhymes with Paul, the first name of Cameroon's incumbent president. This implication is justified when one realizes that Baal curses in Hausa before settling in Ewondo. Here one can easily see Paul represented as Baal, for Paul must have picked up a few Hausa expressions from his predecessor and political mentor, Ahmadou Ahidjo, which he applies before feeling at home in his inborn Ewondo. Baal, accordingly, is Paul. Perceived thus, Besong's stylistic strategy presents as bewildering, as echoes from his dialogues and setting amount to significant colours with which he captures character while communicating. Besong's setting is congruous to the action of his play for together they ably present the plight of an exploited lot of mankind—Besong's thematic concern.

Besong's main theme, the subsequent popular uprising by an oppressed people against an unfeeling felonious regime is topical as well as universal given the situation in his native Cameroon, in particular, and Africa as a whole. If Woman succeeded in conscientizing the youths met in Student, and the unemployed or the underemployed academics and the rest of the proletariat, then Besong's role as teacher and guide to the pupil-leaders in the political backwoods of Cameroon's and Africa's new-found sham of a democracy becomes obvious. To these "unschooled" opposition leaders, Besong's message is conscientizing, for if the suffering masses do not know that their leaders are traitors who are exploiting them, then they would not know what issues to address and who to eliminate if need be. It is because

152

the exploited of Agidigidi are educated about their plight that they free themselves; this is what Besong is doing to Cameroonians and the exploited of the world. Indeed, how true are Isidore Okpewho's words in the University of Ibadan's anthem: "For a mind that knows is a mind that is free" (iv). Bate Besong in *Requiem* strives to free the abused lot of mankind by making them sentient of their plight. This dedication by an artist, of his work, to the plight of the proletariat and social issues that call for concern reveals in Besong a Marxist tendency. From his title, Besong hopes that Baal would be the last Kaiser; quite an appropriate title as he goes on to show how to eliminate and prevent the re-emergence of any such leader again by conscientizing the oppressed whose awareness culminates in a revolution.

Requiem, unlike the other plays, is a play that has identified a social disease and has shown how that disease can be cured effectively. Hence, more than just a source of entertainment and a collection of societal ills, *Requiem* amounts to a literary guerrilla's strategy of liberation for his oppressed peoples.

The Banquet (1994)

That Bate Besong is an avant-garde dramatist within the realms of Anglophone drama is no longer news, and this seems to remain his main stylistic prowess from his earliest play *Zombie* down to *The Banquet*. In these plays, as experimental as his style is, Besong's concern for his country, Cameroon, especially in relation to the fate of the Anglophone-Cameroonian, is paramount. The strategic nature of this remark with relation to Besong's style cannot be overlooked because of the invaluable manner in which everything is done, the style in which message is delivered. Martin Esslin points out: It is a fallacy to think that there is a division between *what* is said and *how* it is said; ultimately form is content and content form…." (*Reflections* 3)

Talking about plot as a dramatic experience in relation to Bate Besong's *The Banquet* would be tantamount to confirming the very free spirit of Besong's creativity, for drama is only a generic form in which this playwright's fleeting, yet ideologically loaded mind is able to waft itself from idea to idea. Yet, in *The Banquet*, Besong has a plot, even if not obviously so because of the influence of the technique of the absurd which is his stylistic core. Besong's plot is inspired and structured by the historical evolution of

153

Cameroon but more especially that of Southern Cameroons, along with the attendant conflicts. This is obvious from the prologue which spans the historical dawn and dusk of the Cameroonian nation by looking first at Southern Cameroon's state as a UN trust territory. During this period, *La République* is not only wooing her leaders but is herself tormented by French presence in Yaounde. Besong revisits the hypocritical ultimatum imposed by the UN on Southern Cameroonians as the sole ticket to their independence, which was joining Nigeria or *La République du Cameroun*; an ultimatum which gave Southern Cameroonians no room towards self-realization. The vatic voices of leading Southern Cameroonians like E. M. L. Endeley and Fon Achirimbi, summarily, spoke against the option given Southern Cameroonians. In contrasting the legal way of doing things in Southern Cameroons as opposed to French Cameroun (*La République*) Endeley observes:

In Southern Cameroons and Nigeria, political differences are settled by arguments and by the ballot box. In Ahidjo's French Cameroun, political differences are settled by the hydrogen bomb and poison... If you vote for Cameroun Republic, you will for ever fail to secure independence for the Southern Cameroons because Cameroun Republic is and will forever remain a colony of France. French troops are still settled in Yaounde and Douala. Mr. Ahidjo cannot drive them out if he wanted to. These French troops are there for two reasons - to prevent Mr Ahidjo's government from being democratic, and to protect the interest of the many thousands of French Cacoubs who have settled there... (ix-x)

Fon Achirimbi, on the other hand, sums up the stance of the people thus:

We rejected Dr. Endeley and his C.P.N.C. party because he wanted to take us to *uneke-egbu* Nigeria. If Mr. Small John Ngu Foncha and his graffi K.N.D.P. want to take us to Ahidjo's French *katakata* Cameroun; We shall also run away from him. *Awawa* Nigeria is water - But - haba! wild French East Cameroun: *Maquisaland* is FIRE! (sic xii)

The prologue, equally, highlights the deeds of French soldiers, businessmen, and politicians which all tend towards painting a picture of France as a

154

notorious intruder into the activities of her so-called former colonies. It is from this historical overview of a prologue that the playwright's work begins with Acts and Scenes emphasizing, even if repeatedly, the activities of *La République du Cameroun* and France in relation to the rebellious Southern Cameroonians. After all, it was Besong himself who strongly advocated that "The significance of any research on the subject should derive from the fact that Anglophone drama be evaluated against its historical surroundings and the fact of the dramatists' life and times" ("Who's Afraid"). He was to reiterate this stance somewhere else when he pointed out again: "The writer from the other side of the Cameroonian bridge, digs into history and uses living historical experiences for the positing of his revolutionary vision. His art is nothing but the truthful artistic response to social reality in revolutionary form" ("New Engagements").

The prologue of the play portrays the existing chaos as we see a French "commando" brutalizing Um Ignace as he parodies the role of a dictator, while CENER[15] agents make arbitrary arrests of suspected subversive elements. Then the problem of today's Anglophone-Cameroon's history comes to light as E. M. L. Endeley juxtaposes the implications of Southern Cameroonians staying with Nigeria, on the one hand, and joining East Cameroon on the other. The former union offers Southern Cameroonians an ostensibly better choice, while the latter is predicted to be tragic. Bate Besong in his prologue, therefore, reviews the options Southern Cameroonians had before joining *La République du Cameroun*. Looking at the summative view posited by Fon Achirimbi, one gets the impression that Besong is suggesting that both options were bad but joining Nigeria could have been somewhat better as Nigeria is presented as water whereas French East Cameroun is fire. Yet, one must not forget that this claim by the playwright looks authentic only because of the unfortunate experience of Southern Cameroonians with *La République* since what could have been, had Southern Cameroonians joined Nigeria, can now only be imagined. This notwithstanding, Besong recaptures Southern Cameroon's dilemma under the auspices of an unfair imperialist ultimatum presented them by a myopic Great Britain and a biased United Nations.

Act I Scene I highlights the prevailing atmosphere of chaos as "*militaires-gorilles*" (1) fire at women and animals who are then to be buried by the grave diggers—three in number—in the company of *Takenmbeng* Women collective. What obtains next is the verbal exchange between the grave diggers, Arreykaka, Um, and Akoko. In their song, "The Road After Foumban" (3) they expose the meaninglessness of the historical come together of Southern Cameroonians and representatives from *La République* as they called the event a bazaar. The charade of today's so-called democracy is aptly put by Arreykaka as he wonders about the meaninglessness of the so-called democratic practices in Cameroon:

> (*in Pidgin English*)... dis democratic avance sef. No be one kind *wuruwuru*? Dis we democratie avancee sef no be one kind *magomago*? (4)

Besong goes on to remember the clash in Bamenda between the years 1990 to 1993 especially as he permits the Second "*militaire gorille*" to declare: "I killed under Colonel Guillaume Pom - with my bare hands," (8) before letting a Voice to present France, ironically, as "the light in a continent mired in primeval economic darkness!" (8). The "*militaire gorilles*" then compare Ahidjo's reign to that of the incumbent—President Paul Biya—in a song:

> *My die-hard*
> *Saboteur*
> *Did we hear*
> *You say: Baba*
>
> *Toura*
> *Mangeait avec*
> *La fourchette*
> *Mais*
> *Lion d'Ezoum*
> *Empiffre*
> *a l'aide*
> *d'un cuillere?* (emphasis Besong's 9-10)

Mention is also made of the economic crisis today tormenting Cameroonians before a warning statement is given to those Southern Cameroonians who now dare to think that Southern Cameroons ought to join Nigeria:

156

(*fires into the air*) To the secessionists who now prefer *uneke-egbu* Mazi
Ajukwu Ekwabam weeping Governor, Ajukwu Mbakwe Sam (*fires into the
air*). For the stupid anglophones who have forgotten the treatment meted
out to them by *uneke-egbu* in the 60's. (12)

First '*gorille-militaire*' subtly hints at the political climate of the country which
has transformed the nation into a "concentration camp without barbed wire"
(13) before insulting Gustave Essaka of the so-called Minorité Presidentielle
– "Did we spray acid on the rectum of pine-apple face Gustave Essaka..."
(13).

Act I, Scene II, offers Besong an opportunity to insult the Cameroon
National Assembly while showing government's intolerance towards
Anglophone-Cameroonians who are demanding equality with their
Francophone counterparts as we see a "*militaire-gorille,*" played by Arreykaka,
firing at them. While other present day miscreants in Cameroon's historical
landscape like Emah Basile and Ibrahim Mbombo Njoya are jibed at, the hell
that this union with *La République* is to the citizenry of Southern Cameroons
is also confirmed:

We rejected Dr Endeley
And his C.P.N.C.
But - *Haba*! - French
Cameroun is FIRE!! (17)

Act II, Scene I, which is temporally set in July, 1992, highlights French
atrocities in Cameroon, a picture which is a reflection of French activities in
their colonies. Cameroon, like the rest of these colonies, is the refuse heap it
is because France cares less about her. As a nation, Cameroon is French
property to be exploited to the benefit of France's waning image. Kitterano's
voice-over amounts to a frightening revelation:

France in the 21st century would be made up of neo-colonial La
République du Cameroun resources or else there will be no Imperial
France!
    We consider La République du Cameroun as indispensable to the
enhancement of the international status of France. (...) ...

All forest resources, cocoa farmer's profits, Sonara oil money and Cameroonian civil servant's (sic) incomes will, continue to pass through circuits like *Carrefour du Development* (sic 19-20)

Act II, scene II expands on Cameroon's relationship with France along the lines of the regime today present in Yaounde. Mbozo'o confirms that the future of La République "will be mortgaged for the next five generations so long as Yawinde breathes ..." (24) before corroborating, with two "*gorilles*," their determined hostility towards Anglophones. Besong here broadens the geographical domain of his concern from Cameroon to Africa as a whole. He observes through First and Second *gorilles* about two incumbent African presidents, although with one's name distorted as it is spelt backwards:

First: (*swelling*) When Amedaye is worth $80 billion in the
   Market place of monstrosities.

Second: (swelling) *Couple* Seko ... Sese Seko my leopard-skin
   Yahoo is nine hundred trillion (*in a sinister tone*) But, what of it if I *Jigida*?
   (27)

As a result, Besong juxtaposes former French colonies as they rival for France's hypocritical attention as revealed by these utterances by Mbozo'o and Ambassador:

MBOZO'O: *Notre Seigneur* will ascend in glory in this
   country, I assure you. The *concordat* with France will last
   till the year 5 million A.D.

AMB: And you have one advantage ... *Mon Coeur Lion
   Dictateur*

MBOZO'O: (*chuckling*) Superior fire power! There must be
   no loosening of the grip! Cameroonians must always
   find themselves looking down the barrel of the gun.
   (*feigning jealousy*) But Bokassa ...

AMB: France will get you, there. (*with a leer*) Mother France
will crown you Emperor. Be patient *mon* President
Field Marshall born on cocoyam leaves a little over
forty years ago (...) *Meme en France!*

MBOZO'O: *Meme en France! (enthusiastically)* As you wish,
Mon Excellence. Mon Excellence,; (sic) if it be Mother
France's sacred pleasure to market Cameroon's oil
wells and forest reserves. Golden Walnut, Iron Wood,
Ebony, Black Afara Obeche, Good timber I assure
you. (30-31)

Again, Anglophone stubbornness is portrayed as the bulwark in the path of
French exploitation of Cameroon's resources. Mbozo'o, meanwhile, goes on
to swear how he will suppress the opposition but just then, there is a
rebellion against French activists in Cameroon:

MALE VOICE: The way of peace is to cultivate JUSTICE.

ANOTHER: Death to the French *colons* murdering our
women and children!

FEMALE VOICE: Death to the French colonial
vulture wrecking our forest reserves!

MALE VOICE: Boycott everything French!

FEMALE VOICE: Hold down Cyclops the Pirate-
ambassador in Cameroon!

ANOTHER: Down with those who confuse and divide our
PEOPLE!

FEMALE VOICE: Away with unscrupulous people who
neither speak our language nor know our culture!

VOICE OF BELLE: Down with pliant creatures and
catamites who draw their window-blinds to shut out
the shameful spectacle of Cameroonians being dragged
through *Avenue Charles de Gaulle!* (34)

The populace is determined to set things right by doing away with that
society "where black is white, wrong is right and shame is pride!" (34). The
scene ends with Mbozo'o repenting and devoting himself towards freeing his
country from the vampirish grip of France while pointing out the emptiness
of French so-called assistance to Cameroon:

...what you call loans are Cameroons savings in France. France is paying
Cameroon's debts for what she has stolen and is still stealing. (35)

As if this devastating revelation is indeed not damaging enough, Mbozo'o
insults French defence deficiency:

... Crataux, you have just been telling me something about loans and *your*
Mother France. You have heard what the voices think about your
renegade country defeated by Germany in three major wars under
seventy-five years. (36)

Act III, Scene I, sets in to emphasize the struggle towards the liberation
of Cameroon. The onus of this achievement is placed squarely on the
shoulders of Southern Cameroonians who are urged to rise up against
"francophonie Re-colonisation" (37). Of course, there is evidence that
francophonie propagated terror is still in vogue.

Act III, Scene II, characteristically, is a cauldron of ideas which, in the
main, springs from the socio-political landscape of Besong's native land—
Cameroon. The idea of rigging in presidential elections comes to light when
Arreykaka, Um's Gestapo hound, tells him about possible election results
and he declares his intentions to win at all cost:

ARREYKAKA: (*coming forward nervously*) C'est grave,
Monsieur le President!

160

UM: (*Looking at him strangely*) Ma wu! Je ne veux *rien entendre*.
Je veux gagner...

ALL: ... Les elections a tout prix! (...) Ma wu Zambe Wam.
(sic 42)

Such corruption is again juxtaposed against the liberating aspirations and final success of the *Takenmbeng* women despite brutalisation from state *Militaire-gorilles*. Through the grapevine, Cameroon's most reliable source of information than even the government media, UM's words above are those of President Paul Biya after the 1992 elections when he was informed that John Fru Ndi, the chairman of the only reliable opposition party then, was winning.

In terms of the logical occurrence of events, Besong's plot can be said to be united although, from time to time, unrelated events, typical of the tradition of the absurd, are mentioned as sequential but not necessarily logical follow ups. Consider how apparently disjointed this dialogue between two "gorilles" is:

FIRST: I'll make you crawl through a concrete pipe that lies
a long the refinery road of Bakassi Crude oil.

SECOND: So you do wear a beard?

FIRST: (*confrontational, grenade in hand*)... I'll hack away at the
beard ... I'll drink your blood to quench my thirst.

SECOND: (*confrontational, grenade in hand*) Taking lumps of
flesh with the hair (...) My friend, you are dragging too
many cans of subversion behind you... Your arms will
be painfully bent backwards...

FIRST: ... and held with wires (...) We are like the Indo
Chinese army...My hobby is choking people to death ...
You see...

161

SECOND: We deal with both the American and
French tanks of demon-crazy! (*the clipped bark of an order*)
Please remit 5.000 frs c.f.a postal fee...

BOTH: ... your brother died of a flu attack. We are sending
you the alabaster with his ashes (Derisive Laughter)

SECOND: (*rubbing his hands with glee*) Mon Lion-Dictateur!

FIRST: Cameroonian's bankruptcy standing there like a
Balladur in the jaws of the Beregovoy tiger!

SECOND: (*in a "pleading" tone*) My hobby is choking
secessionists to death.

FIRST: (*swelling*) When Amedaye is worth $80 billion in the
market place of monstrosities.

SECOND: (*swelling*) *Couple* Seko...Sese Seko my leopards-
skin Yahoo is nine hundred trillion (*in a sinister tone*)
But, what of it if I *Jigida*

(*They sing to the clatter of machine- gun fire from off*) (26-27).

The disjointed nature of the dialogue notwithstanding, the ideas touched on
are focal points of the nation's socio-economic and political blunders. As
individual events they do not relate, yet they give the text a unified whole as
Besong's concerns are the historical metamorphosis of Cameroon as a
nation, coupled with the treasonable and felonious activities of her leaders.

Besong's plot, therefore, turns on the historical, social, and political
plight of Southern Cameroonians, in particular, and Cameroonians as a
whole as the appropriate and satisfactory resolution highlights victory on the
part of the oppressed lot of Cameroonians and true independence for
Southern Cameroonians from *La République's* re-colonisation bid. Whereas
the different Acts and Scenes of the play capture and emphasize the bestiality
of all that France and *La République's* leadership stand for to the Southern

Cameroonian, the end of the play resolves the bloody clashes which are common between government and her citizens; a life-style against which E. M. L. Endeley's prophetic voice had warned. Although these clashes characterise the play all through, the end proves that power is with the people as the oppressed, guided by the women of *Takenmbeng* Collective, win the day.

Besong's characters—and they are the young and the old, men and women—emerge from different groups with equally alienating backgrounds: there are Southern Cameroonians, East Cameroonians and the obnoxious and repugnant Gaullist activists from France. The law-abiding Southern Cameroonians with their love for peace and foresightedness are represented by characters like Dr. E. M. L. Endeley and Fon Achirimbi, while the Francophones with a dwarfing servile attitude towards France are represented by present day political minions-cum-buffoons like Foning, Essaka, Kodock, and the dictatorial Ahidjo. And then there are Rohoboam Kitterano and Omne Crataux, human scum bags, propagators of France's disastrous foreign policy. It is in this light that most of Besong's characters in this play lack personalities as they cut across in the guise of symbols of a people's hope or their failure and garbled destiny, be them the Endeleys and Achirimbis on the one hand or the kodocks, Fonings, and Omnes of "the Communuate Franco-Camerounaise" (40) on the other hand.

It is through the way these characters dialogue that one can see the sages or blood thirsty fools they are as the case may be. Whereas Dr. E. M. L. Endeley sounds like the scholar he was, Achirimbi's English is localised with Arreykaka occasionally relapsing into Pidgin. Otherwise, the language is infused with viciousness, tactlessness, and a show of servitude as the Francophone struggles to display his allegiance to "Mother France" whose true citizens, like the Ambassador, in a condescending manner, instead lord it over the Francophone lackeys. If one were left with any doubts about the origins of Besong's characters, animate or inanimate, after they had vocalised or displayed their concerns, for Besong has a way of breathing life into inanimate objects and landscapes transforming them from mere props into fascinating passive actors, then their names brought a befitting purgation to residual doubts. As Shadrach A. Ambanasom confirms, through suggestive anagramatic nomenclatural reconstructions, one is guided to tell with certainty that Besong has used "Ubae for Buea, Nouayed for Yaoundé,

163

Adoula for Douala, Erooncam for Anglophone Cameroon, Erouncam for Francophone Cameroun," (*Education* 125) and even more, "through the rhythm of their names certain words resemble their originals: Killeran (sic) for Mitterrand, Varis for Paris, Vrench for French, Yzhirag for Jacques Chirac, Reginia for Nigeria, or a completely new word is coined to symbolize another e.g. Prancefraud for France" (125). George D. Nyamndi puts it differently:

> *The Banquet* provides further instances of nominal disfigurement, with the same intention to excoriate.... France is disfigured into 'Prancefraud', Jean-Marie Le Pen into 'Marie le Guenn', Charles Pasqua into 'Caskquoi', Jacques Chirac into 'Risky Yzhirag', and Yvon Omnes into 'Domnes'. ("Therapeutics of Laughter")

Besong's setting, in terms of time, cuts across the colonial era until the present, for he traces the ordeal of Cameroon's historical degeneration until they are liberated by women of the *Takenmbeng* collective. Geographically, Besong goes beyond the boundaries of Cameroon into Africa at large as he jibes frequently at the scum African leadership amounts to while referring to Nigeria, Zaire, and Central African Republic amongst others. This very fertile setting, with colonialism and neo-colonialism as its backdrop, is responsible for the different character-types painted by Besong—the heroes and anti-heroes, the dictators and the oppressed, the foreign exploiters and the exploited locals, some of whom are the traitors betraying their native soil for the offal from the French man's table after he has exploited them. It is because of this setting that Besong is able to paint and sustain the atmosphere of a wasteland that Cameroon and most of Africa amount to with the exploitative activities of the French, which he highlights from time to time around the continent. In the same vein, the action of the play is reinforced by the setting to bring about French confusionist and exploitative tendencies in Africa.

Thematically, Besong is concerned with France's neo-colonial whims, dictatorship, exploitation, and oppression in the main. And these are either explicitly stated or acted out by one character or the other. Because this is still the trend in most Francophone African countries, the importance of Besong's thematic concern needs no emphasis as, all the way, it has been

Besong's ambition to purge his society of socio-political malpractices, especially those sponsored by colonialists and executed by local pawns. In this play, like in others by this playwright, the stage directions are elaborate and invaluable towards a comprehension and staging of the play. Besong's style as a whole, which exploits metatheatrical devices like mime, parody, trance, hallucination and more, amounts to a fictionalized review of a people's history in a bid to conscientize and guide the wretched lot towards their freedom and a total realization of their identity crisis. Kikefomo wan-Mbulai is saying the same thing when he observes of the play: *"The Banquet* then is Bate Besong's bull-headed confrontation with history. It is an artistic testimony in which he indicts and excels; a re-valuation of our travestied past, freezed for futurity"* (11).

As always, Besong in *The Banquet* is indignant at his peoples' fate to such an extent that he taunts, jibes, and insults in an attempt to educate both the oppressed and their oppressors. The concern of *The Banquet* is the plight of today's Cameroon, today's Francophone Africa especially, as they relate to their French puppet-master of a nation. This is so much true of Cameroon and Africa today, hence the topicality of Besong's themes. Besong's works are therefore not intended for entertainment only, if they do at all, as they are crafted to identify weaknesses in society and to educate both the culprits and victims. Besong, as a writer, therefore, is not a disciple of the notion of aesthetic superciliousness above all else as an artistic concern. To him the Euro-modernist idea of "art for art's sake" despite the social, economic, and political topoi surrounding a writer has no meaning as he sees the writer as a prophet who should not only preach but carve out a revolutionary alternative as a means to eliminating the anomie that is typical of the fractured *status quo.*

Besong's stylistic technique, although largely in the tradition of the absurd, is even more pace-setting; this is the saving grace of his art after he would have, in the tradition of the Bayangi *Obasinjom*, purged Cameroon of the warlocks and witches thriving on the socio-political thrones of Cameroon's bloody leadership. His themes may at one time in the future no longer be as urgently relevant as they are today to the Cameroonian predicament, but his revolutionary style would have opened new vistas for further exploration.

In *The Banquet*, Besong has, therefore, revisited history as far back as the early sixties, peaked and flavoured it with more recent historical trends of the

90s before linking it up to the equally tragic yet strangely docile and seemingly flailing present which he rebukes, before predicting a free future. To Besong, it is only during such a future that there can be a banquet indeed as the food is still being prepared, the wine yet to mature and those to feast, victims of caged and tormented consciences which have rendered their palates tasteless from a sequestered existence in political dungeons or an otherwise censored and censured existence for daring to be free, for daring to live. They are yet to be free. The present tide notwithstanding, Besong seems to be predicting the fact that there will, in the end, be a banquet. And this is for sure because virtue pitted against vice will always win in the end.

Change Waka & His Man Sawa Boy (2001)

Bate Besong's *Change Waka & His Man Sawa Boy* (*Change Waka*), amounts to another major graphic splash on his literary canvas re-confirming his convictions about the effectiveness of the theatre of the absurd in addressing the socio-political predicament in society, his native Cameroon, foremost. This category of drama, which undermines logic and virtually delights and flourishes in the unexpected and the unpredictable, is now his stock-in-trade after *The Most Cruel Death of the Talkative Zombie* (1986), *Beasts of No Nation (1990)*, *Requiem for the Last Kaiser (1991)*, and *The Banquet: A Historical Drama* (1994). Besong exploits this dramatic technique to the fullest in his determination to identify and denounce the ills meted on man by man in societies that should otherwise be thriving havens for their now battered and impoverished subjects.

Besong's concern remains the same: the incredible level of corruption, lawlessness, and despair that characterizes the status quo in society, his society especially. All of this, in his play *Change Waka*, is concretized in the symbol of the ballot box which, according to Change Waka, the curious and somewhat enigmatic omenologist, has to be transparent unlike the opaque boxes that are suitable for election fraud. The play revolves around views about the ballot box and electoral malpractices. Focus is on the rigging of elections by any means possible, even through the use of the occult and the supernatural. Ironically, according to the stage directions, Change Waka, who stands for positive change in society, has an appearance that is reminiscent of a sorcerer:

166

The singers are interrupted by a middle-aged, be-spectacled man in
an old-fashioned Victorian outfit. He carries a staff, a crystal ball,
an embroidered robe with a matching cap.
Although he is followed by three assistants, his clothes are in complete
disarray. (10)

Beyond the opaque boxes as accessories of election fraud, there is the signature practice that spells out corruption—the large brown "gombo" envelope exchanging hands between His Imperial Excellency and members of his corrupt administration like the *Sous-Préfets,* and the Kangaroo Judge of State at the Ministry of Elections, Sesekou Daniel Atemengeng. The stage directions make this clear:

(he wobbles to center-stage, halts with his back to audience)…Take these. (offering Justice Atemengeng and the Sous-Préfets a large-sized brown gombo envelope and a sealed ballot box). One will never disturb electoral registers and wipe his hands on walls. (61-62)

In keeping with electoral rigging practices, Change Waka talks of governors collaborating in these malpractices by destroying ballot papers as a way of influencing election results. The grabbing nature of the incumbent political party of Mfawbahep Gknockor Gknockor, the Imperial Excellency of Epeng Ebho, comes across in the fact that it is called the Octopus Party (9); a party with octuple tentacles that can reach out and grab. The extent to which the party will go to grab is revealed by the fact that even the occult is employed in facilitating their grabbing as is obvious in the women's song.

When heresies and strange
gods.
become dangerously
popular
When agents of deeper
darkness; those who want
Victory
Without the cross; send
Down

octopus hands
And hunt down the ballot
box… (9-10)

After the rigging of elections, the Kangaroo Judge, Sesekou Atemengeng, is threatened with being buried alive should he fail to release the results. Corruption then, is the hallmark of the party and her officials.

Besong's fictive setting is the Epeng Ebho society at the head of which is a maniacal leader, Mfawbahep Gknockor. The elections that have brought about ballot boxes are to hold here under the auspices of a whole ministry, the Ministry of Elections a.k.a. MINSO for Ministry of Sorrow. The administrative set-up within Epeng Ebho is flawed given that it is peopled by figures without consciences: from the governors down through the *préfets* to their deputies the *sous préfets* and finally the kangaroo Judge. They are all corrupt, hence the hopelessness of the electoral process. It is a procedure laced with cash-stuffed envelopes to help electoral officers like governors and *sous préfets* distort electoral registers and count in pre-stuffed ballot boxes. His Imperial Excellency's goal is to capture victory at election time at all cost. His methods, beyond the use of corruption, is to cast rivaling political parties, like ordinary citizens, at each other's throats through the injection of fear for each other and the use of divisive language. By this means, potentially daunting forces are kept preoccupied fighting each other instead of the corrupt incumbent, while Gknockor continues to exploit and reign over them. So Change Waka reports:

A gendarme's arm was reportedly chopped off while another had his face bathed with acid. You do not have irreversible glaucoma otherwise you'll see that the cancer has progressed past the point where the drugs could help the pain. Suffocating others. You sabotage fellow competitors, overshadowing others. (*pause*) One of the physicians placed a stethoscope on Rigging's heart. I pronounce the Sawa rogue dead. (10-11)

In like manner, a section of Epeng Ebhoians, in their own society, are not only called settlers but are transformed into threats to be killed by their compatriots. Judge Atemengeng at work rigging elections declares in a most frightening manner: "I believe the only way to reform settlers is to kill them!"

(61). This is a society at its lowest ebb: one without a system nor is there any respect for the citizens and their patriarchy. As a result, the whims of an autocrat Mfawbahep Gknockor Gknockor is let loose on a victim society under the grips of corrupt secondary and tertiary administrators. Not even the officers of law and order are exempt from the practice of corruption as Change Waka reveals: "One day, I was going on the road and one Commissaire asked me for booty. FCFA? I told him to stop being stupid because you are being paid to do your job" (43). Appropriately then, Change Waka recommends a psychiatric test on would-be *sous préfets* to determine the level of their sanity. This is necessary because of the level of subservience they display towards corrupt practices like the rigging of elections. Psychologically balanced people, with some integrity, should be able to reason otherwise and *change their waka;* that is, do things otherwise from the corrupt trend. Change Waka is determined to bring about change in society even if it means dying in the process for he declares about his effort: "I am going to die like a man. Let the ballot-box be without hypocrisy. I'm not afraid..." (11). It is fitting then that the progressives under Change Waka's spell about a decent society had declared earlier on and in the process professing their mistrust for *sous-préfets*:

> Despite insults, abuse, and an ignominious death, we maintain self-control and dignity for we may also receive unsought honour when others observe that we act in accordance with Mister Change Waka's wisdom (...) We fight a war to live in peace, but if you lie down with *sous-préfets*...lie down with *sous-préfets*, you might not wake up...Behind the door lies a corridor with canyons built of human bones... if you lie down with dogs...their teeth marks in the buttocks of ballot boxes... We stand at the very threshold of the fulfillment of Efhiim's decree against Gknockor Gknockor and his system! (13)

If only like Change Waka these corrupt administrators could recognize the transient nature of the worthless power they are going to such lengths to possess, they would certainly change for better, for as Change Waka points out, "I am yet to see where rigging has taken Arahmbuoh to the moon or made an Atemengeng perform head surgery. It will only bring them sorrow, disaster and essentially imperil the life of the electoral register" (18-19).

To react to the political decadence of his society with all the cultic reverberations involved, Besong resorts to a most befitting form—theatre of the absurd. Remarkable for the seeming absurdity that is the style of this dramatic form is its affinity with the tide of events in Epeng Ebho where there is no order in society as is typical of the often irrational acts of dictators. Thus, *Change Waka*, an absurdist play on the state of affairs in society, with frequent seemingly irrational and lengthy interjections about a central issue—the rigging of elections—has no plot nor is there a conflict as such. Thus *Change Waka* subverts the logical and sequenced order of events while relishing the unexpected and the logically impossible. Dramatic conflicts, clashes of personalities and powers are characteristics of a world with an established and accepted hierarchy of values amounting to an enduring institution. Such conflicts lose their meaning in a state of affairs where the establishment and outward reality have become insincere and futile. There is hardly any meaningful action or conversation except when a character moves in a near motiveless manner to and fro while bandying around meaningless or purposeless words all in an effort to expose the helplessly absurd conditions in which a baffled bunch of overwhelmed human beings without drive are wallowing. Hence, all too frequently, lengthy verbal projections, monologues, and soliloquys delivered in dream or trance-like condition are all they vocalize. One of Change Waka's declarations spans pages 22 to 26. The effect is that the characters' utterances are too often long and tortuous while almost virtually eliminating action of any sort.

The result is that Besong's characters are like natural holograms who just externalize words. This explains the pervading surrealist atmosphere about them in their trance-like state or when supposedly hallucinating. This impression is heightened by misplaced semantic utterances that spiral about to no consequence, since effective communication is not immediately achieved because of an overflow of discordant metaphors, and seemingly uncoordinated speech. These characters projected impressions of themselves and society as helpless victims in a meaningless world. Change Waka ends one of his lengthy pronouncements thus:

(A puzzled smile marks his face) You are the unbaptized minimizer of the Iglesia Nueva Apostolica...by Efhiim ... Tarry in Peace. Tarry in war. *(with a half-smile)* I fear you have a difficult task. But I wish you success

170

for, an electoral lie is the truth intrinsically; it holds a lawful place in the state of our Union. ... Numskull, only a fool believes that he can put back the clock. Omenology is dead... and I, an old omenologist, am moribund. Pee Turn Turn ... Mma ahana Mhmu... Mma attem ebuua... Abérèmatics? Mother cook dog ...Okru mbungh-a? Mark time ...Ecoute, Homme SAWA! La prochain fois, le feu. (30-31)

"Next time fire" warns the playwright.

Beyond the characters' awkward use of language, since more often than not they talk while in a trance or while apparently sleepwalking, the playwright's use of language as a whole remains characteristically refreshing. Besong's use of imagery is largely suggestive: the widespread display of enlarged pictures of the despot and king of corruption Gknockor displays efficaciously one method of rigging the elections as he is the only candidate with such a privilege. Consider the effective presentation of the corrupt state as a human mouth with decaying teeth:

We use the front teeth for tearing meat and nyama-ngoróó and then send it to the jaws where there are special teeth for grinding... Decaying teeth smell and we feel ashamed when we laugh in public.... (22)

In other words, just as we are ashamed of a stinking mouth full of decaying teeth, so too must we be ashamed of a nation stinking as a result of corruption, as evidenced in *Change Waka*. Then there are evocative objects and names like the stuffed "gombo" envelope echoing the ongoing corruption which Change Waka confirms when he posits:

Those who record electoral triumphs were doubtless influenced by an apostasy that you and I have not cross-examined. Ninety-eight per cent... Five hundred per cent... Nine hundred trillion per cent. All na lie... My friends, Victory is to be gained through scouring the dead sea of transparent ballot-boxes. Through suffering and not by stratagems and hallucinations of post-electoral amputations. (29-30)

And then there is the transparent ballot box and even the name "Change Waka" all of which hint at the possibility of turning around, that is changing the direction in which the country has been headed, and this happens to be Change Waka's goal in the play. The use of a crystal ball itself, although suggestive of the occult practices in the play, becomes an awkward symbol in the hands of Change Waka, given his positive intentions for society. It is in this light that Shadrach A. Ambanasom points out: "...'Change Waka' is a kind of democratic watch-dog, a defender of the transparent ballot box at a time when the dominant and fashionable 'walking style' is rigging" (*Education* 117). These symbols then, like the evocative words, are in themselves effective ways of enlightening the audience about a lot going on in the society depicted in the play because they go beyond words to bring out the subtle and implied meanings beyond what is verbalized even; this is of primary importance in absurdist theatre.

The name "Change Waka" itself comes out of Besong's childhood years as were other such significant names, although unused by Besong: Nkum-Nkum Massa who went around performing odd jobs and singing to lighten the burden and maintain the work spirit, and Mammy Nkininkini who was considered mental because of her unkempt hair. These were names in childhood lore of the sixties in today's South and North West parts of Cameroon. Although the original "Change Waka" was said to hail from Kumba, there was, seemingly, a Change Waka in virtually every big town of then West Cameroon. Two things stood out about Change Waka in real life: he walked differently from others, possibly due to arthritic pains given his advanced years, and he was graphically vulgar in his insults when called "Change Waka," which he considered an affront. Nostalgia for the good and hope-filled years of his childhood has led the playwright to rejuvenate, with a completely positive connotation, "Change Waka" in his play. Interestingly, Change Waka, in *Change Waka,* is walking in his own direction counter to the corrupt bandwagon like the character in real life walked in his own manner. He wants electoral transparency; hence, he keeps talking of transparent ballot boxes like when he vouches: "I pledge to defend the transparent box with the same fanaticism that Arahmbuoh, Mfornyor Mfornyor has used to serve Loot-dispenser" (37). The ballot boxes in themselves amount to a vocal stage prop that communicates effectively with an otherwise bamboozled audience. As symbols, when the boxes are stuffed, or transparent, they say much about corruption and the bid for change respectively, even more eloquently than words could have done. In like manner, through the Mmoninkim women and their songs, in a manner reminiscent of the informative role of the chorus in Greek tragedy, a lot more meaning is communicated to the reader or the audience:

It is because sycophants have
nothing to contribute
to the making
of elections.

All they do
Is distract attention.

But we of this city
are not doomed
to be ruled

By the might
Of the French
Gun. (27-28)

Beyond the worthlessness of sycophants in elections being communicated by the women's song "The Settler Dirge" (27), the role of the French in the affairs of Epeng Ebho is also highlighted as there is a hint at the fact that the indigenes are being ruled "by the might of the French gun" (28). Besong's concern then is beyond just ballot boxes; it involves all that is influencing, negatively, the otherwise wellbeing of his people: corruption in all its shades and alien influence. For this reason, besides other symbols in Besong's works, the ballot box emerges as a most potent symbol of corruption and decay, hence the need for it to be transparent. Besong's use of symbols is now established: from the lepers as symbols of a tormented society in *Zombie*, through the lavatory as a symbol of total decay in *Beasts*, to the ballot box as a symbol of corruption, which also intensifies the message of decay in society, in *Change Waka*. Of the effectiveness of a symbol as a literary device, Enid Rhodes Peschel observes:

In its largest and most interesting aesthetic sense, symbolism implies at once a rebellion and a re-creation. It is a revolt against the kind of realism that is but the description of things, feelings and people. For the symbolists do not wish merely to describe; instead, they aim to re-create through their words a state of being, a feeling, a glimmer, a vision. They want the reader to sense, and to react to, the experience itself. Seen this way, symbolism is above all an attempt to transmit by means of symbols—frequently by means of a poetic language that the play must invent—the mysteries that palpitate beneath appearances. A symbol is something that stands for or represents something else. It calls attention to itself while also suggesting far more than it is itself (2).

Never before is Besong's language influenced by the proverbial world of his African culture as is the case in *Change Waka*. Besong's proverbs are so heavily loaded with wisdom and delightful literary flavor one cannot help but savor them and in the process think of the poetry of Bongasu Tanla Kishani's or Nol Alembong's in which such enchanting proverbial spells are frequently cast. Here are a few examples to relish: "No matter how skyward the yam tendril may grow, at harvest, the tubers must be dug from the ground" (14); "It is better to recognize that one is in darkness than to pretend that one can see the light" (17); "The frog likes water, but not when it is boiling" (20); "The donkey eats thorns with its soft tongue" (33); "Adversity reminds men of God, so it is said" (43); and finally, "When the squirrel mounts the mahogany, isn't the hunter's game up?" (46). Remarkable! How so richly revealing, didactic, soothing and relaxing to the mind are these unlike Besong elsewhere.

The Anglophone problem in Cameroon is still present in Besong's *Change Waka*, in spite of its being the center piece in his previous plays. The corrupt electoral practices are responsible for keeping the Francophones (mis)governing Cameroon. In the process, the regime has succeeded in implanting suspicion and animosity between the two Anglophone regions so as to be able to continue ruling and exploiting them. As a result, Change Waka declares: "We pray for those pushing mankind into a world of Sawa and La'a kham thermonuclear war. Hatemongers in front, hatemongers behind" (23). The division has taken a slightly different twist this time while serving better the purpose of divide and rule. From the names "Sawa" and

"La'a kham," it becomes obvious now that the Anglophone predicament is being made more complex by introducing the South West region into the larger Sawa commune which includes the Doualas, while attaching together the Graffi of the North West and those in Francophone West and littoral Cameroon together under the "La'a kham" designation. The situation has just become more complicated for Anglophones who have now been separated along cultural instead of historical lines. The implications are more complex than meet the eye. For example, from one perspective, it brings to the fore the so-called eleventh province issue which has to do with those Cameroonians who by upbringing or area of growth can no longer identify with their true roots. For example, there are Anglophone Cameroonians who are from the Francophone zone but found their way into then Southern Cameroons in those years during Ahidjo's persecution of members of The Union of the Peoples of Cameroon (French: Union des Populations du Cameroun - UPC) political party shortly after independence. They have grown up as Anglophones and are now only nominally associated with their different Francophone or East Cameroon roots. Examples are those Basas and Bamilekes who have grown up in Anglophone-Cameroon territory as Anglophones. By fusing these parts of Anglophone Cameroon with their Francophone compatriots along cultural lines, the last two regimes are trying to exploit an approach that they believe will make it more challenging for the Anglophones to leave if they have to secede. This is the case because they will now be focusing more on cultural rather than historical similarities and identities while also wondering what those who are Anglophone by upbringing and Francophone by birth—members of the eleventh province in other words—will do should secession be the preferred outcome. This however, is a failed ploy from the beginning, for with the arbitrary colonial boundaries at the international level, it is known that along international borders a people were just separated in the middle with one half going with the neighboring nation just because a river, for example, was used as the dividing feature. The authorities at the time failed to realize that some of such rivers ran right through the hearts of many villages. Hence, the cultural similarity of most peoples along international boundaries in Africa; this is the case between the people of Mamfe in Cameroon and those of Calabar in Nigeria. They are one people culturally, but history has alienated them as is the case in Cameroon and even the so-called eleventh province challenge. In other words, the cultural similarity between the Douala and the Bakweri, for example, does not change the fact that the South West Region and the North West came into the Union as one people. For this reason, Besong solicits Anglophone unity through Ewube's words: "We are in a painful period, but if we stick together and persevere, things would be good for everybody" (42).

In spite of the seeming meaninglessness of *Change Waka*, the fact is that through this play Besong continues lashing out in his determination to draw attention to corrupt practices such as fraud, bribery, intimidation, and dictatorship in society; hence, the continuous advocacy for electoral transparency voiced by Change Waka himself. He also declares, befittingly, that they would look for an honest means to get into Athens, a metaphor for the Cameroon presidential palace with its Athenian architecture evidenced by the towering attention-catching colonnades supporting a huge roof along with a processional entrance way leading into the lofty structure. "If you agree, Sesekou Atemengeng, Ngutarh, Arahmbuoh, Nfornyor, we will find some way of getting to Athens (…) Once the rogue goes down, what is there? Nothing" (30).

Once Upon Great Lepers (2003)

Bate Besong's *Once Upon Great Lepers* (*Great Lepers*, 2003) immediately brings to mind his earlier play *The Most Cruel Death of the Talkative Zombie* (1986) because of the oneness of their concerns: the state of the Anglophone in the union which has today been hijacked and transformed into a futile monolith. Cameroon's metamorphosis from a partitioned entity with two factions Southern Cameroons and La République into the Federal Republic, then the United Republic, and finally today's the Republic of Cameroon simply has been proven to be no accidental journey. It is indeed the piecemeal realization of a hidden agenda put in place at the dawn of the nation's march towards independence by Ahmadou Ahidjo and the overseeing authorities: France, Britain, and United Nations. The goal has been the slow but certain asphyxiation and ultimate elimination of the Anglophone dimension of Cameroon's colonial values by flooding this people's ideological and geographical landscape with French and francophone values belonging to the majority faction of the union. The Anglophone minority has drunk and feasted on these values without forgetting to regard them as, at best, just another spice to their established

176

Anglophone broth of a culture. The outcome has been an outcry about the violation of the terms of the Foumban talks which, at the least, guaranteed the socio-political and cultural integrity of both factions of the emerging Federal Republic of Cameroon. Bate Besong's *Great Lepers* is concerned mainly with this madness of a political strategy on the part of the Francophone majority and her bigoted leaders. This struggle is also the concern of Besong's *The Most Cruel Death of a Talkative Zombie*. Therefore we encounter, as Shadrach A. Ambanasom has pointed out and rightly so, *Great Lepers* as a sequel to *Zombie* and mindful of Cameroon's history, "the familiar leitmotifs of plebiscite, referendum, reunification and national integration..." (*Education* 119).

In the tradition of Besong's demonstrated drama, theatre of the absurd, *Great Lepers* is without a compliant plot as such. Instead, the characters, essentially, bring up and talk about existing tensions and conflicts which are highly connotative of existing circumstances—the playwright's concern and that of the manipulated, oppressed, and exploited Anglophone minority. These concerns, like in *Zombie*, are generated by two characters who, interestingly, are both from the Anglophone minority unlike in *Zombie* with a character from either side of the union—an Anglophone and a Francophone.

The two Anglophone characters are Ntufam Vikuma Egu Eku and Samndeng Ngufor Akriyé Moghamo. As Ambanasom rightly points out again, whereas these names - the first and the last two of the first set of names can possibly be traced to one South West ethnic group or the other, the name Vikuma is unique and speaks volumes. Anyone with knowledge of West Cameroon politics will remember "Vikuma" is acronymic, with "Vi-" standing for Victoria, "Ku-" for Kumba, and "Ma-" for Mamfe. On the other hand, there is Samndeng Ngufor Akriyé, all names from the North West and specifically the Meta area. Samndeng is obviously a distortion of Tandeng, the middle name of Solomon Tandeng Muna whose political career spans the Southern Cameroons and the West Cameroon days, through the Ahidjo eon into early Paul Biya era. He was Speaker of the National House of Assembly forever during the last two regimes only to degenerate into a laughing stock as it is the consensus through the grapevine that he was never willing to be of help to anyone who was not his own blood and if at all, then the person needing help had to be from his part of the region. Even people of his ethnic group are so bitter that of all the years he was in government

177

the only thing he did for his part of the country was build a modern prison. Ngufor is a North West name too, Akriyé being a form of greeting from the Momo area, whereas Moghamo is also a form of greeting or calling of attention in Batibo Subdivision.

Great Lepers accents the already established discrepancies between the Anglophone's position in Cameroon, and that of the Francophone which was encountered in *Zombie*. However, this revelation takes a step further to establish the recent distrust that has been methodically introduced between the twin Anglophone regions so as to keep them divided while being exploited by the Francophone regimes in place. This comes across in the fight indicated by the stage directions:

> *Ntufam catches Samndeng Ngufor*
> *Akriyé Moghamo with an upper*
> *cut. They fight; yet exchange*
> *meaningful glances. They get up.*
> *They begin to walk again.* (64)

Besong is saying now that the source of the problem has been established, these twin regions should resolve their differences, the one accepting the other, and so "walk again" (64) side by side.

From the onset, Besong's portrayal of these twin characters displays his dissatisfaction with them mindful of their roles as Anglophone political leaders who led us into the union. See the portrait painted of them in this stage direction:

> *The lights pick Samndeng Ngufor Akriyé Moghamo and Ntufam*
> *Vikuma Egu Eku, two gerontocrat lepers in crutches as they*
> *emerge from the South Western aperture through a giant sized*
> *hole in the ground. The legs and faces of these comical*
> *deformities, like primeval men emerging from the dark*
> *confusion of matter and beast, are covered with running sores*
> *and protruding acnes* (11).

But Besong rescues these characters after lambasting them by this portrait like a loving parent who disciplines a child and then re-establishes peace. Besong does this by showing that the founding fathers of our union, on the Anglophone side, are not happy with the way things have turned out, hence Ntufam Egu Eku observes:

You'll notice, mon lepreux
The 20th May corpse-alas!
Bizzarely retains
The position it had during
Couvre-feu (…) (*pause*) Pharaoh
was a magician, while Moses
was a miracle worker. (*a pause*)
Am I as eager for the end of
the present dispensation to come
as I was when I first met
Commandant Mbokaya?
Thirty-three thousand of them fell
In one day. (emphasis mine, 11)

Although a lot of what is happening is presented to the reader and audience through the Anglophone duo Samndeng and Vikuma, the Francophone dimension is equally well represented by Commandant Mbokaya the tyrant and Dr. Obenegou the Surgeon General. Like the Night-soil-men in *Beasts*, the lepers in *Great Lepers* are underlings, already soiled by their degenerative condition as lepers whereas the tyrant and his cronies are those who matter in society and so enjoy all the privileges their society can offer. It is not surprising then that May 20th, a day arbitrarily chosen by government to celebrate or mourn, depending on which side one is, the rescindment of the federal system, is frowned upon by the lepers who see it as the day when the Anglophone population was annexed into a union that is tantamount to madness given its inability to operate efficiently while subjugating them to subordinates in an otherwise union of equals. In the words of Samndeng:

… (*to audience*). On October 1, 1960, I was admitted at

the Centre Jamot de Re-Unification to remove a non malignant tumour near my irrational, *mokhutabag* brain. The surgery, so I was told, was routine and there was little to be concerned about. However, during the surgery a blood clot developed in the brain…Now the corpse is…

BOTH: …oozing out noxious matter Called National Integration (*a Pause*). Don't they owe you an Explanation? (22-23)

Accordingly, mindful of their wish for this hopeless day, Samndeng declares: "We are sending you the May 20ᵗʰ alabaster with her ashes (*a pause*). Rather than have your teeth extracted, you prefer carrying a mouth full of rotten teeth" (27). The result of reunification, according to these words, stink; it is a woeful failure, especially to the Anglophones who came into the union as kings but are now being treated as slaves: "… Mbokaya has dominated man to   his injury. We came as kings, but we are treated as slaves… (30). It is for this reason that not only is the misleading idea of reunification putrid and stinking, it is also considered by the Anglophones an existence in captivity, incarceration preferably, since the society is considered a kind of *political prison* with the continuous analogy to Cameroon's notorious prison in the heart of the city of Yaounde—Kondangui (sic). Samndeng sums up the problem:

National Unity is a complex
Human relationship,
And many enter it with little
Preparation …. (37)

The result is that people are imprisoned and tortured for their political ideas as they critique this whole venture by Commandant Mbokaya. Interestingly, Commandant Mbokaya is presented in the "Ballad of the Party Cadre" (49) as a messiah:

Curse to those who mock

180

A messiah
We'll caress their skulls
In the sand-paper hands
Of the Mantoum *enquêteur*...
We'll scatter
The human manure
Of those who hate a messiah
Whose sensitive organs, we
Plucked.

In the *balançoire*
Of the Foumban ideological
Corveé (sic), whose
Sensitive organs

We manured
At the Foumban
Ideological *corvée*

Curse to those who mock him.
We will machine-gun
Them from
The rear.

 Eternal curse
To those who hate him
We will

Bazooka them
At Tigneré.
For we'll not let those
Who hate him
For no reason, smirk
With delight
Over his sorrow... (49-50).

Typical of the theatre of the absurd, Besong's symbolic characters engage in conversations that come across as meaningless, purposeless, and even stupid sometimes. It is within this cloak of the absurd that Besong sporadically jabs at society in one way or the other as a most significant comment is thrown out there by a leper as if to no effect. By this means, Besong is able to expose the Anglophone perspective of the union as a practice in futility. It is a union that has only brought about further division, misappropriation of public funds, rivalry, and socio-political decadence, with political prisons flourishing all over the country. Act I is a timeless piece, for as indicated by the playwright, the "Time is now, the past and the future" (P11). Indeed *Great Lepers* delves into the past to point out how all this came about, with Commandant Mbokaya, a character reminiscent of Ba'bila Mutia's Commandant Sikamba in *Before this Time Yesterday*, manipulating history to get his way with the union's political structure. *Great Lepers* then focuses on the present to show the collapse of the society's social fabric as we encounter an unhappy citizenry through pronouncements by Ntufam Vikuma Egu Eku and Samndeng Ngufor Akriyé Moghamo. For example, Ntufam wonders about Commandant Mbokaya's stupid deals:

Why does he have a *mitrailleur*
When Akriyé has no hoe?
Why does he import machine guns
And other deadly weapons of
extermination
When Ntufam Egu Eku has no
kunu or sobo
To drink? (20)

A peek into the future is taken through the warning of a potential secession by force:

…The time
is coming, and very soon when
there will be no more lepers in
national integration (…). You are
invalidated out of the Party with

multiple shrapnel wounds. (22)

Remarkable is the fact that instead of those in power looking into the issues raised by the restless faction of society, they always look upon them as ungrateful instead; hence, they are insulted:

> … Ungrateful tombo
> drinking Western Erooncams,
> whether in Wotolo or Ngyenmbo
> are offsprings of Bakogho
> chimpanzee. Stupid and as
> obstinate as a block of wood… (31)

They forget that the Anglophones did not come into the union begging, but as kings with a far advanced democracy. It is one such insult from a then Foumban prince and minister of state that has led to the insult of the people of Foumban through this prurient image here of their women who are said to enjoy being raped in a culture distinguished by the presence of suicide as a common place phenomenon, something that is taboo in most if not all of Cameroon. This prince, at the time a minister of state, had called Anglophones "Biafrans" and "enemies in the house" while urging them to go somewhere else if they did not like it in the union.

Because of Besong's technique, he is able to talk about or reference issues that he might not have been able to bring up in a play with a more traditional structure and a plot unfolding logically from conflict to resolution. Accordingly, he is able to talk satirically while haphazardly throwing in words about the one-sided relationship between the French and Cameroon, with the former benefitting:

> Ungrateful people! How can you
> Speak ill of our elder comrades;
> Civilized Frenschii…? Ungrateful
> and Stone age animals! How dare
> you intend
> To rubbish our *mokhutabag* allies,
> Frenschii?

I say to myself (*pause*). How dare
You?
Can we import
Wine technology and evian water
without the import licences of
Frenschii?
Can we trade or buy palaces in the
casualty I.M.F. *nyama nyama*
market
In Nice and on the International
jaw-jaw
Without the legal tender, the
almighty power
Of Frenschii? Come on.
Admit it! (13)

Besong, by this means, is able to talk about torture, betrayal, the
misappropriation of public funds by hijacking oil money (17), oppression and
the use of torture, dictatorship (27) self-exile (30) secession (36), corrupt
practices by law officers (52), and above all his hatred for the French which is
voiced by Ntufam Egu Eku: "Life is more peaceful / If one is not a
Frenchman" (71).

Thus Bate Besong succeeds in revisiting the Anglophone problem in
Cameroon in yet another effective play. *Great Lepers* is without the filth and
stench of *Beasts* but equally as piquant as it is effective. The smell of shit that
pervades the atmosphere of *Beasts* may be absent but the disgust conjured by
putridness is not altogether nonexistent given the stinking nature of the
Lepers' condition. But the tyrant Mbokaya is worse off such that he pleads
for the Lepers to rescue him by donating blood that would have revived him.
His plea is in vain as these wretched of Mbokaya's beleaguered political
concentration camp of a nation abandon the despot to die not only in
disgrace but in excruciating agony. This is a fate that seems to await these
African dictators who normaly die like dogs in disgrace, repudiated by their
own, and more often in some foreign land where nobody seems interested in
their corpses. It is usually then that reality dawns on most and they see the

meaninglessness of all that they have been about in the name of terrorizing their own nation so as to remain in power for life.

I have, this far, taken a look at the life of Bate Besong and attempted an in-depth study of his works, especially his poems, which, hitherto, have remained a challenge to his audience and critics alike until Shadrack A. Ambanasom even wondered if Besong's poems were too difficult for Cameroonians. Beyond an in-depth appraisal of Besong's works, consequently, I have succeeded in showing why they are difficult while also establishing the fact that opacity is not uniquely Besongese but a normal phenomenon in literature given one's influences and the generation to which one belongs. It is my hope then that this effort will serve as an incentive for many to make their own literary contributions by continuing, in search of meaning, to chip away at these literary structures left behind by Besong. This way, the concerns of this great scholar would stay addressed for as long as they remain relevant cancerous issues eating away at the flesh and soul of the human essence, especially that of the nation he loved so much— Cameroon—or simply milestones in the nation's literary history. As a result of these efforts, Besong would have died, yet he would remain in our midst forever.

This far, one thing is clear to me: creation is indeed daunting, and each time one takes an honest second look, free of pretentions, this fact becomes all the more overwhelming. There is so much out there one cannot fathom, too many questions one cannot answer. An example is how is it that a writer and scholar such as Bate Besong, a man of invaluable strategic importance to his people, dies at such a tender age whereas there are others looked upon by compatriots as traitors to their cause waxing strong as octogenarians? And then one begins understanding vaguely as the words of the Psalmist echo in one's ears: "The ways of the Lord are strange." These facts should render us humble with the realization that there is some superior authority out there in control, otherwise we would not let Besong die, or else we would bring him back to life even, but no, not us. No, as human beings we are on top of the chain, we reason and claim to know so much, and in the manner of toddlers, we play gods dishing out reasons and scientific explanations for whatever puzzle we can identify, yet we know that in spite of this, we are not in control of the very next second of our lives. Else Bate Besong would have spent that night at home assessing the impact, success or otherwise, of the launching of his book *Disgrace*. Something else was summoning and Besong had to answer: he ventured out of doors that fateful night after the launching of his book, like Shakespeare's Julius Caesar to the senate, never to return.

Bate Besong, this versatile, and equally gifted personality—father, spouse, teacher, writer, and literary and social critic—was killed in the company of three of his cherished associates: Kwasen Gwangwa'a, Hilarious Ambe, and Samson Tabe Awoh. In one night and in one sudden swoop many realms were shattered: the family, the intellectual, and that of friends. Too soon and too sudden was his death, yet, in spite of how young he was, comparatively speaking, Besong left behind footsteps deeply embedded in our hearts, in the sands of time. Even then, I am aware of the many storms that blow past repeatedly day in day out, year in year out, dumping layers and layers of sand particles in their wake, which with time would bury the tracks of any colossus; thereby, lodging them into the remote recesses of our minds and concerns. It is with this foreboding then, that I decided on this venture so that as it was said of one of Besong's greatest literary influences—Christopher Okigbo—it may also be said of Dr. Jacobs Bate Besong: may the man not die.

That Besong was enigmatic, eccentric, a puzzle, is true, yet who is not this to one person and that to another, let alone to a third. In coming up with this work, it has become obvious that Besong was a different person at home and a different person at work. From a distance Besong was frosty and seemingly incapable of falling in love, being too far removed from such delicacies of life, trapped in his realm of abstract thinking and creation in the face of mankind's well-being. Yet, he fell in love and his wife speaks of him with fondness and endearment. To his children he was a friend, a role model, and a loving father who did not hesitate to raise his voice when discipline called.

Beyond his home Besong remained a most controversial individual who made and called off friendships with equal ease; an approach to life which, in my opinion, was not being reckless but being principled. And that it wounded him to lose friends comes out in the fact that he became bitter when he had to think or talk of such estranged friends or acquaintances. This once upon a time shy and even withdrawn young man and budding scholar was transformed into a bitter and almost disillusioned and frustrated person by the corrupt sub-standard of his native country's administration which would not employ him, in spite of the need, and when it did, it was only to downgrade Besong by underemploying him, before emasculating him by having him work for years without his salary. This is the mind already bubbly and frothing with literary dreams and desires that turned and channeled all its scholarly might to combat the nonchalance, that languid, blasé disposition that has transformed most Cameroonians into the flotsam and jetsam of their national tide of events, and at best porters for Western pilferers on their own shores, betrayed by the likes of Caliban parading as leaders.

As a poet and playwright, Besong's goal was not to entertain, as such, but to conscientize as his works highlighted the ridiculously arbitrary, fundamentally meaningless, and unnecessarily precarious nature of human life. In this vein, when Besong wrote, he was not at play but at work, at war even, because of his love for Cameroon and the Anglophone-Cameroonian in particular and humankind as a whole. He spoke directly to his audience in his poems despite his denseness, and through his characters in his plays, highlighting their decadent and exploited lot in an effort to jumpstart their dormant essences into a state of awareness leading to some form of action or uprising that could engender positive change in society. His works amount to Cameroon's Hyde Park: discussing them created the opportunity and excuse for the nationally disenfranchised and politically ostracized to engage in the forbidden—conversations and activities about their conditions, about the aberrant and pertinacious powers that be. In his poems, like in his plays, Besong's attack on the perpetrators of injustices and inequalities are implemented in a most scathing manner, with the identities of the culprits barely masked such that they can be identified with little or no effort at all.

Like an enraged spirit from the Bayangi pantheon, Besong swabbed from side to side, chopping here and hacking there at the soulless sons and daughters of evil who enjoy lording it over their compatriots while executing treachery as a way to serve their worthless political god of a failed leader. Besong hunted them down with his damning pen because the welfare of the citizens was not their concern but the longing to maintain their undeserved administrative posts for as long as their voices could be heard echoing throwaway political mantras showering pointless encomiums on quixotic leaders. For his was that romantic conviction that the poet is an inspired soul, a possessed spirit through whose inspiration and guidance society can undergo a rebirth, hence his position to his admirers as prophet, seer, and warrior all couched within the cultural spiritual force he came to be associated with—the Obasinjom warrior. Besong, accordingly, fought against a set-up designed to facilitate the unpatriotic deeds of an idiotic, pilfering, treasonable, moron and type of a leader who spends more time overseas than at home, exploiting the masses and stashing away the nation's wealth in private foreign bank accounts. Besong then was a warrior fighting against corruption, exploitation, tribalism, and the truncation of society's potentials. He fought against those infecting the academic domain with mediocrity because of the interference of political Cyclops in the affairs of academics, a turf far beyond their corrupt, trite, and festering ids.

In his established capacity, Besong could not control his fury against neocolonialist activities in Africa, at large, and Cameroon in particular. His disgust at the French is not a secret as they muddle the political waters of so-called francophonie nations at the head of which are spineless ideologically outdated relics of colonial évolués parading their local landscapes like lords, in diapers, only to publicly acknowledge tutelage to some alien leader who must have been in elementary school when these African political dinosaurs were already ensconced in marbled presidential palaces. These purposeless yet petrifying ageing tyrants exploiting African nations were game for Besong's belittling and equally damning categorization that he hoped could trigger some form of self-evaluation from these retarded stooges who have forgotten to serve their nations and are instead lording it over their citizenry. Interestingly, Besong's main characters in his plays, more often than not, are grumpy pseudocouples, usually two males having a resentful interdependence dominated by garish, ridiculous, yet complex exchanges highlighted by spasmodic vocalizations and non sequiturs. The outcome is the often pervading bleakness and crushing air of pessimism in Besong's works.

To accomplish his mission, Besong decided on a technique that left his corrupt, soiled, and worthless crowned thieves-cum-traitors challenged and groveling in the sands of worthlessness, incompetence. His modernist and absurdist approach at dealing with a disturbed universe was the literary scalpel with which he attacked those who had betrayed the human race, the Cameroonian nation, especially those culprits who are English speaking. For Besong's diction, when not coined, was contorted almost beyond recognition even as his absurdist approach to theatre splashed shit on his human targets leaving them fumbling about and choking in incomprehension from the stench of their own transgressions, his intention being to set right mankind who had failed to overcome his own innate vices. While being greatly influenced by the theater of the absurd, Besong went further stylistically in that beyond just isolating man's failure, he, uncharacteristic of this theatre, went on to recommend a solution—an uprising more often than not. Besong's works reflect the spirit and tensions of the eras that led to their creation. True, his style is opaque, with the common denominator being his critical approach. This, however, was because the fountains of his stylistic inspiration were far apart in time and setting, from the classical to the present, from Greece to Cameroon and more so from his personal if not private experiences. Norman N. Holland has pointed out that to critics, the style is the man (225), before going on to explain what literary critics seem to include into this literary broth called style. First of all, according to him, when critics talk about style, they mean the writer's way with words; secondly, they take into consideration a writer's choice of his material and his characteristic form of handling it, and thirdly, his way of dealing with his audience. In this light, as already established, Bate Besong's style was most complex given his exceptional way with words, the choice of his material, and his way with his audience. Besong's poetic and theatrical aesthetics and vision must then be approached with this awareness in the background and before long tiny rays of comprehension will begin darting across the landscape of his intimidating and nerve-wracking creative genius which was, despite all else, too often prophetic. Apt, then, is the description of Besong by many as a genuine intellectual and seer.

Of the genuine intellectual as seer, Cameroon's literary grandmaster and iconoclastic authority of the classics, the late Bernard Fonlon, had this to say:

If the thinker scholar is verily a Seer, one of the foremost things on which he will inescapably, relenthlessly (sic), have to focus the searching light of his eye and mind will be on the nature of good and evil, of right and wrong, of justice and injustice, in the living of private lives, in the conduct of public affairs; and, since man is corrupt from conception, helpless at the enticements and the seductions of evil, more often than not; more inclined to wrong than to right, to injustice than to fairness; since the holders of office, the wielders of power, will be tempted more

190

surely, more irresistibly, to its abuse than to its judicious and salutary use; the genuine thinker scholar, if he is faithful, if he is *integer vitae scelerisque purus* – pure of life and free from sin – he must become, inevitably, the *keeper of the Public Conscience*; indeed he will have to be the very Conscience itself of Society. If he is really genuine, far from being a cynical, supercilious, haughty, self-righteous and self-appointed judge of weak and erring men, he will become a humble votary of Truth, Goodness and Justice: ever conscious of his own weakness and short-comings, full of sympathetic understanding; but yet a determined, unflinching, dauntless combatant in the war of truth against falsehood, of good against injustice, of humaneness against wickedness, of freedom against tyranny; he will become a tireless crusader-persuader urging men by word and deed along the road to right; a goad and gad-fly, ever pricking, ever stinging society in order to rouse its conscience to shun evil and seek the good; a fearless defender of truth and injustice ever ready to front 'the frown of the great,' to bide 'the tyrant's stroke.' (133-134)

What a summation of the world in which Besong lived, and the type of scholar Besong tried to be. Mindful of what this master of the classics has opined of the genuine intellectual and seer, it is true then that Besong was a faithful and genuine intellectual and seer; alas, one whose vision and integrity was occasionally blighted by the tendency to superciliousness and self-righteousness as already indicated. However, like every human being, in the imitation of Christ the King on this *Via Dolorosa* called life, we fall and do all to try and rise again; so too did this intellectual and seer rise again after falling. His life was like that of a prophet who came to turn mankind from his evil ways only to end up like a voice in the wilderness as man's decadence even after him seems to be thriving instead. I dare suggest that before his death, Besong had identified and risen above his own flaws that tainted his vision as a genuine intellectual and seer—occasional superciliousness. Of our state upon death, the Bible reveals of what the Lord has decreed:

The one who has sinned is the one to die....
   If the wicked, however, renounces all the sins he has
committed, respects my laws and is law-abiding and upright, he
will most certainly live; he will not die. None of the crimes he

committed will be remembered against him from then on; he will most certainly live because of his upright actions. (*The New Jerusalem*, Ezekiel 18: 4, 21-28)

In the manner of the Almighty, therefore, one must accord Besong his merit as a genuine intellectual and seer, his past flaws notwithstanding; otherwise, show me that human being without a flaw in his or her character.

And so for as long as these horrors perpetrated by man on man live on, for as long as the Anglophone struggle in Cameroon thrives, atrocities against which Besong fought and died fighting, may he never die as his ideas, through his ink, continue passing on, inspiring and stirring generations after generations until victory is achieved. Even then, may he live on as each time joy is to be celebrated, when somehow Anglophone-Cameroonians would finally have acquired professional identity cards, his vision and struggles that paved the way will also be remembered and celebrated with libations poured in his honour as a sign of our gratitude for a brave and true patriot who once lived and gave up his life fighting for his people's wellbeing in their homeland hijacked, derailed, and transformed by felons into a circus, a jungle even, where only the fittest survive by any means as the laws and dignity of the people and their land thaw into nonsense even as the years come and go.

All said and done, as a spouse and parent, Bate Besong loved and was devoted; as a friend he listened, disagreed, quarreled, and then made up or looked forward to it; as a scholar, writer, and critic he was blunt, indignant at times even, and above all fearless, armoured by the truth; as a Cameroonian he loved his roots so much, hence he wept so often for his people whose plight became so personal. It is these different dimensions of Besong's essence that amounted to the unique poet, playwright, and critic that he was, with a style that was equally inimitable. His style suited well his times and the ideological battles he fought. And so through his works and efforts such as this—*The Obasinjom Warrior: The Life and Works of Bate Besong*—may his spirit rage and blaze on like Caesar's at Philippi, until Anglophone-Cameroonians, whom he loved in a special way, are free again, together with their Francophone counterparts or apart should the need arise. Besong, *Aja-oh-o*!

Notes

Part I

1. There are frightening stories from students about how they were victimized by faculty for bizarre reasons and made to repeat exams over and over until they were frustrated. It was also said teaching was carried out in French only, in spite of the presence of Cameroonian students who were not fluent in French and so they failed in their numbers, an unfortunate situation that seemed to please rather than trouble the authorities. Stories abound about the institution as a literary sinkhole for Anglophone students than the institution of learning it should have been.

2. In 1949, Arthur Miller put forward his views of what he considered a new kind of tragic hero. In an article titled "Tragedy and the Common Man" Miller challenged Aristotle's idea that the hero must be a "highly renowned and prosperous" figure who has a tragic flaw. According to Miller, in contrast to a disorder within the personal traits of the hero, this modern hero suffers from a clash between the character and the environment, especially the social environment. To Miller, each person has a chosen image of self and position and so tragedy results when the character's environment denies the fulfillment of this self-concept. The hero, therefore must no longer be born into the nobility but gains stature in the action of pitting self against cosmos. The tragedy is "the disaster inherent in being torn away from our chosen image of what and who we are in this world" (McMahan 770)

3. Biatcha's letter:

A l'occasion des rencontres théâtrales de Yaoundé, le théâtre Universtaire Anglophone dirigé par Monsieur Bole Butake, a représenté la pièce intitulée 'Beach (sic) of NO Nation' de BATE BESSONG le 26 mars 1991 à 21 heures, dans l'amphithéâtre '700' de l'Université de Yaoundé.

Cette representation à laquelle j'ai assisté appelle les observations ci-après:

Il s'agit d'un véritable pamphlet politique dirigé contre le régime en place qui est tenu pour responsables de la crise économique par la corruption; le favoritisme, et l'exportation des capitaux vers les banque étrangeres.

L'auteur soutient que les Francophones au pouvoir sont responsables de la crise économique parce qu'ils entretiennent la gabégie et les détournements des fonds. Parmi les francophones (frogs), un accent particulier est mis sur les Beti, amis et frères du Président Biya, qui sont plus responsables de l'état actuel au Cameroun.

L'auteur affirme également, et ceci est la philosophie principale de la pièce, que 'les Anglophones au Cameroun, sont marginalisés et confinés dans des rôles indignes comme celui de 'ramasseurs d'excréments'. Ils n'ont aucun statut propre et sont même dépourvus de toute carte d'identité professionnelle, qu'ils réclament sans succès.

Pour Monsieur BESSONG (sic), l'Anglophone au Cameroun est considéré comme un traître et un esclave. La pièce s'achève par une incitation à la révolte et au refus de l'ordre régnant. A la fin de la représentation, l'auteur de cette pièce est monté sur scène pour déclarer publiquement que l'avenir au Cameroun est énigmatique et que le chaos peut intervenir à tout moment, surtout de l'autre côté du Moungo. Il a par conséquent lancé un appel à l'audience, à prédominance Anglophone, pour qu'elle sache se mobiliser en vue d'opérer ses choix.

Après avoir enduré cette pièce, j'ai dû en guise de protestation, me lever, accompagné du Chef du Service des Associations et Clubs Culturels Estudiantins pour quitter la sale, au moment où Monsieur BESSONG terminait ses propos incendiaires de la fin.

Lorsque nous quittions l'Amphithéâtre '700', j'ai été hué par les 'man no run' et 'Owona' 'Owona'.

Je pense, pour ma part, qu'au moment où des efforts constants et soutenus sont déployés par les pouvoirs publics pur faire du Cameroun un pays uni où les deux communautés cohabitent en toute fraternité, il est anormal et inadmissible que des intellectuels aiguisent et favorisent la scission et les conflits. En tout cas, l'"Université ne devrait pas servir de forum à ce genre d'entreprises mal intentionnées.

Malheureusement, le programme des rencontres théâtrales qui a été conçu par le Ministère de l'information et de la Culture ne nous a pas permis de lire au préalable cette pièce dont j'ai acheté une copie, à la sortie de l'Amphithéâtre.

A la lecture de cette pièce, je me suis d'ailleurs rendu compte que certains passages ont été modifies par Mr Bole Butake dans le sens d'une réactualisation pur rendre ce pamphlet plus caustique.

Cette expérience qui est, il faut l'avouer, assez choquante et décevante servira de leçon davantage de vigilance à l'occasion de toutes les autres manifestations culturelles qui se dérouleront dans le campus universitaire. Jean
Stéphane Biatcha (1991:11)" (sic Ambanasom, *Education* 94 - 98)

194

Translation

"On the occasion of Yaoundé theatre performances, the Anglophone University theatre, directed by Mr. Bole Butake staged a pay entitled *Beasts of No Nation* by Bate Besong on March 26, 1991 at 9 p.m. in Amphi '700' of Yaoundé University.

The performance, which I watched, calls for the following observations:

It is a clear political pamphlet directed at the regime in power, that is held responsible for the Economic Crisis through corruption, favoritism and capital flight to foreign banks. (sic)

The author holds the thesis that Francophones in power are responsible for the Economic crisis because they are producers of waste and embezzlers of public funds. Among the Francophones (frogs) special emphasis is placed on the Betis, friends and brothers of President Paul Biya, who are more responsible for the present state of Cameroon.

The author equally affirms, and this is the central thesis of the play, that 'the Anglophones of Cameroon are marginalized and confined to undignified roles like that of 'carriers of excrements'. They do not have any professional identity cards, which they are asking for in vain.

According to Mr. Besong, the Anglophone in Cameroon is considered a traitor and a slave. The play ends with an appeal for rebellion and the disregard of the present authority. At the end of the performance, the playwright took to the stage and publicly declare (sic) that the future of Cameroon is uncertain and that chaos can set in at any time, especially from the other side of the Mungo. Consequently, he appealed to the audience, for the most part Anglophones, to get themselves ready in order to carry out their choices.

After enduring this play, I had to get up, by way of protest, accompanied by the Chief of Service for Students' Associations and Cultural Clubs, to quit the hall just at the time when Mr. Besong was concluding his fiery exhortations at the end.

While we were leaving the hall, I was booed in these words: 'man no run' 'Owona'. I think, in my opinion, that at the time when the government is exerting great and constant efforts to make Cameroon a united country where the two communities coexist in all brotherliness it is abnormal and unacceptable that the intellectuals should promote divisions and conflicts. In any case, the University ought not to be the forum for such ill-intentioned ventures.

Unfortunately, the programme of theatre activities that was conceived by the Ministry of Information and Culture did not allow us to preview this play, a copy of which I bought at the exit of the Amphitheatre.

On reading this play, I even realized that some passages have been altered by Mr. Bole Butake to make the play more current and critical. This experience, which I must admit, is shocking and disappointing enough will serve as a lesson for the future and will help me to be more vigilant and diligent with regards to all the other cultural activities that will take place on the university campus.

Jean Stéphane Biatcha."

Part II

1. According to Yoruba mythology, Ogun had a covenant with God to advance humanity and obey the laws of God. Ogun is said and believed to be creative and proficient in all that he set his mind to do. Because of his covenant with God to obey all the ten commandments which he wants all his followers to obey, he is said to detest all forms of immorality including cheating, falsehood, stealing, mudslinging and fornication and so much else. Hence Besong's allusion to Ogun because of Soyinka's reparative mission).

2. "Aro," as of the time Besong was writing, was a mental hospital at Ibadan, and a term used by students of the University of Ibadan of the eighties to indicate they believed something was mentally wrong with anyone whom they referred to as "Aro!" Anyone who behaved strangely no matter who the person was, was also referred to as "Aro." It was a term used by students both seriously and when joking around poking fun at each other. For example, a student could dress up in a way other's thought was out of place and someone in the group or surrounding area would shout out "Aro!" and students would laugh at the joke having understood what was implied.

3. The shuttle was an English newspaper intended for disseminating

political ideas as did the *Kidderminster shuttle* a century before in England.

4. "Criminal" because in spite of the long years they spent in office, decades, during which they made huge personal financial gains, they did nothing to benefit the nation but themselves and members of their privileged families.

5. The positioning of this poem in the volume mindful of the previous ones may make this seem like a contradiction in the poet's approach to things but that is not the case; it is simply that this poem should have come earlier on in the volume than now.

6. *Évolué* is a French term of reference that was directed towards members of colonized peoples who were said to have "evolved" or "developed" by acquiring the education and overall culture of the colonizers (the French in this case) while accepting their values as superior. These characters were usually considered second generation French men and women and they could hold white collar jobs at the level of clerks and nothing more. They were considered elite and so superior to the other locals who were yet to "evolve."

7. "Rdpc" is an acronym for "Rassemblement démocratique du Peuple Camerounais" in French and "Cameroon People's Democratic Party" (CPDM) in English. The party's uniform is usually cloth material designed with the party's colors and logos on it along with the portrait of the leader of the party who is usually the head of state. Whereas the men tailor their uniform in the form of a simple shirt of "jumpa" women sew theirs mainly in the style of a free size gown known as the "kabba ngondo," by the coastal peoples of Cameroon. The material is usually supplied the members of the party free of charge—paid for by the tax payers since the money comes out of the country's treasury.

8. The Aboem à Tchoyi commission was appointed by President Paul Biya to look into the student strikes that took the University of Buea by storm in 2005 when Dorothy Njeuma was Vice Chancellor.

9. Even though Besong has not mentioned the name of the dead Mayor and the people whose Sultan he is referring to, these facts are not hidden to the Cameroonian.

10. *"Ennemies dans la maison"* or "enemies within" is another derogatory term of reference for Anglophones, the English speaking Cameroonian. So a city is happy when government delegates who exploit and steal the wealth

from Anglophone-Cameroon territories die. These government delegates function as mayors to these cities.

11. "Ghana must go" was a type of plastic bag that was sewn in Nigeria initially, then locally from some kind of colorful plastic material much like salt bags. It earned its name because it was put into use heavily in Cameroon and Nigeria at a time when Ghanaians who were in Nigeria illegally were asked to leave. The bag was light in weight, cheap, yet sturdy enough to contain a lot without ripping, unlike more expensive bags.

12. Alemji looks at the idea posited by some within his society that Cameroonians, unlike in other African countries, do not seem to read at all, before going on to explore the invaluable role played by literature and writing in society.

13. By eleventh province, Cameroonians are referring to those who are Cameroonians but displaced from their provinces of origin for one reason or another and so can pass as members of another province whereas, indeed, they belong to another province. There are examples of the Bamilekes who were originally Francophone but immigrated into then Southern Cameroons for political reason, who have long settled down and brought up their children as Anglophones even though they are Francophones. Some have completely lost touch with their roots and so can only go with the present English speaking regions to which they now belong, although they were from the Francophone part of the country originally. Then there are people from somewhere else, other countries, who have become Cameroonians but are from none of the ten provinces officially. Both these categories will pass for members of the eleventh province. This expression was popular when Cameroon was still divided into provinces for administrative reasons. Today provinces are called "regions".

14. In Cameroon, "frog" is a derogatory term of reference for Francophones whereas Anglophones are, in return, called "anglos."

15. CENER is the French acronym for Cameroon's secret service.

Works Cited

Achebe, Chinua. *Arrow of God.* New York: Anchor, 1969. Print.

Achingale, Douglas. "Homage to a Literary Colossus (Remembering Bate Besong Five Years After)." *Bate Besong: Freedom Inked.* Bate Besong, 8 Mar. 2012. Web. 3 Apr. 2014.

Achobang, Fon Christopher. "Bole Butake Crosses Moungo to Bali." *Modern Ghana.* MG Media Group, 9 Jan. 2014. Web. 24 Apr. 2014.

Adegbamigbe, Ademola. "How Babangida Murdered Mamman Vatsa." *Ocnus.net.* Ocnus, 4 May 2007. Web. 3 Apr. 2014.

Alembong, Nol. *Forest Echoes.* Mankon-Bamenda: Langaa, 2010. Print.

Alemji, Mbe Nkemawung. "The Role of Literature in Cameroon." *Up Station Mountain Club.* Up Station Mountain Club, 23 June 2008. Web. 14 Apr. 2014.

Ali, Richard. "Denudation: Remembering Dr Bala Mohammed Bauchi (1944–81)." *Pambazuka News.* Pambazuka News, 4 Apr. 2010. Web. 7 Apr. 2014.

Ambanasom, Shadrach A. *Education of the Deprived (A Study of Four Cameroonian Playwrights).* Bamenda: Unique Printers, 2002. Print.

- - -. "Is Bate Besong's Poetry Too Difficult For Cameroonians." *ALA Bulletin* 28 3/4.summer/fall (2000): 43-50. Print.

Ambe, Hilarious N. "Shit and Stench as Dramatic Strategy: Bate Besong's *Beasts of No Nation.*" *The Literary Criterion* XXXIX.3 & 4 (2004): 185-97. Print.

Anastaplo, George. *The Artist as Thinker: From Shakespeare to Joyce.* Chicago: Swallow, 1983. Print.

Ashuntantang, Joyce. *Landscaping Postcoloniality: The Dissemination of Cameroon Anglophone Literature.* Mankon-Bamenda: Langaa, 2009. Print.

Bamikunle, Aderemi. "Problems of Language in Understanding Soyinka's A Shuttle in the Crypt." *African Literature Today.* Ed. Eldred Durosimi Jones, Eustace Palmer, and Marjorie Jones. London: James Currey, 1989. 77-90. Print. Vol. 16 of *Oral and Written Poetry in African Literature Today.*

Beckett, Samuel. *Endgame.* New York: Grove, 1958. Print.

- - -. *Waiting for Godot.* New York: Grove, 1970. Print.

Besong, Bate. *The Banquet.* Ibadan: African, 1994. Print.

- - -. *Beasts of No Nation.* 1990. *Three Plays (The Achwiimgbe Trilogy).* Yaounde: Editions CLE, 2003. 81-143. Print.

- - -. *Change Waka & His Man Sawa Boy.* Yaounde: Editions CLE, 2001. Print.

- - -. *Disgrace: Autobiographical Narcissus.* Limbe: Design, 2007. Print.

- - -. *The Grain of Bobe Ngom Jua (Poems).* Yaounde: Drapoe, 1986. Print.

- - -. *The Most Cruel Death of the Talkative Zombie.* Limbe: Nooremac, 1986. Print.

- - -. "New Engagements in Cameroon Literature: The Other Side of the Bridge." *Bate Besong: Freedom Inked.* Bate Besong: Freedom Inked, 10 Apr. 2004. Web. 19 Apr. 2014.

- - -. *Obasinjom Warrior with Poems After Detention.* Limbe: Alfresco, 1992. Print.

- - -. *Once Upon Great Lepers.* 2003. *Three Plays (The Achwiimgbe Trilogy).* Yaounde: Editions CLE, 2003. 7-81. Print.

- - -. *Polyphemus Detainee & Other Skulls.* Calabar: Scholars, 1980. Print.

- - -. *Requiem for the Last Kaiser.* Calabar: Centaur, 1991. Print.

- - -. "Who's Afraid of Anglophone (Cameroon) Theatre?" *Bate Besong: Freedom Inked.* Bate Besong, 6 Mar. 2008. Web. 19 Apr. 2014.

Besong, Bate. Interview by Elvis Tah. "Bate Besong: The Family Remembers." *Bate Besong: Freedom Inked.* Bate Besong, 5 Apr. 2007. Web. 3 Apr. 2014.

Brutus, Dennis. *Letters to Martha.* London: Heinemann, 1968. Print.

Burris, Sidney. *The Poetry of Resistance: Seamus Heaney and the Pastoral Tradition.* Athens: Ohio UP, 1990. Print.

Butake, Bole. "Bate Besong: The Silent Volcano." *Bate Besong: Freedom Inked.* Bate Besong, 19 Jan. 2011. Web. 3 Apr. 2014.

Camara, Mohamed. "Sékou Touré: Guinea's Hardline Hero or Visionary Villain?" *Think Africa Press.* Think Africa Press, 19 Dec. 2013. Web. 3 Apr. 2014.

Chumbow, Beban Sammy. Foreword. *Disgrace: Autobiographical Narcissus.* By Bate Besong. Limbe: Design, 2007. Print.

Conrad, Joseph. *Heart of Darkness.* New York: Chelsea, 1987. Print.

Dipoko, Mbella Sonne. *Black and White in Love.* London: Heinemann, 1972. Print.

Doh, Emmanuel Fru. "Dipoko's 'Ntarikon Blues': Poetry or Anticlimax." *Cameroon Post*. Tuesday, July 23, 1996: 9. Print

Elimimian, Isaac I. "Poetry as a Vehicle for Promoting National Consciousness and Development: The Example of Four Nigerian Poets." *Oral and Written Poetry in African Literature Today*. Ed. Eldred Durosimi Jones. London: Heinemann, 1973. 111-23. Print. Vol. 16 of *African Literature Today*.

Esslin, Martin. *Reflections: Essays on Modern Theatre*. New York: Double Day, n.d. Print.

- - -. *Theatre of the Absurd*. Revised ed. New York: Anchor, 1969. Print.

Fandio, Pierre. "Memory Lane - Anglophone Cameroon Literature at Crossroads: An Interview with Dr. Bate Besong." *Bate Besong: Freedom Inked*. Bate Besong, 9 Mar. 2007. Web. 9 Apr. 2014.

Fishkin, Benjamin Hart. "A Costly Gift to the Receiver." *Fears Doubts and Joys of Not Belonging*. Ed. Benjamin Hart Fishkin, Adaku T. Ankumah, and Bill F. Ndi. Mankon-Bamenda: Langaa, 2014. 175-96. Print.

Fonlon, Bernard. *The Genuine Intellectual*. Yaounde: Buma Kor, 1978. Print.

Futcha, Innocent. "Bate Besong: Jeremiah In Cameroon." *Up Station Mountain Club*. Up Station Mountain Club, 24 Mar. 2007. Web. 8 Apr. 2014.

Gwangwa'a, Kwasen. "Bate Besong as Seen by Kwasen Gwangwa'a." *Bate Besong: Freedom Inked*. Bate Besong, 13 Mar. 2007. Web. 3 Apr. 2014.

Hardy, Thomas. *The Mayor of Casterbridge*. Oxford: Oxford UP, 1998. Print.

Heywood, Annemarie. "The Fox's Dance: Staging Soyinka's Plays." *Drama in Africa*. Ed. Eldred Durosimi Jones. London: Heinemann, 1976. 42-51. Print. Vol. 8 of *African Literature Today*.

Holland, Norman H. *The Dynamics of Literary Response*. New York: Columbia UP, 1968. Print.

Home be Home. Composed by Prince Nico Mbarga. Decca Studios/Rogers All Stars Nigeria Limited, 1978. CD.

Ikiddeh, Ime. Introduction. *Polyphemus Detainee & Other Skulls*. By Bate Besong. Calabar: Scholars, 1980 1-3. Print.

"Introduction to the Prophets." *The New Jerusalem Bible*. Standard ed. London: Darton, Longman & Todd, 1985. 1157-89. Print.

Izevbaye, Dan. "From Reality to Dream: The Poetry of Christopher
    Okigbo." *The Critical Evaluation of African Literature*. Ed. Edgar Wright.
    London: Heinemann, 1973. 121-48. Print.

Jack, Ian. *The Poet and His Audience*. Cambridge: Cambridge UP, 1984. Print.

Jumbam, Martin. "The Open Quarrel I Never Had With BB." *Martin
    Jumbam.Com*. Martin Jumbam, 12 Apr. 2012. Web. 3 Apr. 2014.

Konings, Piet. *Neoliberal Bandwagonism: Civil Society and the Politics of Belonging in
    Anglophone Cameroon*. Bamenda: Langaa, 2009. Print.

Kunene, Daniel P. "Language, Literature & the Struggle for Liberation in
    South Africa." *The Question of Language*. Ed. Eldred Durosimi Jones,
    Eustace Palmer, and Marjorie Jones. African World Press: Trenton,
    1991. 37-50. Print. Vol. 17 of *African Literature Today*.

Mbarga, Prince Nico & Rocafil Jazz International. "Home Be Home," *Family
    Movement*. Rogers All Stars. Ontisha, Nigeria. 1981. LP.

McMahan, Elizabeth, et al. *Literature and the Writing Process*. Ninth ed. Boston:
    Longman, 2011. Print.

**Moore, Arthur K. *Contestable Concepts of Literary Theory*. Baton Rouge:
    Louisiana State UP, 1973. Print.**

Mutia, Ba'bila. *Before This Time, Yesterday*. Seine: Editions Nouvelles Du Sud,
    1995. Print.

- - -. "Besong: The Man, His Ideas, His Vision and His Life." *Bate Besong:
    Freedom Inked*. Bate Besong, 5 Apr. 2007. Web. 9 Apr. 2014.

- - -. *Coils of Mortal Flesh*. Mankon-Bamenda: Langaa, 2008. Print.

The New Jerusalem Bible. Standard ed. London: Darton, Longman & Todd,
    1985. Print.

Ngongkum, Eunice. "Revisiting the Play that Won the 1992 ANA Award."
    Cameroon Post [Limbe] January 27 - February 9 1993: 12. Print.

Ngwane, George. *Bate Besong (Or The Symbol of Anglophone Hope)*. Limbe:
    Nooremac, 1993. Print.

Niane, D. T. *Sundiata: An Epic of Old Mali*. Trans. G. D. Pickett. Revised ed.
    England: Pearson / Longman, 2006. Print.

Nwachukwu-Agbada, J. O J. "The Language of Post-war Nigeria Poetry in
    English Expression." *The Question of Language in African Literature
    Today*. Ed. Eldred Durosimi Jones, Eustace Palmer, and Marjorie

Jones. Trenton: Africa World, 1991. 165-76. Print. Vol. 17 of *African Literature Today*.

Nwoga, Donatus I. "Obscurity and Commitment in Modern African Poetry." *Poetry in Africa*. Ed. Eldred Durosimi Jones. London: Heinemann, 1973. 26-45. Print. Vol. 6 of *African Literature Today*.

Nyamndi, George D. "Bate Besong or the Therapeutics of Laughter." *Revue Lisa/Lisa e-journal [En Ligne]*. Presses Universitaires de Rennes, 1 Jan. 2008. Web. 3 Apr. 2014.

Okonkwo, Juliet I. "The Missing Link in African Literature." *Retrospect and Prospect*. Ed. Eldred Durosimi Jones. London: Heinemann, 1979. 86-105. Print. Vol. 10 of *African Literature Today*.

Okpewho, Isidore. *The Font: University of Ibadan Anthem*. Ibadan: Spectrum, 1988. Print.

Olaogun, Modupe. "Graphology & Meaning in the Poetry of Christopher Okigbo." *The Question of Language in African Literature Today*. Vol. 17 of *African Literature Today*.Ed. Eldred Durosimi Jones, Eustace Palmer, and Marjorie Jones. Trentoon: Africa World, 1991. 108-30. Print.

Opio, Azore. "Farewell Master of Obscurantism." *Bate Besong: Freedom Inked*. Bate Besong, 24 Mar. 2007. Web. 3 Apr. 2014.

Oyono, Ferdinand. *The Old Man and the Medal*. London: Heinemann, 1967. Print.

Peschel, Enid Rhodes. Introduction. *Four French Symbolist Poets: Baudelaire Rimbaud Verlaine Mallarmé*. By Enid Rhodes Peschel. Trans. Enid Rhodes Peschel. Athens: Ohio UP. 1981. 1-63. Print.

Segal, Erich. *The Death of Comedy*. Cambridge: Harvard UP, 2001. Print.

Shakespeare, William. *Julius Caesar*. Cambridge: Cambridge UP, 1988. Print.

- - -. *Macbeth*. New Haven: Yale UP, c2005. Print.

- - -. *The Tragedy of King Lear*. Ed. Jay L. Halio. Cambridge: Cambridge UP, 1992. Print.

Sophocles. *Oedipus the King*. c. 1942. *The Complete Greek Tragedies,* Vol. II of *SOPHOCLES*. Ed. David Grene and Richmond Lattimore. Chicago: U of Chicago P, n.d. 11-76. Print.

Soyinka, Wole. *A Dance of the Forest*. Oxford: Oxford UP, 1963. Print.

- - -. *Kongi's Harvest*. London: Oxford UP, 1967. Print.

- - -. *Madmen and Specialists*. New York: Methuen, 1971. Print.

- - -. *The Road*. Oxford: Oxford UP, 1965. Print.

Steane, J. B., ed. *Christopher Marlowe: The Complete Plays*. Middlesex: Penguin, 1969. Print.

Stevenson, W. H. Foreword. *Polyphemus Detainee & Other Skulls*. By Bate Besong. Calabar: Scholars, 1980 n. pag. Print.

Tah, Elvis. "Bate Besong: The Family Remembers." *Bate Besong: Freedom Inked*. 5 April 2007. Web. 28 April 2014

Tande, Dibussi. "In Memoriam: Mbella Sonne Dipoko - The Bard Who Dared to be Different." *Dibussi Tande: Scribbles from the Den*. Dibussi Tande, 17 Dec. 2009. Web. 2 Apr. 2014.

- - -. "Mbella Sonne Dipoko in His Own Words: The Luxury of Memory." *Dibussi Tande: Scribbles From the Den*. Dibussi Tande, 26 June 2006. Web. 3 Apr. 2014.

Tangwa, Canute. Letter to *CamLit* forum 25. Feb. 2014. TS

Tanla-Kishani, Bongasu. *Konglanjo*. N.p.: n.p., 1988. Print.

Ugah, Ada. "Bate Besong: A Dramaturgy of the Oppressed Workers." *Bate Besong: Freedom Inked*. Bate Besong, 7 Dec. 2004. Web. 3 Apr. 2014.

Vakunta, Peter. "Bate Besong: Why the Caged Bird Sings." *Up Station Mountain Club*. Up Station Mountain Club, 21 May 2013. Web. 5 Apr. 2014.

Wan-Mbulai, Kikefomo. "Bate Besong's Re-valuation of History in 'The Banquet.'" *Cameroon Post No. 0020* [Limbe] August 13-19 1996: 11. Print.

Wellwarth, George. *The Theater of Protest and Paradox: Developments in Avant-Garde-Drama*. Revised ed. New York: New York UP, 1971. Print.

Widmer, Kingsley. *The Literary Rebel*. Carbondale and Edwardsville: Southern Illinois UP, 1965. Print.

Wimsatt, W. K., Jr, and Monroe C. Beardsley. "The Intentional Fallacy (1946)." *Modern Criticism: Theory and Practice*. Ed. Walter Sutton and Richard Foster. New York: The Odyssey, 1963. 248-57. Print.

INDEX

207

210